T0208799

The
COSMIC CANCER

Effects of Human Behavior on Life of Our Planet

David Louis Sussman

iUniverse, Inc.
New York   Bloomington

The Cosmic Cancer
Effects of Human Behavior on Life of Our Planet

iUniverse books may be ordered through booksellers or by contacting:

iUniverse
1663 Liberty Drive
Bloomington, IN 47403
www.iuniverse.com
1-800-Authors (1-800-288-4677)

ISBN: 978-1-4502-4726-9 (pbk)
ISBN: 978-1-4502-4727-6 (cloth)
ISBN: 978-1-4502-4728-3 (ebk)

Library of Congress Control Number: 2010910812

Printed in the United States of America

iUniverse rev. date: 7/29/2010

For
Claire
Ellen, David, Rona, Michael
and particularly for those most affected by the outcome:
Caitlan, Daniel, Emma and Nicholas, their
contemporaries and successor generations

Contents

Acknowledgements

I am deeply indebted to Reg Morrison, who graciously agreed to review an early manuscript, and whose critique of content and structure was instrumental in helping me to reorganize and improve the presentation; and also for allowing me to 'stand on his shoulders' while peering at the subjects of his seminal work on human behavior, *The Spirit in the Gene, Humanity's Proud Illusion and the Laws of Nature.* Michael Sussman also reviewed the manuscript and provided invaluable suggestions for improvement. Had I followed their advice to the letter, this would undoubtedly have been a much better piece of work. Those listed in the bibliography were mainly involuntary participants in the process of shaping my own thoughts on the human condition and its consequences, whom I thank profoundly for sharing their ideas through their published works. None of these individuals can in any way be held responsible for errors, omissions or misguided conclusions, which are strictly of my own doing.

Preface

It will become clear presently why I am compelled to explain my motivation for this probe into the underpinnings, characteristics and consequences of human behavior by someone with my history and constitution. Fundamentally I am driven by a personal feeling of identity with nature, under assault by a rogue species that it spawned perhaps 5-7 million years ago when the first glimmer of the hominid line split from a common ancestor with our primate cousins.

My 'epiphany' stems from a simple occurrence at Bear Mountain Park, in New York State at the age of 12 or so. To gain respite from the ordinary turbulence of our family life, my father would pack my mother and the brood of 6 or 7 siblings into the old Hudson Terraplane and wheel over to the park on a Sunday morning. Once there we would picnic and have the run of that beautiful rolling and verdant terrain. On one of these occasions – a pleasantly warm and otherwise magnificent summer day beneath a cloudless and brilliant sky - I happened to lie down under an enormous spreading shade tree, whereupon I suddenly felt at one with my surroundings, and have never been the same since. Despite other feelings of insignificance and ineptitude, this has provided a level of serenity that has overridden most of the tribulations typically encountered as we shuffle through this mortal coil.

As a young boy, the greatest imprints upon my psyche were images of magnificent creatures tromping majestically through bucolic rain forests of Asia and Africa. The urban setting of my youth seemed like an aberration, an anemic choice of habitat for humans, whose life experiences would be so greatly enhanced were we to share the jungle with our fellow earthly inhabitants. Going to a zoo with my parents and siblings was a painful experience, as it seemed to me that perfectly innocent cousins were incarcerated for no reason other than perverse pleasures of misguided people, and whose bizarre behaviors could easily be understood with a little role reversal.

Since we humans have only the *illusion of choice*, a theme that permeates much of this discussion, it is necessary to explain how it happens that I have 'decided' to set down my thoughts for those who might someday take notice. As evolution has bestowed on *Homo sapiens* (*H. sapiens*) both outsized braininess and sexiness, at the same time it has made us masters of self-deception, so it's natural to behave as if we have the power to chart our own course, appearing to make not only day-to-day decisions, but even planning for posterity. My explanations of purpose are therefore suspect, but unfortunately there is no alternative.

Although my deep and abiding fascination with life is the impetus for attempting what is essentially a treatise on human behavior and its consequences, my personal history does not appear to lend authority to this endeavor – no educational or professional involvement in sociology or any of its derivate specializations: soldier, student, engineer, college teacher, farmer, international business consultant, (inept) basketball player[1]. In fact, rather than attempt to surreptitiously poke a foot into the domain of this esoteric discipline, I must rather confess disdain, mainly because most of its practitioners have stubbornly failed to take into account the most fundamental basis for social phenomena, our multi-million year evolutionary history.

In truth I have been a student of human behavior for over seven decades, starting from the day at age 5 when I pondered why my aunt apprehensively observed my doings while sitting on the bathroom potty of her Coney Island apartment. Subsequently, in the course of my work over seven plus decades, I have personally witnessed how behavioral patterns in most all civilized societies have resulted in despoliation of virtually every corner of this once beautiful orb.

There are multiple paths to knowledge, not only the institutional approach of formal education, a system that in many ways stultifies thinking. In my days as a teacher, engineer and manager, on many occasions I interacted with students and colleagues who defied the conventional path to understanding, who were regarded as anything from oddball to incompetent but who were, in fact, leading the pursuit of knowledge. On one occasion, while guiding a class of aspiring engineers in a two-semester foundation course, I was permitted by the college president (who recognized the potential value of unconventional learning) to accept a consulting job that would spill over into the second semester, leaving my students to fend for themselves for the first month or so. In preparation, the students and I discussed only where they 'needed to go', but without a prescribed structure for getting there. Upon my return I learned that they had met as a group during scheduled class sessions, with one or another taking the lead in discussing the topic of the day. Their 'progress' would have been awesome had I not realized that they dance best who follow their own inner rhythms.

As un-anointed social analyst for a starter, certainly the breadth of issues addressed appears presumptuous, at the very least. However, in my view there is no dimension of life that is irrelevant to the basic issue of human impact, which is determined by the pattern of behavior upon which all mutually interdependent human characteristics have a bearing. All dimensions of human life, as for any other species, are manifestations of an underlying nature honed through millions of years of evolutionary history, and which may still be in a state of flux.

From the outset I have to point out that over time a trend toward misanthropy, more distrust than hatred, has gradually ripened with life experiences, not because I am not enamored with humanity and all other life forms, but because humans have been such a disappointment. This may seem like a strange assertion considering some of the viewpoints expressed herein, specifically the notion that we humans are not in control of our destiny, either singly or as a group. In our usual state of consciousness we certainly feel that we can choose, but my contention is that this is illusory. In a created universe the assumption of human choice suggests a kind of paradox: an omnipotent creative superpower grants choice to humans; if one is human, then one is capable of affecting her destiny; then the superpower lacks omnipotence. But even if the absence of will is acknowledged, in everyday life we cling to the delusion that what we think or do is a matter of choice, a delusion that makes life in a sense livable. Were it otherwise, many of us would be inclined to give up any pretense of making the world a better place, and either focus on self-aggrandizement or simply accept our fate.

It is a strange position to be a traitor to one's species. But to this I must admit. The despicable behavior of humans toward their fellow travelers on Planet Earth is at the root of my misanthropy. What would we think of a passenger on a train who hogged all the seats, imposed his obnoxious ways on the others aboard, and in the end dispatched to oblivion a good number of them for pure enjoyment?

An outgrowth of our complexity is that we are not one-dimensional. We exist at many levels, sometimes at the peak of the mountain and at other times in the vale of tears. So it isn't possible to continually survey the human scene as if we are in a gigantic zoo. But I must say that at times as I walk the streets of a city, not only the emperor loses his clothes, but everyone in sight, and movements and gestures of the passing gallery take on the aspect of a primatorium.

For anyone who cares to notice, humanity has inflicted great harm to our planet and to the many species that have accompanied us on this journey through the eons. We can tinker with possible solutions – environmental awareness, acknowledging sustainable capacities of Earth, appreciating the value of other forms of life - but so long as we remain the same kind of animal the outcome will likely not change very much. Our patterns of behavior are too well ingrained, reinforced by the notion that we can fix whatever we break so long as we have the will. What is needed instead is something transcendental, ascendency to a completely new plane of understanding about what makes us tick.

Here in the twilight of my life, I can only hope, as part of this process, to shed some light on the hazardous path that humanity has taken, and, in some small measure, to influence corrective adjustments. This may likewise be delusional, but it may be an early inkling of the kind of alteration in human consciousness that may bode well for the future of life.

What follows, then, is merely a minor manifestation of a chain of cosmic forces extending from time immemorial. As Omar Khayyam so aptly expressed the phenomenon in 1120 A.C.E. (Quattrain 71)[2]:

The Moving Finger writes, and having writ,
Moves on: nor all your Piety nor Wit
Shall lure it back to cancel half a line,
Nor all your tears wash out a Word of it.

According to the gospel of Luke (23, King James version). Jesus utters on the cross "Father, forgive them, for *they know not what they do* (italics added)." Nothing more aptly describes humankind as unwitting instrument of nature, created and directed by forces beyond the control of any living organism.

But we are so accustomed to functioning as if we have some say in the matter, that it seems essential for communication to slip over occasionally into the vernacular, or common parlance, predicated on the view of ourselves as thinking and deciding independent agents. If you 'choose' to listen, I beg your indulgence for one who really can't help himself.

Chapter 1

INTRODUCTION

Every one of us has exactly two parents. We probably have four grandparents, but not necessarily - in fact, we could have only one maternal and one paternal grandparent if our parents brought us into this world incestuously.

If we assume the normal pattern of parenthood, five generations back we would have 32 ancestors. Go back 10 generations and there would have been 1,032. Fifteen generations ago our ancestry, numbering 32,728, would have trouble finding seats in a modern sports arena. Beyond this our parentage begins to assume the proportions of the modern industrialized state - 33 ½ million at 25 generations. At 50 generations, approximately a millennium, the numbers approach the astronomical at a little more than 1,000 trillion!

Modern humans have a history of about two hundred thousand years (about 4000- 8000 generations). It is clear that the assumption of two distinct parents for each ancestor of anyone alive at this juncture and doubling the number of progenitors in each generation backward in time is patently untenable. In fact, there were only about 100 million humans in the year 1,000 A.D.

Over the span of modern human history there obviously has been a great deal of mixing and matching. How closely any two of us alive today are related can only be approximated, using the currently available state of the genetic arts. Considering the intermingling brought about by war, migrations, pilgrimages and the like, for all but the most isolated human populations, each of us is of uncertain parentage beyond a relatively minor span of history. We stand on the shoulders, or under the foot, of our ancestors, the great preponderance completely unknown. The amalgam of genetic and cultural strains, of which each of us is comprised, is beyond conventional analysis.[3] Recent experience tells only a very small part of the story and is woefully incomplete at best, and in fact can be highly misleading. Any inferences drawn from analysis of behavior in a current social milieu fails to take into account the great river of history that resides in each of us. As Scottish biologist Richard Dawkins points out (River Out of Eden), we are all progeny of an unbroken string of survivors, those who had what it took in their respective eras to stay alive at least to the point of producing offspring. In another work (The Selfish Gene) Dawkins explains the relevance of kinship to what is commonly considered altruistic behavior, which compels us to think about the potential benefits of spreading knowledge about human relationships to the minds of every child in the world.

Steve Olson (2002) explains how race and other categorization of human populations tend to overstate divisions among us. We are much closer genetically than meets the eye. For example, he points out that every one of European origin living today had at least one common ancestor within the last few thousand years. If altruism were linked to kinship, one would anticipate far less strife among national and ethnic groups. The fact that we are more militant and contentious than might be expected is, to say the least, a disappointment.

For these reasons it seems inappropriate to analyze one's personal history. What can be learned in this way, when knowledge of such a large proportion of the underlying behavioral influences is lost forever? The 'choice' is rather to reveal impressions of human existence, for what they are worth, and little of the life experiences from which they were gleaned. This may appear presumptuous, but we all are inclined to have others see the world from our perspective, even though we do not fully understand it. There is no help for this - atavistic forces are at play.

We are limited by our own experience of birth and death to insist that there is a beginning and an end. But suppose that there isn't any *isn't*, that there is only what *is*. Then what nature provides may be the only game in the universe, which, despite all our attempts to intervene, to the contrary goes on its merry way without being constrained by our limited perceptions. 'God' may have created and may even be controlling things out there, but our rational faculties do not lead us inevitably to its existence.

The delicious part of this mélange is that our fate is not sealed, despite our inability to do anything about it. Nature plays her tricks with the billiard balls of life (see Chapter 3 *A Matter of Choice*), games of chance that obviate predictions about how they will respond to physical and 'emotional' interactions. For the observer this is the only interesting part of the panorama. This is what makes immersion in the currents of life a worthwhile endeavor.

There seems little doubt that humankind has now reached a state in which its numbers and consumption patterns have remarkably altered its habitat, comprised of virtually every corner of Planet Earth. Pundits have warned that humankind is in imminent danger of extinction. In fact, the rate of extinction of other species is now greater, from all evidence, than it has been since the disappearance of the dinosaurs 60 million years ago. There is little doubt that the culprit is humankind. Mass extinctions in the past have been associated with cataclysmic environmental events. This is probably the first instance of such extinctions resulting from the lifestyle of one of Earth's inhabitants, and there is little doubt that these other species are so many 'canaries in the mineshaft', harbingers of what is in store for humanity itself.

Something has happened to the feedback loop. Normal instincts of self-preservation, even in the absence of will, would be expected to precipitate individual countermeasures to avoid catastrophe, which would be reflected in the collective response. But knowledge about symptoms of imminent danger such as urban mayhem, children murdering children, alienated people reeking of hatred and seeking to inflict violence, even hysteria in music and other art forms, do not appear to register or elicit any serious response that would tend to alleviate them. We have 'selected' a path that we know to be wrong, but continue its traverse because we are powerless to correct, driven by forces stronger than rationality. The culprit is a form of dual personality disorder, epitomized by the words of *Pogo*, Walt Kelly's[4] comic strip character: "We have met the enemy and he is us!"

A reading of any period in the annals of humankind reveals the same litany of wanton disregard for the health and welfare of others, whether of kindred beings or those other species whose presence completes the tapestry of life that billions of years of evolutionary honing have produced. And yet there is more. It is not sufficient to destroy those whose extermination either materially or symbolically furthers the quest for power and possession, but there is all too prevalent in the record instances of a diabolical step beyond, a sadistic streak that seeks to inflict pain for the sheer pleasure of witnessing its effects.

What makes humans unique as a species is at the same time its badge of dishonor. Most characteristics are shared to some degree by other species, bipedal primate cousins and birds, stereoscopic vision of many mammals. Consciousness of self, on the other hand, fashioned over the eons by natural forces as surely as the neck of the giraffe or the appendages of the octopus is, in humans, quantum leaps beyond that of any other species. This characteristic not only magnifies for the individual its own significance, but also provides a channel for imposing one's will on others through psychological devices from simple rejection to the use of terror. Pain experienced existentially and images displaced in time heighten the impact of both physical and emotional assaults, providing for the power-seeker a very effective mechanism of dominance. In many instances potentially subservient beings are destroyed in the process, but there are others to fill the gap and whose servility will be more assured by the fate of those destroyed.

A review of recent human history provides many examples of the use of terror for the purpose of dominance. Any place we start is like coming in at the middle of the movie. Annihilation of native Americans in the 19th century by the military and vigilantes; the enslavement and cultural destruction of Africans from the 17th to the 20th centuries; the holocaust in Europe of WWII; Vietnam, the Balkans, Rwanda, Barundi, Sierra Leone, Mexico. It is only necessary to mention the sites of such atrocities – modern media are proficient at disseminating the gory details to every corner of the globe.

No, it is not easy to love humans. On the other hand, it is quite easy to find us despicable, both individually and collectively. The inclination of the individual to go beyond mere dominance, to inflict pain and suffering gratuitously or as a means of gaining and perpetuating advantage, is all too prevalent. As if the exercise of dominance is not sufficient, a lasting reminder is needed to indelibly imprint the subjugated with the desired degree of subservience. The hapless participants in this ancient dance play their parts faithfully, like well-seasoned veterans of a long-running theatrical tragedy.

The truth is that it is all beyond our "poor power to add or to detract". We live under a grand illusion of independence from natural forces, exacerbated in western industrialized countries by a material cocoon, woven with the threads of exhaustible capital resources whose limits we deny. We do what we do what we do, deluding ourselves that we could do otherwise under the circumstances.

Are we to blame for our shortcomings? There is the fundamental issue of the motive force behind what our rational capacities tell us is out there. There seems to be order in the universe, as far as we can tell, some rules for nature's behavior that are immutable. For example there is conservation of energy, the Uncertainty Principle, relativistic time dilation and the like. At first glance it looks as if there is some structure to the universe that, from our perspective of cause and effect, demands acknowledgement of a prime mover or designer. Why, for example, are there neat mathematical forms that so precisely describe the behavior of physical processes? Why are there inverse square laws with a perfect '2' for the power of distance?

The apparent order in the universe coupled with our propensity for mysticism tells us that (a) there must be a creator for what apparently exists, who is (b) omniscient and (c) omnipotent. Over the course of time, the creative force loosened the reins to attribute choice to humans, a gambit that provides a framework for clever exploiters to expand political influence: choice allows for good and evil thoughts and deeds, with gods and their earthly interlocutors ready and willing to accordingly praise or condemn, and with monumental consequences. Who could more effectively gain our attention and allegiance than those whose judgments conduce to eternal Eden or Hell?

Is humanity approaching a dead end? Is evolution over?

The evolutionary process of beneficial genetic modification conferring selective advantage may be either arrested or at least attenuated as human culture has progressively intruded, and integrated with, the physical side of nature, imposing survival influences such as legal and moral codes (e.g. operational ethics and religious strictures), social safety nets and other public programs that result in survival outcomes for humanity different from what nature 'red in tooth and claw' alone would produce. Our cultural and genetic trajectories are too interdependent to be considered in isolation.

An evolutionary process that depends solely on genetic variation will not determine the future of humanity. Culture has become such an intrinsic dimension of the human organism that its effects on behavior can't be discounted. Traits that unite us are much greater than those that divide us. Civilization itself is a cultural phenomenon that has now permeated the most remote segments of human society; differentiating cultural traits are only skin deep, in some cases literally.

Feedback, not only in the form of mere survival, may yet have its effects in altering the nature of humanity to a more sustainable path, even though it may well be true that we are not in control. Since cultural modifications often spread like wildfire, in sharp contrast to the sluggish pace of physical evolution, we may yet see humanity transmuted into a species at one with its environment, in harmony with nature and all of her mysterious inclinations, and before we would otherwise consign ourselves, and our planetary wards, to oblivion.

In fact, we have witnessed time and again how culture has engendered redeeming qualities that militate against total condemnation and loss of hope. Too many individuals have been acculturated to transcend narrow parochialism and to act magnanimously and heroically, even to the extent of sacrificing their lives for ideals - heroes made, and not born.[5] There are undoubtedly legions unsung, which have brightened the landscape over the millennia. During the World Wars of the 20th century the prevailing sentiment of Americans who answered the call to military service was predominantly to save the world for democracy.[6] Women and men were inspired to put their very existence on the line for a principle – abhorrence of totalitarianism – and suffered over a million casualties.[7] In the 1960's many Americans rose to challenge apartheid, facing physical danger and death in the cause of promoting equal opportunity for their fellow citizens. If only this were the norm!

The issue of man's place in nature - the capacity to choose, i.e. free will as the central characteristic that separates man from beast - has been pondered by many philosophers of the past few centuries. Almost invariably the conclusion is that a human being does have the capacity to chart one's own course, to opt for the 'road not taken' for example.[8]

Recent researches on motivations for human behavior increasingly attribute actions and attitudes to conditions in the brain and other parts of the body that are described in biochemical and biophysical terms, in other words, following natural imperatives. There does appear to be some reticence by the 'scientific' community to cross the line by acknowledging that there may be some justification for asserting that all human behavior, as well as that of all other organisms, is strictly determined by forces that channel interactions between matter and energy. Why this is so would be puzzling, were it not for the realization that they are merely acting out their destinies under the influence of the very phenomena that they relegate to irrelevance. 'Scientists' are conditioned to follow a code of conduct that rejects metaphysical speculation and insists upon adhering to the code's rigorous methods involving hypotheses and experimentation. The question of human control is not only too large, but also too hot to handle.

What settled the issue for me was Desmond Morris' *The Naked Ape*, published in the 1960's, which presented humanity as nothing more (or less) than a primate in clothing. Although he refrained, from modesty and sensitivity, to bind humanity inescapably to its animal roots, he made it clear through clinical analysis that there is no reason to suppose that we humans have transcended our natural underpinnings.

Why assign to humans the epithet 'Cosmic Cancer'? So long as we 'choose' to restrict our presence to our mother planet and the stratosphere, though we may continue on our path of excess and violence, the impact is negligible in the unimaginably vast reaches of space. Now we have not only undertaken missions to the other planets of our solar system, but some space probes have already penetrated into the reaches beyond. Space flight has become a commercial venture: scientists and adventurers see the planets and galaxies as the new frontier to be conquered, oblivious of the devastation we have wrought on our own planet, perceiving no harm in extending it to whatever bodies in the cosmos might have the misfortune to encounter us as guests or even settlers.

The proposal that humanity has cancerous behavioral characteristics is not original, although conceived independently. Dr. Alan Gregg (1955), presented a clinical analysis of the explosion of human population as analogous to metastasis, preempting my claim to discovery, although at that time he focused upon what was occurring on our own planet:

"...I suggest, as a way at looking at the population problem, that

there are some interesting analogies between the growth of human population of the world and the increase of cells observable in neoplasm (cancer). To say that the world has cancer, and that the cancer cell is man, has neither experimental proof nor the validation of predictive accuracy; but I see no reason that instantly forbids such a speculation......
What are the characteristics of new growths? ...they exert pressure on adjacent structures...within closed cavities (they) exert pressure that can kill, because any considerable displacement is impossible. ... Metastasis ...describe(s) another phenomenon of malignant growth in which detached neoplastic cells ...lodge at a distance from the primary focus or point of origin and proceed to multiply without direct contact with the tissue or organ from which they came. It is actually difficult to avoid using the word *colony* in describing this thing that physicians call metastasis."

James Lovelock (British atmospheric chemist) postulated the Gaia hypothesis (Lovelock 2000), that Earth is a single, self-regulating, living organism. Earth's internal management system, in a manner suggestive of homeostasis in humans, regulates interactions of biota and biosphere with Earth's other physical elements (land, seas and atmosphere), with the capacity to maintain conditions supportive to all of life. His concept is supported by knowledge about life's origins, apparently a singular event about 4 billion years ago, shortly after Earth's formation, in which self-replicating molecules developed in the primordial mix of organic material in water. For billions of years these simple organisms were the only life forms, until environmental conditions propitiated the formation and replication of the first pre-cellular DNA (deoxyribonucleic acid), which gradually evolved into single, self-replicating cells that derived sustenance from its ocean surroundings. Gradually, over millions of years, the string of genetic coding increased in complexity and length, providing for the production of nutrients from basic materials and replication of cells with multiple forms and functions.

All of the resultant life forms, except for bacteria, share the same fundamental structure, chemistry and building blocks. Andrew Knoll (2004), Professor of Natural History and Earth and Planetary Sciences at Harvard University: "It's pretty clear that all the organisms living today, even the simplest ones, are removed from some initial life form by four billion years or so, …the first… much simpler than anything that we see around us. But they must have had that fundamental property of being able to grow and reproduce and be subject to Darwinian evolution." Plants and animals are comprised of eukaryotic cells having a nucleus that allow for the production of multicellular organisms. Our cousins, the bacteria, have prokaryotic cells without a nucleus, and are therefore 'condemned' to a relatively simple life, although the symbiosis between the two is essential for continuation of life as we know it.

As a component of Gaia, humanity would do well to observe its own responsibility to self-regulate. But the truth is that we do not observe the 'rules', and have created problems for ourselves and for the rest of life. Humanity appears to be an element of the system out of control, much like cancerous metastasis. As a consequence of our special natural endowment, we have the propensity to procreate beyond sustainable bounds, to expand numerically to the point that in order to maintain our accustomed mode of existence we attempt to seize the space and resources of other communities; in some cases we send our excess population packing so that they are not only someone else's problem, but also that their expansion in that remote setting does not adversely impact upon our standard of living. The solution is before our noses, but unrecognized or otherwise dismissed: that is to adjust our fecundity to the available resources so that the standard of living is not only maintained, but also has the opportunity for non-materialistic advancement.

Attempting to intervene in nature's inexorable but uncertain trajectory while, at the same time, acknowledging that none of us has any say in the matter is a fundamental paradox, something like being condemned to a life sentence behind bars without the possibility of parole but continuing to dream and plan what we will do when released. Nature plays the cards that it has dealt to all of us who share the vast majority of the human genome, and to every other particle of matter/energy in the cosmos. Part of our hand is the illusion of control. The paradox is perhaps akin to what Lewis Carroll had in mind as he created *Through the Looking Glass* in 1872, as Alice climbs through the mirror over the mantel and then becomes privy to what lies beyond her ordinary consciousness.

We are faced with our irremediable condition and its behavioral consequences. The former is covered in Part I, and includes an exposition on choice (Chapter 2), of which the absence is the fundamental human condition. The attendant inclination to blame and praise almost certainly dooms humanity to an early demise, as nature exacts its penalty arising from widespread employment of this ruse to gain control of others. Chapter 3 is a review of inordinate growth in human population, already far beyond numbers that can comfortably be accommodated by the sustainable capacity of the one planet available to the vast majority of humans living now and, more than likely, in the future. Population growth is not strictly an imperative, and yet is so fundamentally a conditioned response to nature's prodding that it is treated as part of the foundation for humanity's behavioral repertoire.

Part II deals with selected behavioral features intended to illustrate and to seek solutions to these salient, but by no means all-inclusive, imperfections in the human constitution – our collective predilection to almost invariably do the wrong things - with unfortunate, if not fatal, consequences. The principle criterion for selecting behavioral patterns for scrutiny is their impact on prospects for the continuation of life on Earth. It may appear at first as an eclectic array of topics, but they are unified by their indubitable interrelatedness as contributors to the mayhem that humanity has spawned and by their potential for accelerating the demise of our species and other innocent bystanders. The failure to cherish and to properly nurture our youth is a universal characteristic, doting mothers notwithstanding, virtually assuring a buildup of ignorance and hostility in future generations (Chapter 4). A derivative effect of political machination is the endorsement of rights of potentially devoted followers, rather than inculcation of responsibilities, thus setting faction against faction in proclaiming their due perquisites, and furthering social disharmony and ultimate disintegration (Chapter 5). Civilization has destabilized sexual expression through codes and standards that have little bearing on maintaining social order, resulting in rampant sexual abuse on a global scale. Media moguls have channeled the sex drive into a force to generate profits, with attendant aberrations and resultant social tensions (Chapter 6). Religionists and politicians have learned and conspired to inject large doses of mysticism into the affairs of an already excessively prone species, greatly impeding social maturation (Chapter 7). The pursuit of knowledge has been largely relegated to specialists whose primary identity is 'scientist' rather than member of society, and who peer with laser-like intensity at ever subdividing areas with little concern for larger consequences, a type of myopia that will shortly, barring a perceptual transformation, complete the great job it has been doing in despoiling Earth (Chapter 8).

There are many other issues that could be fruitfully scrutinized in this fashion – one obvious candidate is the proclivity of humans to wage war to the death, rather than settling differences with less draconian methods. Confrontations between most animal adversaries are settled with displays of one sort or another and rarely lead to death or dismemberment. Humans tend to take confrontation over the brink, undoubtedly the outcome of frailties already identified, at root an outsized self-consciousness. Whether in one-on-one or in collective confrontation, scenarios depicting circumstances and events from biased to highly imaginative perspectives take over, in which perceived threats easily assume unacceptable proportions. In collective settings a scenario that serves the interests of a charismatic leader is often propagated, mutually reinforced in the collective frenzy so that it permeates the marrow of each and every member. This is how genes overcome prudence, whereby the emotional response trumps rationality.

Patterns of human behavior, honed during eons of physical and cultural evolution, are wreaking havoc on our planet.[9] As a component of the biosphere, *H. sapiens* plays out its role as nature dictates, in its current form with disastrous consequences. All of our interconnected behavioral elements are derived from the strategic plan devised by nature for the individual organism interacting with its external environment – most shared by all people throughout the world. How these inclinations are manifested is variable in ways that are significant for the future of life. Modifications are necessary if there is to be a semblance of decent life for posterity, which can come about with greater understanding of the roots of behavior and their consequences. The primary need is for enhanced depth perception, greater concern for the far-reaching consequences of individual and collective attitudes and actions. The topics examined herein are examples of where we have gone astray, the first step toward developing a more wholesome behavioral repertoire.

Part III (Chapter 9) is an attempt to assess the outlook for humanity and for all of life on Earth. Our condition, nature's essentially immutable bequest (within a critical timeframe), is related to the likelihood of fortuitous behavioral changes and their consequences.

PART I
THE HUMAN CONDITION

Chapter 2
A MATTER OF CHOICE

Most of the time, as we wend our way through life, events seem to follow a logical pattern. If it rains, we get wet; if the sun is shining, it is a warm summer day and there are no immediate household impediments, we may decide to go to the beach. If the number one team in the league is playing against number ten, almost certainly number one emerges victorious.

Occasionally events take an unexpected turn. Although there are showers in the area, a patch of clear sky follows us overhead, so all but we are drenched. Conditions are perfect for a sojourn at the seashore, but we decide to read a book. The number ten team annihilates number one.

Would the unexpected outcome be explained if we only knew all of the antecedent conditions and circumstances? Are we really free to choose, and if we cannot, is the future foreordained?

Although these questions have been debated for millennia, it is very likely that choice is an illusion, and also that its contraposition with determinism is a false dichotomy, i.e. absence of free will does not imply a predetermined future (these contentions are supported empirically and through reason, as will presently be explained). There is too much indeterminacy built into the natural world of which humans are a part for our future to be cast in stone individually or collectively. The same uncertainties affecting human life apply to all matter and energy of which all things are comprised. Although no organism is in control of its destiny, neither is that destiny foreordained. The 'choice' is not between strict determinism and free will. Even if all uncertainties arising from antecedent events could be resolved by greater observational and reasoning power by humans (or perhaps some other species), the behavior of any organism at a given time and place is essentially unpredictable within certain ranges. Indeterminacy remains and, as far as we know, is a fundamental characteristic of nature, and concomitantly, all that exists.

Granted the proposition that choice is illusionary may be wrong, but it has the potential to vastly improve the landscape on Earth. If we would face this condition head on, it would lead to a number of healthy developments. For one thing, we would function with humility rather than pomposity, and perhaps forever relinquish claim to hegemony over other forms of life that has been so destructive of our fellow Earth-mates and the planet in general. Secondly, we would discontinue the practice of blaming and praising, devices intended, in our uninformed state, to coerce vulnerable souls to do our bidding, and acknowledge that no one can fundamentally be held accountable for anything. We would be more prone to respond objectively to threats, without absolving anyone of the responsibility to do the right thing. Menaces to society could be dealt with, even in rather harsh ways, not from malice, hatred or vengeance, but to allow for orderly societal functioning and progress.

Choice

In a chapter *Free Will* of his recent work *13 Things that Don't Make Sense*, author and physicist Michael Brooks (2008), describes investigations of neuroscientists concerning the effects of electromagnetic brain stimulation on motor responses of subjects. In the 1990's Itzhak Fried, a neurosurgeon at Yale University School of Medicine was able to elicit motor responses in epileptic patients by stimulating brain sites with electric charges. Responses at certain sites were first sensed as 'urges' at low stimulation followed by action with greater stimulation. Patrick Haggard, professor at University College, London's Institute of Neurological Sciences, has done similar experiments, convincing him that "...there is no such thing as free will" since these studies seem to link actions with physical brain phenomena.

Psychologist Steven Pinker believes that "free will is a fictional construction, but it has applications in the real world." In other words, the supposition (and fear) is that general dissemination of this knowledge could jeopardize our entire social structure, built upon the idea of individual responsibility, and that it would lead to dismantling our legal and cultural frameworks. In a Time Magazine article (Jan. 29, 2007) Dr. Pinker, Johnstone Professor of Psychology at Harvard University, discusses the origin of consciousness. He alludes to behavioral links with areas in the gray matter of the human brain, leading to his speculation on the identity of mind and matter. He asserts that recent studies indicate behavior predicated on evolved physical processes, that all of our thoughts and actions are manifestations of material events in the brain. Consciousness must have evolved in the same manner as any other feature of an organism, and made of the same stuff. "For many non-scientists this is a terrifying prospect. Not only does it strangle the hope that we might survive the death of our bodies, but it also seems to *undermine the notion that we are free agents responsible for our choices* (italics added) - not just in this lifetime, but in a life to come." Popular media do not often deal with such esoteric subjects, particularly when the conclusions could shake some of our most fundamental ideas and beliefs.

Aside from those with dubious claims of extrasensory perception, most of us, like Missourians, want to be shown. All we are sure of is what we are *told* by our senses. Our sensory apparatus receives physical information, which is processed by organs and their components obeying the laws of nature. However, not only our sensory apparatus is subject to its own physical variability, but also the information it receives is transmitted across a nebulous void. The human body (and every other physical entity) never actually touches anything. Our cells, as those of any other physical object, are comprised of molecules and atoms, each of which is surrounded by orbiting electrons of uncertain physical nature expressed more accurately as waves rather than physical entities. The laws of physics preclude two electrons in precisely the same location. Forces of repulsion would rise to the infinite if the distance between any two reduced to zero. So physical contact is impossible. For other sensory impressions we rely on intermediaries. Sound, for example, is a complex of pressure waves processed mechanically by the tympanic membrane (eardrum), which activates a mechanical linkage that signals the auditory nerve, which in turn sends chemical and electronic pulses to the brain. Whatever humankind has discovered for itself from observation is physical in nature. Metaphysical perceptions only arise, so far as we know, from the peculiar characteristics of humans acquired through long history of evolutionary development.

Philosophical underpinnings of free will

Philosophers from the ancient Greeks to recent times have pondered the existence of free will. Through the 20th century, before revelations concerning the composition of the genome and discoveries of neuroscience, almost invariably philosophers ultimately came down of the side of man, in some measure, apart from nature.

Hegel traces human consciousness through its evolutionary stages, and at some point proclaims the existence of free will. Mind is regarded as the goal of nature; whatever is in nature is manifested in a higher form in the mind that derives from nature. But once precipitated in its processes, mind rises above the limitations of nature and becomes free to exercise itself through art, religion, and philosophy, and to create its own reality. Kowalski (2004):"It is in virtue of being a 'free will', a being who is 'for itself', that a person gains consciousness of his duty to self to endow his free will, with external concrete determination such that it can realize individual freedom."

Kant also postulates morality predicated on the existence of an autonomous free will, from which moral action derives and which is universal among humans as an outgrowth of our commonly shared rational faculties. Rummel (1975): "For Kant, freedom is an independence of the will of motivations, character, and external causes. It is more than just the power to choose. Freedom is the power to fulfill our moral oughts (ought implies can), to will as reason directs, to be a first cause of events."

David Hume (1993) combines liberty with causality deriving from natural imperative. He posits two types of liberty, the power to act or not act according to determinations of the will. One is 'hypothetical', which is thought to be a characteristic of everyone who is not otherwise constrained (e.g. incarcerated). Another type is 'liberty of spontaneity', which a person may enjoy but still be denied 'hypothetical liberty'. You may decide to attend the opera, but you may not have the price of a ticket.

John Locke, in 'An Essay Concerning Human Understanding' of the 17th century, proposed the *tabula rasa* or blank slate theory for human development, in which the rules for acquiring and interpreting information are derived from sensory experience. The mind, character and soul are thereby free and self-defined under the constraints of an immutable human nature. Sigmund Freud also alludes to the concept of *tabula rasa* in his psychoanalysis, where environmental history plays the major role in the development of personality and character. In *Three Essays on Sexuality* (1915), Freud outlines the stages in child development (oral, anal, phallic, latency period, and genital), each responding to libidinal urgings that largely determine the adult personality.

The existence or absence of choice has politico-religious implications. Paul, the disciple of Jesus, parlayed the ancient idea of free will into a formula for expanding the reaches of Christendom. His appeal was to co-opt the minds of those whose sufferings could be relieved only by willfully accepting Jesus as the savior of mankind and following his precepts. There could be no promise of heaven against the threat of everlasting hell if one did not have choice. " Thou comest not to the father but by me". Accept my word or suffer the consequences. It is well within your powers.

Charles Darwin believed that heredity and environment *together* determine all feelings, thoughts and actions. Although some philosophers argue for 'soft' determinism – a notion of freedom somehow compatible with unbridled cause and effect - in one of his notebooks Darwin confessed that "one doubts [the] existence of free will" and concluded that humans deserve neither credit nor blame for their actions. Viorst (1998) points to tacit acknowledgement of his material perspective on humanity: "Thought, however unintelligible it may be, seems as much function of organ, as bile of liver. This view should teach one profound humility; one deserves no credit for anything. Nor ought one to blame others."

On the other hand, proponents of the 'existentialist' philosophical movement[10], whose central theme is the uniqueness of the individual, postulate that a human being is free to define herself. The existentialist Paul Sartre (*Existentialism is a Humanism*): "man first of all exists, encounters himself, surges up in the world – and defines himself afterwards." One can choose her course of action, e.g. to be magnanimous rather than cruel, but one is not thereby defined.

It is axiomatic that you can't build a solid house on a shaky foundation. Philosophers through the 19th century had only little awareness of the evolution of human development, DNA or links between physical, chemical and biological processes in the body and behavior. They otherwise might have been less prone to think of humanity as somehow insulated, and even isolated from nature.

Do we really need science and inconsistencies in politico-religious dogma (Chapter 7) to tell us that the will is not free? How could it be otherwise? Life for humans is a process begun with a sexual encounter that, even if willfully undertaken by its collaborators, certainly could not, in the wildest of our imaginings, have involved the willfulness of the zygote produced. Does a child decide to be born? Even granting the infusion of will from the time of conception, certainly the mere fact that the all-important choice - to be or not to be – is denied by definition to any living being countervails against the significance of choice in the course of a human life. Even the Buddha's concept of reincarnation does not attribute rebirth to the will of the unborn.

What we call *choice* is the behavioral response of an individual to her external environment. For such a complex organism, the environment is both immediate and remote. The immediate environment is everything within range of the senses, including what is available through the appurtenances of modern technology. The remote environment consists of the range of images and scenarios derived from knowledge, experience, conjecture – in short, all of the conceptual mechanisms within the human mental arsenal.

The compactness of that great human invention, mathematics, can be called upon to succinctly express the idea that behavior follows from a virtually infinite stream of antecedents that brings the organism to its present state, upon which its response to an external stimulus is completely dependent (for those not mathematically inclined, the next four paragraphs may be skipped without missing a beat; they are simply an imperative arising from the author's own history).

So differential behavior (the instantaneous response to a stimulus) might (audaciously) be expressed in the following mathematical form:

$$\frac{dB}{dt} = \Psi(g, \Delta g, e, s)$$

dB	differential behavior, or instantaneous response
dt	time differential
g	genetic endowment
Δg	genetic mutations during lifetime of organism
e	environmental, or experiential history
s	spiritual bequest
ψ	stochastic (probabilistic) function

This equation expresses the relationship between instantaneous change in behavior of an organism over time, as a function of genetic endowment, environmental or experiential history, genetic mutations that occur within the cells of the living entity, and perhaps a spiritual[11] bequest. It allows that whatever spiritual qualities are conferred upon the individual may be transformed by subsequent experience or adjusted according to nature's program.[12] It should also be noted that the relationship is stochastic[13] or random, the main source of uncertainty residing in the quantum mechanical character of nature as discussed below.

The character of an organism, at an instant of time, is a product of the cumulative effects of the above factors. The equation states that, in the same sense that "we are what we eat", we are what we have accumulated as a consequence of the program established by our genetic makeup, genetic mutations within specific body cells that may affect behavior, the sum of our experiences in the world outside the limits of our own physical being and perhaps a spiritual component that provides some moral (or immoral) foundation for behavior.

Behavior of an organism is considered a continuum, comprised of differential elements that only in the macroscopic scale of time reveal a pattern that we can discern. It may well be that macroscopic responses are, in fact, more discrete in their elementary nature, perhaps packaged in 'quanta' that determine minimal neural response intervals. It can be argued that triggering of synapses, which control neural functions, is inherently digital in nature[14]. It is also possible that only a finite sequence of neural operations constitute a meaningful experience, which thereafter comprises an incremental effect of an organism's environmental history. In either case, the response to a stimulus is essentially instantaneous, and subsequent response elements are conditioned by all previous differential behaviors, with feedback further conditioning the elements suggested in the above function.

Consider a newly born human infant. It has a genetic endowment, and some limited experiential history in the womb. Piaget[15] and others tell us that the character of a child is substantially formed at a very early age by the nature of its surroundings, and before there is any chance of having an influence on those surroundings. Neither was the child's genetic makeup of her own choosing. So the factors that formed the child's character were essentially beyond its control.

So far as we know, the infant had no parental choice, maternal or paternal. The external environment certainly is not under the control of so helpless a creature. Whether or not it is yet the recipient of some spiritual bequest is uncertain - even if so, it is not of its own doing. So, none of the factors upon which its response (or choice) is predicated is under its control. At this point it is probably not very controversial to assert that free choice is not an option for a newborn infant.

In a subsequent instant, not long after the first, the infant remains a product of its history. This is an inescapable fact, even into adulthood. Every differential behavior evokes its own external responses, which form part of the organism's external history. There is a virtually continuous interaction between the physical organism and its external environment, so that at any instant of time none of the factors that could influence behavior are under its control. Neither the older child, nor the adult that carries the same historical baggage, is completely free to choose its course of action.

At any instant of time, the organism exists, molded only by its endowment and its history. The history invariably involves phenomena with elements of randomness, so that up to the instant of exposure to a stimulus its nature is fundamentally indeterminate; its environment is similarly affected by randomness. This is what makes life, as we perceive it, interesting. If we had evolved in a deterministic universe we might be automatons, with immutable models wired into our brains rather than what passes for reasoning.[16]

But analysis of differential behavior is not necessary to confirm the absence of choice or free will in humans or in any other living organism. Derived from natural forces as any other animal, our rational faculties don't lead us to the existence of choice, nor can we rely on our inherently suspect mystical visions. Considering the mayhem inflicted on the rest of life by this most dangerous creature ever to walk the Earth, only a malevolent god could have conferred such a property on humans, a possibility that is anathema to believers.

What should be comforting is at once a source of unease if not terror. What demonic forces will be unleashed if no one is responsible for anything, even the most heinous crime? Religionists and sociologists are terrified that if the word gets out, a species totally unprepared for its consequences could easily run amok. What mayhem would result if unrepressed masses got the notion that they can't, or at least shouldn't, be held responsible for anything?

Intuition tells us that we can calmly accept this information without panic (although not without a program for a change in our priorities). If a child is caged an early age, abused continually and deprived of all that children need to grow up secure, sane and otherwise healthy, it's clear that barbarous acts committed by such a person could not be held against her. On the other hand, a person reared with all the support elements necessary to allow for identity with, and full participation in, her social milieu would be most unlikely to commit antisocial acts (but is similarly undeserving of praise or blame).

We can live contentedly in the knowledge that we are devoid of free will while pursuing our everyday lives as if we did. At the same time, we are likely to be, in a sense, more compassionate knowing that no one is really responsible for bad behavior. We can punish, and even commit miscreants to the most severe penalties under extreme conditions, but with understanding and never with malice or hate. If we are able to adopt as our goal enlightenment of populations around the world, this can be a liberating process. The more people are disabused of their mythical notions the more likely it is that rational processes will lead us to a better way of life. Man does not live by bread alone. We are multidimensional and so can live in the day-to-day world while at the same time being acutely conscious of our inescapable identity with nature.

Spirit

The spiritual quality is defined as a moral foundation divinely conferred, from which the individual can choose among behavioral options. This 'spirit' has to be differentiated from the inexorable spirit (the 'libido' or life force) that resides in every organism. For this reason, the term 'élan' (or 'élan vital' – a term first used by philosopher Henri Bergson in 1907) is used to signify the latter, and is further discussed in Chapter 7. Each of these must be distinguished from 'soul', an ethereal entity in which the spirit purportedly resides and which succeeds the material body after death (see Chapter 7 *Ensoulment*).

However, if an omnipotent force exists, either it has the power to direct the future of everything, and free will (choice) does not exist – so that the spirit is superfluous – or it confers the power of choice upon its creations and thus relinquishes omnipotence. In the latter case there is the possibility that choice is granted incrementally, either as new organisms appear or as they mature, so that in each exercise only a portion of omnipotence is relinquished. In either case, the capacity of the omnipotent force both to set behavioral benchmarks and to exact retribution for transgressors seems logically inconsistent, i.e. lack of omnipotence would appear to nullify the capacity to exact retribution.

If human morality, the aspect of our spiritual characteristic that purportedly causes us to behave altruistically rather than exploitatively, is the essential quality that separates man from beast, it is interesting to speculate concerning the precise point in human evolution that such a quality was conferred.

Whether the nature of the evolutionary process is continuous or punctuated, there is general agreement that reproductive success of a trait introduced by genetic mixing or mutation is the basic mechanism. Could the spirit have evolved under the guiding hand of a creative force? Paleontology tells us that we derive from very simple organisms whose behavior could only be instinctive, responding to external stimuli as determined only by their genetic endowment. Speciation is generally attributed to physical isolation of a segment of a population that changes genetically to the point that fertile breeding between the original and isolated population is no longer possible. The omnipotent force (or the choice-conferring creator) would have had a very difficult time deciding at what point in the evolution or speciation process the offspring of a remote ancestor qualified for human-hood, and thus to be infused with moral fiber. Was it at the point of the genetic mutation, or when the mutation was first expressed in the body of an offspring? How about siblings, some of whom received the non-mutated allele from the sex cell of the parent and some who did receive the crucial mutant? Some are on the path to human-hood, and thus conferred with moral fiber, and others free of the terrible onus and thus at liberty to continue their beastly ways without fear of final retribution.

The possibility remains that the spiritual fiber could have been conferred incrementally. For example, the process could be linear. If there are so many variants in the genetic makeup of humans as compared with our remote non-human ancestor, then the buildup could have occurred in direct proportion to the percentage of transitional variations realized at a particular stage of the process. Human spirituality could have grown in intensity as we approached the fully modern human state. During the transition phase, the standard by which the omnipotent force would then either absolve the individual of blame or exact retribution would perhaps be proportionately adjusted.

As evolution is an endless process, we humans may still be only partially held accountable for our thoughts and deeds. If spirituality is conferred only at the fully developed human genetic state, we may still lack the property. However, we may be at the end of the evolutionary trajectory, in which case we may already enjoy (or suffer with) all the morality we will ever have. A cursory review of recorded human history, invariant over time in its behavioral gamut of tyranny, mayhem, murder and exploitation leaves one with the impression that this is one gift horse that should be looked in the mouth.

But it isn't necessary to conjure up the notion of spirit to understand altruism. In fact, the concept of spirit is a distraction from a more comprehensible and supportable basis for cooperation. A practical way to comprehend the incidence of moral behavior is reciprocity. In an enlightened individual, capable of sensing the infinite stream of behavioral ripples that emanate outward from any thought or action, the rational faculty invokes operational morality based upon analysis of consequences. Essentially something like the *quid pro quo* concept embedded in the Golden Rule acts as a guide for individual behavior and for conditioning the external environment, fostering advancement of individuals who similarly sense the benefits to be enjoyed when they and their neighbors are mutually well-intentioned.

Indeterminacy

Uncertainty surrounding future events is the delicious part of human existence. It is the flavor and spice of life. However, even the genius of Albert Einstein, as expressed in a letter of 21 March, 1942 to Cornelius Lanczos[18], could not fully accept it: "You are the only person I know who has the same attitude towards physics as I have: belief in the comprehension of reality through something basically simple and unified ... It seems hard to sneak a look at God's cards. But that he plays dice ... is something that I cannot believe for a single moment."

Einstein's collaborators and friends, Banesh Hoffmann and Helen Dukas (1981) expressed his unwillingness to accept indeterminacy in physical processes: "We see here Einstein's vivid way of looking at and expressing dissatisfaction with the quantum theory, with its denial of determinism and its limitation to probabilistic, statistical predictions. He was himself a pioneer in the development of the quantum theory, but he remained convinced that there was need for a different understanding."

Despite Einstein's reservations, virtually all of the scientific community now accepts the reality of indeterminacy. George Johnson (1995), a science journalist of the New York Times, in his masterful exposition on the common roots of science and mysticism very neatly categorizes and sums up the sources of uncertainty in physical processes. Uncertainty is perceived as randomness, whether or not the underlying mechanism is random. First is apparent randomness arising from complexity of a system that we cannot adequately model or analyze. Second is 'chaos', a characteristic of complex systems: a salient feature of chaotic systems is that they are critically dependent on initial conditions - a minor difference or change in distribution of particles or temperature, for example, in China can cause tidal waves on the east coast of N. America. Even if the system is essentially deterministic, the final outcome is basically unpredictable. Third is quantum uncertainty as explained by Heisenberg and Bohr, which operates at the subatomic level. Johnson confirms (citing scientific authorities) that micro uncertainty could produce macroscopic effects.

In a 1998 conversation with Dr. Jeffrey Mishlove[19], Professor Murray Gell-Mann, Nobel Laureate in physics, describes the link between the principle of indeterminacy, which occurs at the subatomic level, and free will that humans seem to experience. Subatomic phenomena follow the rules of quantum mechanics, in which uncertainty is a fundamental characteristic. As a rule in the scientific community, specialists in one field are loath to express their views concerning others. However, Gell-Mann, ventures to extend his understanding of physical process to the domain of behavioral science by linking indeterminacy, which is a fundamental characteristic of matter and energy, to the behavior of organisms, including humans. If the mind/matter duality is an illusion - that all is matter/energy - then choice is not logically possible, since matter – atoms, pions, muons and quarks – are not attributed with any sort of choice, even though there may be variations in the way processes are carried out because there are inherent uncertainties in nature.

However, Gell-Mann doesn't "… actually adopt the point of view that our subjective impression of free will, which is a kind of indeterminacy behavior, comes from quantum mechanical indeterminacy." He suggests that it has other derivations, such as partial information, but mentions the link as a "logical possibility". "…quantum mechanics gives us fundamental, *unavoidable indeterminacy* (italics added), so that alternative histories of the universe can be assigned probability. Sometimes the probabilities are very close to certainties, but they're never really certainties."

According to Gell-Mann, the fundamental basis for indeterminacy in behavior of the universe is quantum-mechanical uncertainty. An organism, a component of the universe, must be similarly affected. Even though quantum-mechanical uncertainty is operative at the subatomic level, which might involve a photon exchange within the human brain, there are macroscopic implications. One mechanism might involve small quantum-mechanical fluctuations amplified in some cases by the classical phenomenon of chaos, where the outcome of a process in a complex system, say the human brain, is highly sensitive to changes in its initial state. There are also uncertainties in the sensory information received. A further source of indeterminacy in behavioral response to a stimulus from interaction with the outside world is that the information it receives is never complete.

There is an understandable hesitancy in Gell-Mann's assessment of a possible link between free will and physical processes, as he is stepping outside the bounds of disprovable claims that Karl Popper insisted as necessary for a scientific theory. Popper (2002) suggests that "A theory which is not refutable by any conceivable event is non-scientific. Irrefutability is not a virtue of a theory (as people often think) but a vice." To 'scientifically' test that all human behavior is linked to physical processes and that an essential spirit or morality does not exist is probably beyond the realm of possibility.

That there are macroscopic effects of inherently uncertain subatomic phenomena is indisputable. According to Peter L. Bernstein (1996)[20], Berkeley computer scientist James Crutchfield, "estimated that the gravitational pull of an electron (quantum) randomly shifting position at the edge of the Milky Way, can change the outcome of a billiard game on Earth." Could not a photon from Betelgeuse trigger a neuron (with quantum uncertainty) that can alter the behavior of an organism, even one in the shape of a human? If the Copenhagen interpretation of quantum theory is correct - that nature is characterized by probability waves so that there is fundamental uncertainty at the subatomic level and that subatomic particles only reveal their nature when they have to do something - doesn't it follow that there is no objective reality, or more to the point, no objective reality upon which the future is predicated?

If there is no objective reality, can the absence of free will be far behind? Paul Watzlawick (1976) suggests three possibilities: (1) reality has no order and confusion reigns, with life a "psychotic nightmare"; (2) we invent an order and then delude ourselves into thinking that there is something out there for us to choose; or (3) there is an order created by some higher being with whom we long to communicate. Watzlawick asserts that if we believe that choice, like any other event, is predetermined from all causes in the past, then free will or choice is an illusion. Even if one thinks there is an alternative, that thought is an echo from the past events. "It does not matter how I choose, for whatever I choose is the only thing I *can* choose. There are no alternatives, and even if I think there are, this thought itself is nothing but the effect of some cause in my personal past." Whether as perpetrator or recipient of an action, the event is determined by antecedent events even though "...I may call (it) causality, the Being, the divine experimenter, or fate."

Two tenets of psychoanalysis support the contention that free will is illusory: that what we do or think is strongly influenced by past events, and that we are driven primarily by instinctive needs and unconscious impulses. John Bargh and Ezekquiel Morsella (2008) point out that "There are a multitude of behavioral impulses generated at any point in time derived from our evolved motives and preferences, cultural norms and values, past experiences in similar situations and what other people are doing in that same situation." These impulses provide unconscious motives, preferences and behavioral tendencies in response to perceptions about others' behavior. " There certainly seems to be no shortage of suggestions from our unconscious about what to do in any given situation." If history and unconscious impulses are such influential factors in behavior, can free will exist?

But there is a tendency to insist that people have to be held accountable for their actions, that in spite of genetic disposition or unwholesome experiences, some standards of behavior have to be maintained to keep us on the straight and narrow.

If humans and other living organisms are not responsible for their behavior, is blame a legitimate concept? Reg Morrison[21] asks: "If our growing environmental problems are truly attributable to human activity, do certain individuals or groups deserve our special condemnation, or have we all behaved badly? Is it possible that this successful species of ours also embodies one or two heritable flaws against which we have no defense, flaws embedded in the wiring of our brains, or hidden in the coils of our massive DNA?"

Morrison suggests that the delusion of free will and the duality of mind and matter are essential to humanity's survival. "It has been argued that something called 'genetic determinism' is a suspect concept in that it offers too easy an excuse for past actions. ...This argument fails to account for the fact that we could only take cynical advantage of those excuses (that behavior is a product of genetic determinism) if the central proposition were *untrue*. As it is, however, even that degree of free will remains unavailable to us, and for very good reason. If we were not continually at the beck and call of our genetic code, and if we did not instinctively believe in the duality of existence (the body and the spirit) and act accordingly, then our mythically driven civilization would grind to a halt. In other words, our delusions of spiritual autonomy are essential to the survival of our species...a proper understanding of our genetic subservience would also rob us of all our heroes and villains, since they too are governed by their genetic imperatives and no more worthy of reverence or condemnation than the rest of us."

The vagaries of nature allow that any person at any time can commit any conceivable act. It is only a question of statistics - the bell curve - and time. The monkey at the keyboard will eventually tap out an etude of Chopin. If the synapses line up in a certain way and a photon from Alpha Centauri happens to impinge upon the sensory apparatus at the proper time, anything can happen in the cranial recesses of an individual, with behavioral consequences. Princes might beg, and paupers dispense good tidings.

Darwin explains that the underlying imperative for individual behavior is essentially security and survival. Constrained by that framework, behavior is indeterminate, normally within ranges that do not raise eyebrows, but occasionally off the wall, the equivalent of rare celestial alignments that cause earthquakes and tidal waves.

The absence of free will, and the indeterminacy that characterizes future events, does not recommend passivity. We do what we do what we do. We have to play out what is in us and hope that it leads to something better.

So evil, obstinacy and other despicable traits are to be pitied rather than despised. When we regard self-aggrandizing performances of politicians, antisocial behavior of criminals, pompous assertions by scribes, insensitive treatment of fellow species by hog-butchers or terrorist acts of fanatics, we can best try to correct their waywardness, but not blame them for their transgressions from good sense. As Jesus admonished in his most godly utterance, "forgive them, for they know not what they do". Pity the bastards, and put them away if necessary, but humbly - because they are only blindly subservient to the vicissitudes of nature.

Despite overwhelming evidence to the contrary, manifestations of free will abound:

Free will on Earth:
"Alice, I would like to kiss you. Would you allow me?"

"By all means, Henry, but only if I am allowed to allow you
to."

"Fine Alice, but only if I am allowed to allow you to allow
me to."

"Great, Henry, but only if I am allowed to allow you to allow
me to allow you to." ....

Free will on high:

"Lord, I would like to dishonor my father and mother."

"You are free to do as you please, but if you do you will incur
my wrath and go to hell!"

"But if you are a benevolent god, you would not allow me to
perpetrate this dishonor."

"But then I would have no reason to tell you that you will
be condemned to hell for doing so. In fact, I would be
superfluous."

We have no choice

Although it is counterintuitive, there is no reason to assume that
humans are endowed with free will or choice. Certainly it 'feels' as if
we can choose, but so far as we know this can only be one of the traits
that nature has bestowed through the process of human evolution.
The importance of widespread acknowledgment of the true capacities
of *H. sapiens* can't be overstated, particularly regarding the matter
of choice - the basis for assigning blame and dispensing praise that
are so effective as social polarizers. Our failure to acknowledge the
absence of choice is an impediment to social progress and a grave threat
to life. This illusion is behind much violence among humans, mass
extinctions of other species that have shared our trek across the eons,
and devastation of the planet that is our common home. Recognizing
our limitations does not have to diminish the richness of life's tapestry;
instead, it has the potential to transform us into a much more tolerant
and accommodating animal, with positive benefits for the quality of
our lives and for those of our travelling companions.

Chapter 3
HOW MANY OF US
ARE TOO MANY?

At this point in time there are about 6.8 billion humans on Earth. In the course of one lifetime, the proverbial threescore and ten (70) years, human numbers have increased to this level from about 2.3 billion, an average rate of growth of a bit over 1.5% that has produced about three times as many alive now as compared with 70 years ago. Projections by the United Nations Population Fund (UNFPA) indicate that there will almost certainly be 9 billion or more of us by mid century and perhaps as many as 12 billion by the year 2100.

By the most conventional measure of prosperity, in the face of this expansion, world real per capita growth in Gross Domestic Product (GDP) has average a little more than 2% over this span[22]; nevertheless, over one billion people worldwide currently live on less than $1 per day. Despite the apparent income improvement, disparity is growing:

"In Eastern Europe and the CIS countries the per capita income of the highest quintile is 7 times that of the lowest quintile - in Russia 14 times. In industrial countries the per capita income of the highest quintile is 7 times that of the lowest - in Japan only 4 times. Although no figure was available for Sub-Saharan Africa as a whole, income disparity is significant in some countries of the region. In Lesotho the per capita income of the richest 20% is 22 times that of the poorest

20%. For South Africa the figure is 19 times, and for Kenya 18 times."[23] In the US, the top 300 thousand people had about as much income as the lowest 150 million.[24] The top group's average income was 440 times that of the lowest group, nearly twice the disparity that existed in 1980.

Increasing income spreads between 'haves' and 'have-nots' are a reflection of excessive world population. Producers of goods and services, abetted by their political and religionist collaborators, salivate at the surplus wealth to be skimmed from growing minions of workers and consumers ready and willing to play their respective roles. Rather than work to attenuate the looming threat of unsustainable population growth, they seek optimality with respect to their own corporate objectives. Technology has permitted global marketing reach, while disseminating information that ironically has the impact of reducing fertility.[25] Overall, these developments have been positive for powerful market players, permitting concentration and more capital-intensive production. The result is widening of income disparity[26] and increasing numbers of destitute people, whose rate of procreation tends to increase with the degree of uncertainty in survival of their offspring.[27]

Conventional measures of prosperity distort the true impact of changes in income distribution. Subsistence farmers, for example, have little cash income, but through hard work and good husbanding practices can maintain a simple but adequate lifestyle. As land is divided among siblings, increasing numbers are forced to seek wage income, usually at the lowest rate permitted by the supply/demand relationship. This now appears statistically as an increase in the wages of low-income workers, whose life qualities have actually deteriorated as a result.

While on the surface things are getting better according to World Bank indicators, most of the reduction in poverty in the decades since the early 1980's is attributable to rapid growth in China.[28] GDP in that country has been growing by over 9% per annum and should surpass the US economy in a decade or two, though the relationship may be distorted by China's manipulation of the official rate of currency exchange to the US dollar.[29]

Even much of this apparent prosperity is attributable to spending on the credit card. Budget deficits in the world's largest economies feed into consumption of the integrated global economy. In 2010 projected budget deficits for some of the leading economies, as a percentage of their GDP's are as follows: Germany 6.5, Italy 6.2, USA 9.0, UK 7.1, Japan – a staggering 170. Deficits in the USA are projected at about the same level for the second decade of the 21st century.

Advocates of a hands-off policy on world population argue that there is little evidence that present numbers can't be sustained by tapping Earth's resources, that alarmists on population have been 'crying wolf' for decades without the predicted catastrophes. They point to the power of the global economic system to adjust to change, substituting one material for another in short supply, for example.

Jeffrey Sachs, Director of the Earth Institute at Colombia University, and architect of "shock therapy"[30] for economies of the former Soviet bloc in the 1980's, apparently believes that the trend toward increasing poverty in the 'Third World' can be overcome. In developing his exposition on the theme, a plan to put an end to global poverty, to reduce disease, armed conflict and environmental degradation within 20 years, he proposes market solutions.[31] According to Sachs, it is the responsibility, as well as in the self-interest of industrialized countries, to assist the less-developed countries in achieving a path to peace and prosperity by helping them to develop market-based systems for production and consumption. More mouths to feed and bodies to clothe does not factor into his calculus.

Little has been reported concerning a link between climate change, which many experts predict will have dire consequences for the future of life, and human population. In its State of the World Population Report of 2009, the UN Population Fund does suggest that human numbers may be relevant:

"Although its role is difficult to quantify amidst the many factors contributing to emissions growth, population growth is among the factors influencing total emissions in industrialized as well as developing countries. Each additional person in a population will consume food and require housing, and ideally most will take advantage of transportation, which consumes energy, and may use fuel to heat homes and have access to electricity." The report points out that the impact of population on emissions is greatest for those countries with the highest levels of per capita energy and material consumption - the industrialized countries. For those countries with population declines, e.g. Japan and Italy, the International Energy Agency projects emissions to be lower in 2030 than today.

How do we know that the world is overpopulated? To borrow the phrase of Supreme Court Justice Potter Stewart (regarding pornography), it's not easy to define, but we know it when we see it. One only has to observe the multitudes of desperate people around the world, who will never have access to the dream world of poverty alleviation that Sachs suggests is just around the corner, if only...... That the prerequisites for his rosy scenario are impractical and unachievable does not seem to faze Prof. Sachs, nor does the fact that sustaining 6 billion or 9 billion or even 12 billion humans on Earth with anything like a decent standard of living is a pipe dream.

Extinction

Indicators of excessive human population are in plain view. For one thing, the rate of extinction of species that have for eons shared the path to development along with humans is the highest since the dinosaurs disappeared 60 million years ago. Some estimates have the extinction rate as much as 100 times the 'background' rate, which would occur in the absence of human impact. "Although the extinction of various species is a natural phenomenon, the rate of extinction occurring in today's world is exceptional -- as many as 100 to1,000 times greater than normal"[32] Fossil evidence confirms that many large mammalian species occupied North America at the time of the human appearance about twelve thousand years ago and rapidly became extinct (before entering from Siberia across the land bridge that existed at that time, it is very likely that no human had set foot on the American continents, although this is in dispute).

Most paleontologists believe human intervention was the cause. Humanity has continued to adversely affect survival prospects for many species, large and small, albeit not through the same mechanisms as the early Americans. Most threats to the continued existence of other species is the result of habitat intrusion, as massive numbers of humans seek living space and exploit the remaining land for crop production, mining resources and disposal of human wastes. As brilliantly explained by Rachel Carson (1962), whose pioneering work has been continued by many others, much of the extinction is attributable to contamination of Earth's land, air and water.

Food supply and space

Although cultural patterns differ in this regard around the world, most people seem to enjoy a little breathing room, enough space around them to be able to sit quietly and take in the beauty of nature. While the US population has trebled in the course of one lifetime, Mexico's has quintupled in the same time span. Between 1960 and 2010 Pakistan's population nearly quadrupled to 180 million. The UN projects that Pakistan will add 66 million people within the next 15 years, and become the fourth most populous country in the world, behind India, China and the United States. By that date, the average land area per capita for Pakistan compared with the US will be (sq. km. per capita): US 0.024, Pakistan 0.003. In other words, Pakistan will be *eight times* as densely packed as the US.

It has been argued that there is plenty of room left on Planet Earth for many more humans, that if all the current world population of about 6.8 billion moved to Australia, the average allotment would be about a quarter acre. However, one only has to observe how humanity is presently accommodated to realize how misleading is this observation. To put that in perspective, Australia's ecological footprint (see definition below) was 7.8 hectares[33] or 19.2 acres per person. In other words, to maintain their lifestyle, the average 'Australian' would need 76 times the area allotted.

The available land surface area of the six habitable continents (excluding Antarctica) is about 45 million sq. miles, if water surfaces are excluded. However, only about a quarter is arable, or about 12 million sq. miles – the remainder is too frigid, arid or mountainous for ordinary cultivation. This leaves a little more than an acre per capita but only about half is actually under cultivation - little more than a half acre per capita, a square of about 150 ft. on a side. If the human population increases to 9 billion by mid 21st century as predicted by the UN Population Fund, this will be reduced to a plot of about 135 ft. on a side. About one sixth of the world's population is chronically malnourished or starving, which should indicate how adequate is the land available for food production. In the United States, about 1.2 acres per capita is required for food production, while population growth projected at 2050 (500 million) will reduce available land to 0.6 acres.[34]

The most obvious indication of an impending food crisis is the increase in prices, averaging almost 32% globally in 2007. Of the trends driving the strain on food supply and consequent price increases, actual and anticipated population growth is the central factor. By 2050 UNFPA (UN Population Fund) projects a population of 9.2 billion – many more mouths to feed and less arable land for food production. Some impacts of inordinate population growth[35]:

- Increasing prices for fuel and the consequent diversion of food crops for fuel production (biofuels); higher oil prices affect cost of food production at many levels, from farm to consumers (currently 20 per cent of the United States corn crop goes into ethanol production – a figure likely to rise to 32 per cent by 2016);

- Greater demand for meat, dairy and fish in developing countries with high and increasing populations and rates of economic growth, e.g. China and India;

- Climate-related decrease in food production, e.g. drought in Australia, cold weather in US and Europe; high rates of erosion and desertification of croplands attributable to intensity of cultivation;

- Export restrictions by some major grain producers – imposed to secure domestic supply;

- Inelastic production system, i.e. slow response of production capacity to increases in demand for foods; IFPRI (International Food Policy Research Institute) estimates that aggregate agricultural supply increases by about 1-2 per cent for each 10 per cent increase in price - and by even less when processes are so volatile.

According to a report of the United Nations Food and Agriculture Organization, despite its 12-year concentrated effort, an increasing number of people - 1.02 billion this year - are hungry, almost a sixth of the world population. "Scientists and development experts across the globe are racing to increase food production by 50 percent over the next two decades to feed the world's growing population, yet many doubt their chances despite a broad consensus that enough land, water and expertise exist."[36] The global financial recession of 2007-2010 added at least 100 million people to the ranks of the undernourished.

Will the situation get any better in the future? World leaders often evoke the green revolution of the 1960s and 1970s as a model for progress. The original 'revolution', inspired by the work of agronomist Normal Borlaug, was predicated on the introduction of new crop varieties, increased use of fertilizers and irrigation in Asia and Latin America to stave off famines. Impressive increases in yields and reductions in maturity periods were realized, and greater resistance to climate extremes and disease.

However, the new technology required hybridized seeds, which are sterile. Farmers could no longer save seeds for the next planting cycle, but rather had to purchase them from suppliers. Farmers were also faced with increased costs of non-renewable fertilizers and pesticides. Herbicides were needed because the more intensive fertilizer application has also stimulates weed growth. High yields and the use of artificial fertilizers often led to degraded soils. As groundwater supplies are depleted from overexploitation, irrigation becomes an increasing problem. Larger farmers operating on a commercial scale generally profited from the 'revolution', but small farmers were primarily disadvantaged. Furthermore, the green revolution is probably not replicable in much of Asia and Africa, if only for the lack of irrigation - only about 7 percent of these farmland are irrigated. Another downside is that rents for land producing higher yields became too costly for tenant farmers, denying many of them a livelihood.

Genetically modified organisms (GMO) are another issue, promoted as the next revolution in food production that will stave off world hunger. However, there is widespread concern that GMO are a health hazard. Borlaug stated in a 2002 interview that biotechnology (i.e. use of genetically modified crops) was an extension of the green revolution.[37] Even though the World Trade Organization has declared the practice illegal, the European Union has established rules limiting the use of GMO. Some member states have invoked the 'safeguard clause' (Art. 23 Dir. 2001/18/EC) to restrict use or sale of GMO, but must justify the action on grounds of risk to human health or the environment.

A report of the US Department of Agriculture in 1999 indicates that "…it would not be unrealistic to expect the global land resources of being able to support a population between 9 to 20 billion persons. There will be an adequate supply of grains to feed the 9 billion persons who will inhabit the Earth in the year 2025; this does not imply that all will be fed."[38] It suggests that countries with poor quality land, incapable of sustaining even subsistence agriculture, and which are most greatly afflicted by endemic poverty and hunger, can be assisted through proper planning and cooperation at the international level. The study concludes that the absence of political will is the only impediment to avoiding famine and starvation of people of these impoverished countries, and not the capacity to produce the necessary quantities of food.

However, such rosy scenarios, even if political impediments were removed, are unlikely to be realized. Resource constraints, particularly fossil fuels that are needed in virtually every component of industrialized agriculture that now produces the bulk of the world food supply, will most likely preclude adequate food supplies for the world's growing population.

A presentation prepared by the Society of Petroleum Engineers, Gulf Coast Chapter[39] shows how crude oil production increases are more than offset by steep declines in production of key existing fields in many producing countries, and that new discoveries are generally smaller than existing fields. Significant new finds, such as the Tupi field in Brazil, are in ultra-deep water and in unusually difficult drilling conditions so that extraction will be very expensive. Large shale oil fields have been discovered in North America, the Baaken Formation and Williston Basin in Dakotas and Saskatchewan and the Utah/Colorado formation. In 2008 the US Geological Service (USGS) announced that the Baaken discovery "has potential to eliminate US dependence on foreign oil." Subsequently, in April 2008 USGS estimated that Baaken contained about 3-4 billion barrels (not 300 billion as had first been announced). At the current US consumption of about 19 million barrels per day (B/D), the Baaken Formation would be depleted in about half a year. Oil shale of Utah/Colorado contains trillions of barrels, but the technology to extract liquid hydrocarbons from kerogen, a rock-like solid containing organic compound in which it is embedded, is extremely difficult and energy consuming. "It is impossible to substitute unconventional oil (e.g. shale) for high flows of sweet oil – high energy requirements, low flows and oil often of low quality."

In December 2009 Fatih Birol, chief economist of the International Energy Agency (IEA), stated that absent significant discoveries "the output of conventional oil will peak in 2020 if oil demand grows on a business-as-usual basis."[40] This was a "new and striking claim" coming from the IEA, whose analysis of world energy markets is closely followed. Additional challenges for US oil production are the high rate of consumption (plus enormous amounts of coal and natural gas), and the state of the oil infrastructure, old and rusting and in need of huge capital investment. Also, natural gas production declines are even steeper than for oil.

In a 2009 news article Tom Whipple, a retired CIA analyst and columnist, predicts major changes in American agriculture resulting from depletion of fossil fuels:[41] "With shrinking amounts of increasingly expensive fossil fuels, the American way of agriculture is going to be severely tested. Throw in some climate change and our food producers are going to have trouble keeping up with the demand. Many are worried about depleted soils, and the vast amounts of energy required to grow, store, process, and transfer food raised thousands of miles from the consumer..." Whipple associates the decline in agriculture with the outbreak of social unrest as foods become scarce and expensive. In contrast to the 1960's "This time riots will be for food and jobs rather than for civil rights and against the draft. The unrest will change everything."

Lester Brown, of the Earth Policy Institute, links the prospect of peak oil production with world food security, as modern agriculture depends heavily on the use of fossil fuels either directly or through the power grid for operating cultivating and stationary machinery.[42] Natural gas is the source of ammonia as the foundation of nitrogen fertilizers. Production and distribution of the other major fertilizer components, phosphate and potash also depend heavily on fossil fuels. In fact, the entire food system is largely energy-dependent. Only 20% is consumed in cultivation, and the rest in distribution, processing, packaging, marketing and preparation in home and food service outlets. "In short, with higher energy prices and a limited supply of fossil fuels, the modern food system that evolved when oil was cheap will not survive as it is now structured."

Over the next few decades, agriculture in the US and other major food exporting countries will undoubtedly hit a wall. Fourteen industrialized countries, including the US, are responsible for about 67% of global food exports. If some degree of political stability can be maintained throughout the world during this period of transition to a more sustainable system of food production, we may be able to work our way out of this mess. But with over 1 billion people already near starvation, increasing population and widespread armed conflict and terrorism, the problems seem almost insurmountable. If it is not too late to start to convert to more local production of foods using renewable resources, there is certainly no room for delay.

Water

One of every six humans lacks access to potable water, and one-third lack adequate sanitation.[43] Millions die each year from water-borne diseases. The supply of potable water is significantly reduced by pollution and contamination from agricultural runoff, untreated sewage and industrial effluents. It is true that much fresh water is wasted. Agricultural use, which accounts for about 87% of fresh water use globally, is widely inefficient, with much irrigation water lost to evaporation and runoff as a result of poor planning. Water is usually underpriced, with subsidies diminishing pressure for conservation. Nevertheless, demand for clean water increases with growth of human population, with about one third currently experiencing water stress.

There is widespread concern that availability of fresh water will reach crisis proportions in many parts of the world in the near future. Per capita availability of water in Asia, heretofore an abundant resource, declined by 40-60% between 1955 and 1990. Availability of clean fresh water is expected to be severe within the next decade or two. Other parts of the world are even in worse condition, e.g. Africa, where desertification and population increase will create stress, scarcity and vulnerability in huge swaths of the continent by 2025.[44]

Forest cover

Another obvious signal of overpopulation is the loss of forest cover. The annual net loss of forest area between 2000 and 2005 was 7.3 million hectares - an area about the size of Sierra Leone or Panama - down from an estimated 8.9 million hectares between 1990 and 2000.[45] Now each day at least 80,000 acres (32,300 ha) of forest disappear (about 12 million ha. per annum) and an equal area degraded, with as many as several hundred species going extinct. Loss of forests is accompanied by increases in atmospheric carbon and loss of topsoil to erosion. Tropical forests, which provide habitats for a myriad of species, have experienced an increasing rate of deforestation, 8.5% higher in 2000-2005 as compared with the 1990s. Even though natural reforestation and plantings may make up the difference, much of it still represents a considerable loss of biodiversity, as plantations do not reproduce the diverse habitats lost to a multitude of species when the primary forest that they replace was destroyed.

Migration

During the decade of the 1990's, according to the Census Bureau, 33 million people were added to the US population. About half of this growth is 'natural', and the rest attributable to immigration, more than 1 million legal and a half million or so undocumented. By most estimates from 12 – 20 million undocumented persons reside in the US at the beginning of the 21st century.

Before considering the US population situation in isolation, it has to be regarded as just one part of a global migration phenomenon attributable largely to the wide disparity in income distribution around the world. Some of the migration is the result of geo-political changes such as the breakup of the former Soviet Union during the 1990's. On the surface the number of migrants as a percentage of world population does not seem overwhelming. International migrants represented 2.5% of population in 1960 and 2.9% in 2000, about 175 million. Some migration resulted from economic liberalization, income disparities among nations, increased access to transportation and demographic disparities between developed and developing nations. People migrate mainly for economic reasons, although many seek asylum from persecution and other forms of terror. According to the International Organization for Migration (IOM)[46]:

"The most significant changes in recent years have been an increased concentration of migrants in the developed world and in a small number of countries. There have also been significant shifts in the poles of attraction for labor migration, for example to East and Southeast Asia, and a remarkable contribution of international migration to the population growth of receiving countries experiencing low fertility levels [to serve as low-paid workers]."

According to this report, 17 million refugees [ostensibly fleeing persecution] in the world represented 9.7 per cent of all international migrants in the year 2000 as compared with 4.5 million or 5.5 per cent in 1970, the majority having found asylum, not in the industrialized countries, but rather in the developing countries of Africa and Asia.

The IOM assists from about a half to one million migrants per year, but to put this in perspective, census figures confirm that there are at about 1.5 million immigrants annually to the United States alone. At this point the US has the highest rate of population growth of any industrialized country by far. Why is this a concern, for a country purportedly the wealthiest in the world?

So long as the United States, as titular world leader, fails to acknowledge through public policy that population is a global issue, little will likely be done about it. A rate of population growth of one percent or so for the country or world does not seem excessively large with economic growth typically in the 3% or greater range in the U.S. and even larger in some of the developing countries. However, conventional measures of economic growth don't take into account costs of resource depletions, notably petroleum, that the world will face in the near future, nor environmental degradation. Nor is economic growth, even by conventional measures, likely to match what has occurred in the past.

It seems compassionate to permit the downtrodden of the underdeveloped countries free access to the industrialized and ostensibly prosperous nations such as the United States. One argument in favor is that migrants will take up places in the economy that are shunned by its citizens. Even in the unlikely event that this is true, can the U.S. or any other country comfortably accommodate over 1 billion people worldwide who are living on the brink of starvation, all of those who face only bleak prospects at best, and who would surely opt for better opportunities if given the chance?

The problem of excessive migration becomes more apparent in periods of economic recession. Although there are certainly refugees driven from their mother countries by oppression, for whom the developed countries have a moral obligation to provide a haven, most migrants leave their home countries because their economies are incapable of absorbing their increasing populations.

Countries in North America, Europe and Africa are experiencing serious tensions - to the extent of murderous attacks - between their own unemployed citizens and workers from South Asia, Africa and Latin America, mainly undocumented, who are competing for low level jobs. In the U.S. for example, "..recent studies have begun to document, in rising levels of detail, the tension that has emerged between immigrant groups and lower-skilled American natives......"[47] In San Diego in the summer of 2000, five Mexican workers were beaten, stabbed and otherwise terrorized by local 'skinheads'. A few days earlier, in the same area, a worker was beaten and lynched, his body thrown into a nearby ravine.[48]

Despite attempts to provide minimum work standards, the law of the market often controls: an excess of supply tends to drive down the price. Expectations of migrants are also unfulfilled: as expressed by an exasperated entrant to the U.S. from the strikingly beautiful (and peaceful) Himalayan country of Bhutan: "Nothing works without a job! I have no way to pay the bills. I am healthy and strong; I was a teacher at home. I need to work but there is nothing. I want to take care of my family, but I can't do it without a job."[49]

The real problem is the failure of world leaders to promote sensible family planning. The need was apparent decades ago when there were numerous indications that global population increases were unsustainable, e.g. environmental degradation, growing destitution. As matters now stand, it is very unlikely that the current world population can be accommodated with anything like minimally acceptable standards of living for all.

Rather than rely on the rest of the world to produce low paid workers, it will be far better for industrialized populations to learn to do what they have to do for themselves. With unemployment rampant in these countries, there are undoubtedly sufficient numbers willing and able to do whatever jobs are necessary, so long as they are paid a living wage. Highly skilled workers in demand by these countries would much more fruitfully serve needs in their countries of origin, even if not specifically in the areas for which they were trained. There is really no need in the receiving countries, which have the wherewithal to upgrade capacities of their own populations to fill whatever jobs are necessary. The claim of insufficient workers is essentially a ruse to increase the supply of potential employees to a level greater than demand, for reasons that are all too obvious.

Promoting excessive growth in population, or its tacit equivalent – ignoring or opposing family planning measures - is a dangerous and destructive game. The world is rife with episodes of violence arising from the poverty and ignorance of economic deprivation that occurs when, as in any market including labor, too much supply compared with demand has the effect of depressing wage compensation. The situation is exacerbated in a global economy geared to rapidly depleting cheap fossil fuel, with inevitable economic recessions and depression that have the greatest impact on the massive numbers of humans living in dire conditions.

Michael Klare[50] explores the relationship between economic downturns and increased civil unrest and ethnic strife. "As people lose confidence in the ability of markets and governments to solve [global crises], they are likely to erupt into violent protests or to assault others they deem responsible for their plight, including government officials, plant managers, landlords, immigrants, and ethnic minorities......It is entirely possible......that, as the economic crisis worsens, some of these incidents will metastasize into far more intense and long-lasting events: armed rebellions, military takeovers, civil conflicts, even economically fueled wars between states."

Violent protests erupted in Cameroon, Egypt, Ethiopia, Haiti, India, Indonesia, Ivory Coast, and Senegal as a consequence of rising food prices in 2008. Civil unrest in Indian-controlled Kashmir resulted from allegations of discrimination in jobs, housing and land use. Nomadic shepherds around the city of Agra (location of the Taj Mahal) closed roads and railways as a protest against infringement on their means of livelihood, leading to civilian deaths as police fired into the crowd. Impoverished citizens in Assam violently resisted the influx of even poorer, mostly illegal immigrants from Bangladesh. Economically driven unrest occurred across much of eastern China in 2008, protests by workers over sudden plant shutdowns, lost pay, or illegal land seizures.

Success of the growth mantra, largely responsible for the excess of human population, arises from the natural inclination to procreate, exploitatively conjoined with mercantile, political and religionist interests. It is a convenient device for those who seek short-term advantage at the expense of impacts on future generations. However, there are ways to grow aside from numbers and consumption amounts. Societies can try to develop better human beings, and in the process learn to live more in tune with irrepressible and undeniable nature.

Wealthier countries have to continue serving as havens for the oppressed, but should otherwise determine immigration policies in the light of world conditions and their long-term impacts. Limiting access to the U.S., for example, may cause some governments (e.g. Mexico, where population growth is essentially out of control - a five-fold increase in the span of a single lifetime) - to take more seriously the constraints of their own living environments when they determine their own population policies.

Migration is a major factor in the global population problem. So long as countries with excessive population growths are permitted to dump them through the safety valve of the developed countries, there will be little incentive for these governments to deal seriously with their burgeoning populations. Former U.S. president Richard Nixon actually commissioned a study on world population and planned to promulgate a US population policy, but the church and industrial leaders undercut his idea to serve their own population agendas. At issue is not 'immigration', but rather massive human migration from lands with unsustainable rates of population growth. Ecological excesses engendered by human demands on Earth are the real threat, on the verge of straining an already overloaded system of natural resources to the breaking point.

Rather than tarring with the brush of racism or lack of compassion for the downtrodden those who view loose immigration standards as a globally dangerous policy of encouraging further growth in human numbers, better to admonish political leaders to promote family planning efforts throughout the world as the surest path to avoiding global environmental catastrophe.

Optimal world population

A number of objective approaches to determining the optimal world population have been proposed. One is the 'ecological footprint', in which the amount of land necessary to sustain the average lifestyle of an economy as determined from its productivity is compared with the actual land available. The approach attempts to measure the amount of land and water area required by the population to provide the resources consumed and to absorb the waste produced. The world apparently crossed over the sustainable threshold in the 1970's, when world population was about four billion. We now consume about 1.4 Planet Earths to sustain today's population level, and will need about two to sustain the projected population by mid-century (2050).[51]

Another similar objective approach is 'carrying capacity', the largest population size of a species that can be supported in a specific area without reducing its ability to support the same species in the future. It is the number of organisms in the area that can be supported by the amount of renewable resources available.

Ultimately, availability of energy will determine Earth's carrying capacity. In a 2007 paper based upon the World Energy and Population Model, Paul Chefurka relates energy available at any point in time to average annual global per capita consumption, currently at about 1.7 toe (tons oil equivalent).[52] In the model, this declines to a level of 1.0 toe by 2100. "To put that in perspective, the world average in 1965 was 1.2, so the model is not predicting a huge decline below that level of consumption. An increase in the disparity between rich and poor nations is also likely, but that effect is masked by this approach." According to the availability of non-renewable and renewable energy sources compared with average energy consumption to sustain a minimal lifestyle, world population will peak at under 7.5 billion by 2020 and then decline to under 2 billion by 2100. "...if the model is correct, there will be no ongoing overpopulation problem at all, as natural processes intervene to bring our numbers back in line with our resource base." This is at odds with the UN Population Fund estimate of about 9 billion by mid 21st century, but Chefurka's energy constraint may not have been sufficiently taken into account.

The decline in human population predicted by this model is staggering: "...it's safe to say it will be catastrophic far beyond anything humanity has experienced. The loss of life alone beggars belief. In the most serious part of the decline, during the two or three decades spanning the middle of this century, even with a net birth rate of zero we might expect death rates between 100 million and 150 million per year." In contrast, during World War II, from 1939 to 1945 (six years) there were 10 million excess deaths (above the normal death rate) per year, so the carnage resulting from the energy dearth could be 10-15 times worse, without taking into account the social upheavals that would result.

Even if Chefurka's energy peaks for various sources are postponed, or his rates of decline are overly precipitous, certainly within this or the next century his scenarios will play out. The 'ace in the hole' seen by some analysts is nuclear power generation, but fission is a Faustian bargain at best, where the devil will eventually have his due, and fusion appears to be a pipe dream. The outlook for humanity and the rest of life on Earth would be well served if we would take our heads out of the sand, but our propensity for allowing myths to predominate in our calculations are overpowering, particularly when they serve short-term aspirations.

Overpopulation denial

Why is it so difficult to accept the idea of overpopulation?

Economists tend to believe that there are no limits to resources. They create optimization models assuming that resources are infinitely available, and then prescribe policies accordingly. What's the difference if current sources of energy are finite? There is the sun, wind, tides, nuclear – we'll figure out a way. Why should we be concerned with the amount of arable land for food production? There is always a green revolution at hand, fish farming, hydroponics.

People are inclined by evolutionary imperative to covet offspring. From this perspective, humanity can't be criticized for being in a state of denial concerning its propensity to proliferate. We can't help ourselves, because our internal programming dictates the production of progeny as part of our survival strategy, a manifestation of the life force in every living thing. Even though our collective fecundity is a threat to life on Earth, as individuals the urge to procreate is overwhelming, often precluding rational analysis of its collective consequences.

Capitalists, who rule the roost, want multitudes of willing hands at the factory gate clamoring for employment, so that they can pick and choose according to their criteria and play one against the other in their quest for more services at lower cost. They also want hordes of devouring consumers, the better to amass surplus value out of the flow through their production machinery.

Politicians want larger and larger constituencies, particularly within special interest groups - mainly ethnic and social classes - upon whom they can focus their appeal as a means of continuing to maintain their incumbencies, which by one means or another usually confer privilege, prestige and, most importantly, wealth.

Religionists want more parishioners to maintain and extend their influence and to support their esoteric lifestyles. They have the advantage of declaring practices that would tend to limit human numbers as immoral and even sinful, such as reproductive control mechanisms and abortion of fetuses, with everlasting consignment to hell as the penalty for transgression.

On the other hand, it is amazing that there appears to be so little concern about increasing numbers of humans presently inhabiting our planet. Although approximately 75 million new souls are added to the throng each year[53], approximately another Egypt or France or Germany, crises of food supply, water, or clean air are almost never attributed to our growing numbers. It seems that there is a reticence among politicians and the media in particular to suggest that limiting population might be one way to address the global, national and regional ills to which they constantly call attention. It is as if they have purged from their consciousness the fact that there are limits to the numbers that our small planet can sustainably and adequately support. How about the law of exponents? For example, the human population is presently growing at about 1.1% per annum. Should this rate continue for another century there would be approximately 3 times the present 7 billion or so trying to scratch out an existence in the year 2110.

A visit to any major city, for example mingling with frenetic New Yorkers, oblivious for the most part of the looming threat, exemplified by the equanimity with which they apparently accept nose-to-nose packing density on subways and at other public venues and belied by the glamor and lights of tinsel town, is a reminder of how precarious is the existence of humankind. How can urbanites who rule the roost, insulated for their entire lives from the foundations of nature by municipal services, theatre, subways and the like, be aware of their indispensible links to the natural world? Of course, even the trappings of urban society, as the handiwork of a class of its constituents, are part and parcel of the natural world, but would rarely be recognized as such. Even E.O. Wilson (2003), noted Harvard University zoologist and exponent of socio-biology, defined nature as "Everything that we see in the cosmos with the human impact extracted...If all mankind were to disappear, the world would regenerate back to the rich state of equilibrium that existed ten thousand years ago. If insects were to vanish, the environment would collapse into chaos."

The only problem is that nature is the only game in town, so isolating humans from nature is like defining a giraffe as an animal with a short neck.

With 6.8 billion of us occupying this space that was meant for no more than 2 billion or so and our fellow species mates on Planet Earth (who generally have enough 'sense' to keep their numbers in check), and increasing by 75 million or so annually – no issue seems more daunting than the need to diminish our presence. This would most peaceably be achieved through attrition over extended periods of time, but our procreative proclivity does not make this a good bet.

Insensitivity to the consequences of our 'choices', including procreation, has been attributed to duality, for which our propensity is most decidedly expressed in childhood – the more dualistic, the more childlike we are. The most obvious manifestation of dualistic thinking is dividing people into 'them' and 'us'. It is quite satisfactory if benefits for 'us' are at the expense of 'them' - at root is the most fundamental ontogenetic human imperative. Duality has many other conceptual manifestations: body and spirit, man and nature, good and evil, black and white, happiness and depression. Its origins likely reside in our bicameral brain and horizontal symmetry. Our lack of vertical symmetry may also play a role. Earth's gravitational force is probably responsible for the up-down dichotomy that reinforces our dualistic perceptions. Unity in all things is only within the province of Bodhisattvas.

The human race seems be saddled with a very short planning horizon, ignoring long term trends for the most part. This syndrome is demonstrated repeatedly: industry typically plans for 3 years or less, ignoring socio-economic trends and cycles of much longer duration; politicians seek primarily to retain their incumbencies, trading short-term popularity for long term economic peril; individuals buy now and leave the issue of payment aside, in the hope that providence will intervene. Similarly, what is surely happening to the world's climate and its implications, the impending energy crunch that will have dramatic consequences for life styles, the state of the world's underprivileged at the root of our security threats, any major issue with long term implications - is treated as an insignificant blip on the radar screen. We seem to respond meaningfully only when there are obvious signs of distress (e.g. bodies piling up in the streets).

It is possible to have too many of us?

Virtually all segments of every society covet new additions to their populations. Parenting is a natural inclination, a most basic imperative of any organism. Productive elements of civilized society, e.g. commerce, industry and agriculture, seek abundant workers and consumers. Politicians and religionists thrive when there are minions to proselytize and bind. Economists neglect limits to resources in their models, thereby anesthetizing people to the possibility of over-exploitation from excessive demand. The result is ever-growing numbers of human beings, increasingly straining the carrying capacity of our planet. All of the interlinked problems threatening life are related to inordinate growth in human population – militarism, terrorism, climate change, environmental degradation, economic boom and bust, mal-distribution of wealth.

Excessive population is, in essence, part of the human condition. Even our consciousness of the problem does little to alleviate it. Our propensity to procreate is overwhelming, which can be attributed solely to nature, particularly if we regard population exploiters, and their devious machinations, as hapless subjects of its ubiquitous influence. Behavioral transitions that may alleviate the condition are not out of the question. After all, we were once much simpler creatures with very different habits, who may still have been present had a mastodon stomp obliterated the deviant gene that ultimately gave us to the world.

PART II
PATTERNS OF BEHAVIOR

Chapter 4

THE JEWEL IN SOCIETY'S CROWN

As a derivative of their inherent inclination to grow intellectually, emotionally and physically, children are the fresh nutrients with the potential to restore and rebuild societies. No weakness is more debilitating to its health, nor is any issue of greater concern to a society seeking long-term survival and elevation, than that its youth are deprived of opportunities to develop and exercise their full capacities. And yet this tautology is ignored in most corners of the world. Rather than being delicately and painstakingly groomed as society's future pillars, with all the care and resources that can possibly be brought to bear, children around the world are neglected, exploited, abused and even murdered to satisfy aspiration, convenience, whim and sadism of their elders. There does not appear to be a self-correcting mechanism that adjusts for what is tantamount to societal suicide, and in the process wreaking havoc on other forms of life by sending out into the world young people too stressed to think about the wider implications of their actions. This testifies to our corrosive presence within nature's domain.

In the United States, for example, school boards throughout the country typically are driven by the imperative of creating a competent workforce to serve industry and commerce. Children are looked upon as potential engines of prosperity. They need to 'learn the basics' so that they can get good jobs and generate income for the community.

Rather than look upon each child as a budding treasure to be cultivated to her highest potential, school systems typically are employed to filter children through sieves that segregate the promising from the also-rans. This is no less true in 'higher' education than it is in the K-12 system. Misguided priorities and denigration of the needs of children in the minds of politicians and the general public in the United States is reflected in its allocation of resources: of the $2.9 trillion budget for 2008, only 1.9% is dedicated to education while 16.8% is allocated to the military. Other public agencies directly or indirectly impacting the lives of children garnered another 3.6% of the budget (housing 1.2%, health and human services 2.4%).

If universal peace, prosperity and justice are ever to reign, or even become the norm, and if the future of life is to be secured as our natural heritage is preserved, nurturing children will have to become the first priority of society, above economics, military prowess, adult health care or any other activity or program for which society budgets resources. The reason is that each child deprived of the opportunity to reach her highest potential intelligence and mental and physical health, becomes to that extent a drag on society. Only when children are nurtured so that they identify with societal goals and with nature, of which they are indelibly a part, will humanity reach a state of sustainability that is essential for attaining these goals. This is the surest path to lasting security.

Early life

Humans enter life in a state of immaturity or neotony, with decidedly infantile traits such as relatively small brain size and physical weakness. Ours is the only species on Earth that enters life so ill prepared for it, with utter dependence on parents or other caregivers for survival. Were humans to come to full term in the manner of most other mammals, we would be born perhaps at eighteen months rather than nine. Our purported intelligence is somehow to blame for this condition, as the birth canal could not enlarge evolutionarily so quickly to accommodate our rapidly increasing brain size as we transited from primordial form to modern human. As a consequence, post-natal nurturing is a more significant component of the life support system for humans than for any other species. This is something we have to live with, at least so long as our evolutionary path has not yet either sufficiently broadened the hips of females to accommodate a more mature brain case or more efficiently packed our neurons and synapses to allow for a smaller cranium.

Pulitzer Prize science writer Ronald Kotulak (1997) compiled much medical and psychological research information dealing with the effects on human biology of genetic makeup and environmental influences, and their behavioral consequences. Researchers have since amassed an enormous amount of information concerning the biological effects of pre-natal and early childhood experiences on behavior patterns, but are so enmeshed in the strictures of their professions that they are incapable of proposing the dramatic actions that are indicated to ameliorate or eliminate the deleterious effects of typically deficient rearing processes. The totality of human expectations, the complex of influences - nutrition, security, intellectual stimulation, social orientation, etc. – that determine character are wired into the brain very significantly from the womb to the age of three.[54] Lesser, but strongly significant impacts, occur up to the age of 12, but continue at a reduced level indefinitely. Much of the misery that children currently endure, and its social consequences, are created and exacerbated by ignoring developmental needs and often subjecting children to abuse, which has indelible physical and psychological impacts that affect outlook and character.

In the United States of America, consumption at the cost of investing in children is the Faustian bargain. One of the dire consequences of the resultant neglect is that children bear children. In 2007 approximately 40% of American births were to single parents, many of them teenagers (about 10.5%)[55], who are by and large incapable, under the social structure, of proper nurturing. This is creating a virtual nightmare for the children (and ultimately for society) of these child procreators, who understandably lack the wisdom and other capacities to serve the comprehensive needs of their offspring.

As an illustration of the effect of intellectual stimulation on the outlook for children, David Weikert[56], President of Pre-School Study in Ypsilanti, Michigan, conducted a study in late 1960's in which two groups of black children born in poverty were exposed to two different learning methodologies for two years starting from the age of three. One method involved what was termed 'direct learning', which consisted of direct teaching of academic skills, enforced attention and reward for correct answers. The alternative was the 'self-starting' method, where the group of children planned, executed and reviewed their own activities and engaged in active learning with people, materials, ideas and events. Although there were early signs of improvement in cognition in both groups, by age 23 there were large differences between the two groups (direct learning vs. self-starter) in treatment for emotional problems (about half vs. 6%), felony arrests (39% vs. 10%), plans for a college education (27% vs. 70%).

The study concluded that the brain has the capacity to rapidly reorganize in response to external stimuli during early life, as brain cells are being created and broken down at a rate much greater than in later life. "These windows of development occur in phases from birth to age twelve when the brain is most actively learning from its environment. It is during this period, and especially the first three years, that the foundations for thinking, language, vision, attitudes, aptitudes and other characteristics are laid down." After this early period when much of the brain architecture is completed, development opportunities presented in early life attenuate markedly, particularly after the age of twelve.

There is widespread (but by no means universal), agreement among neuroscientists, psychiatrists and behavioral scientists that imprints of experiences in early childhood have long-lasting and perhaps indelible consequences. Kotulak (1999) cites findings from a number of experts in the field:

Felton Earls, Professor of Human Behavior and Development, Department of Society, Human Development, and Health at Harvard University: "A kind of irreversibility sets in. There is this shaping process that goes on early, and then at the end of this process, be that age two, three or four, you have essentially designed a brain that probably is not going to change very much more."

Neurobiologist Martha Constantine-Paton, Investigator, McGovern Institute; Professor of Biology and Brain and Cognitive Sciences, Massachusetts Institute of Technology: "The aspects of brain development most closely tied to human behavior can be affected for better or worse by the care we give our children... the actual structure of the brain can be adversely affected by neglect."

Torsten N. Wiesel, Nobel Laureate in Physiology or Medicine 1981, formerly of the Harvard Medical School and President of Rockefeller University: "There is a very important time in a child's life, beginning at birth, when he should be living in an enriched environment - visual, auditory, language and so on - because that lays the foundation for development later in life."

Bruce McEwen, Alfred E. Mirsky Professor at the Harold and Margaret Milliken Hatch Laboratory of Neuroendocrinology of Rockefeller University,[57] identifies our behavior and misbehavior as the greatest problem for humanity in the future, alluding to their dependence on the social and physical environment on our bodies and brains. Genes are a significant influence on behavior, but the environment regulates how genes are expressed.

David A. Hamburg, Professor of Psychiatry and Behavioral Sciences and former President of the Carnegie Corporation of New York, emphasizes the adverse consequences of child abuse regarding fulfillment of developmental potential, "For all the *atrocities* (italics added) now being committed on our children, we are already paying a great deal ... in economic inefficiency, lost productivity, lack of skill, high health care costs, growing prison costs, and a badly ripped social fabric."[58]

Evidence that a child's environment is crucial to development is overwhelming. A comprehensive review of recent findings concerning prenatal and early childhood development is contained in a study by the UCLA Center for Healthier Children, Families and Communities.[59] The consensus is that the development of the individual in terms of personality and intelligence is greatly influenced by these early experiences. A newborn child has twice as many synapses[60] as she will have as an adult, which are rapidly adjusting to environmental influences. "The human brain is fundamentally an adaptive organ, whose physical organization is shaped by the environment. In this sense, learning is the process by which the brain responds adaptively to the environment in which a child is reared." Anecdotal evidence supports the notion of a window of opportunity for young children. For example, their ability to learn properly accented language is well documented - typically children of expatriates learn local languages much faster, and with far less foreign accent than their parents. Many studies have confirmed that children have an advantage over adults in acquiring a second language, and that the ability diminishes starting from very early age, and even more sharply at the close of puberty.[61]

President-elect Barack Obama in 2008 indicated that early childhood education would be one of his top priorities, although he alluded primarily to the formal system of education rather than the complex of experiences that comprise proper nurturing. Some communities have instituted programs that address one or more nurturing issues. In Illinois, "Character Counts", a program promoted by the non-profit Josephson Institute, focuses on character-building in communities and school systems by inculcating social responsibility through promotion of its 'six pillars of character': trustworthiness; respect and tolerance; responsibility and perseverance; fairness; caring and compassion; and citizenship. But as a rule, there has not yet been a serious attempt to develop a comprehensive program of adequate nurturing comprised of all of the elements that are necessary for the fulfillment of a child's potential (see *The Essentials of Nurturing* below), for even a small percentage of American youth, and much less for the children of the world. School boards at the local level, and politicians in state capitals, in Washington, and throughout the world, appear to have little cognizance of their most important responsibility.

How can it be that professionals in the field of child development are not demonstrating for comprehensive nurturing for every child in the United States and the rest of the world, intended to allow each to fulfill her potential, insisting that this must be the number one social priority, making enough noise so that political forces will sit up and take notice? Perhaps it is the unfortunate consequence of their own nurturing, during which their perceptions were stultified by deficiencies in the system in which they were raised and 'educated'. A serious impediment is the compartmental nature of our academic system, where 'subjects' and 'disciplines' are treated as separate and distinct components of knowledge, ill preparing even the most perceptive teacher or mentor to take an organic view of their professional involvement.

These practices hinder development of intelligence, as young minds are passed through the academic meat grinder and segregated into distinct lines of knowledge to conform to convenient departmental structures defined by academics and educational administrators (see Chapter 8).

'Flawed' children

In the US, children are becoming increasingly disaffected. As youths traverse the bewildering path from a state of dependency to self-awareness and identity, clearly something is going awry. Not only are children's needs and motivations neglected, but also influential political and community leaders woefully misunderstand them.

The concept of a relationship between early childhood environment and subsequent social attitudes and behavior is not universally shared. Tom DeLay of Texas, former Republican member of Congress and once House Majority Whip, in an article for the Washington Post attributed child crime to the "fact that we enter this world flawed and inclined to do the wrong thing, as the Judeo-Christian tradition has taught."[62]

The "flaw", according to Mr. DeLay, is a sinful nature, which can be held in check only by two forces: the restraint of conscience and the restraint of the sword. "Tolerance, as the guiding moral imperative (of the misguided social engineers) forces acceptance and understanding of even appalling behavior as the product, not of our flawed (sinful) selves, but of flawed processes." Mr. DeLay makes clear his attribution of 'conscience' to religious teachings: " Our Founders were right when they insisted that self-government is suitable only to people with a restraint of conscience that flows from accepting absolute standards grounded in religious conviction."

Atrocious behavior on the part of youth is, then, attributable solely to the inherent unconstrained sinfulness of humankind arising from the absence of conscience that might have been instilled only thorough the inculcation of religious values. Attribution of antisocial behavior as a consequence of 'flawed processes' of a youth's environmental experience is to be disregarded as misguided tolerance.

In one fell swoop Mr. DeLay has clarified a centuries-old controversy, the attribution of bad behavior to a sinful nature, with little or no influence of the environment in which a child is nurtured, or to her genetic endowment. If humans were inherently inclined to 'do the wrong thing', it is unlikely that any of us would be here to tell the tale. In fact, the numerous kindred species within the hominid line doomed to extinction apparently *did* enter the world inclined to do the wrong thing, at least in relation to survival value. If it is wrong to survive then we humans are, indeed, inclined to do the wrong thing, as we have been the most successful survivors among the multitude of larger species that have inhabited this Earth through the ages. However, cultural developments that increasingly exploit rather than cherish youth as society's treasure trove have significantly diminished the odds on our survival.

Mr. DeLay and others of his persuasion find it convenient to ignore their own complicity in the failure of American youth, and through the unfulfilled opportunity of U.S. leadership, the youth of the world, to rise to their full potential. Only by acknowledging, and acting upon, links between the nurturing process and the quality of citizens will a future for life, with world peace, justice and prosperity be possible.

The Essentials of Nurturing

There are some things that science does not have to tell us - certainly not that the assertion about children having to overcome inherent universal 'flaws' is chimerical. Nor do we have to be told about the ill effects of deprivation and other forms of abuse during a child's early years - this is all too obvious. Life experiences and good sense inform us about what children need to reach their full potential - not only good educational opportunity, as promoted but misconstrued by members of school boards across the country[63], but an array of complementary support services equivalent to a chain whose weakest link determines its overall strength. It is all too apparent that failure to provide any component of a nurturing environment diminishes the effectiveness of other positive influences, perhaps to the least common denominator. This list of elements may not constitute the whole package, but none of them can be ignored if we are interested in rearing healthy, intelligent and socially responsible citizens:

- Adequate nourishment
- Comfortable shelter
- Freedom from violence, threats and other forms of abuse

- Protection from exposure to real or simulated (media) violence
- Emotional support
- Wholesome social interactions
- Intellectual stimulation – development of cognitive capacity
- Inculcation of democratic values
- Reinforcement of identity with nature

That most, if not all, of these elements are essential for proper nurturing is probably incontrovertible, but the last two might elicit some skepticism. Regarding democratic values, first, it is axiomatic that a democracy cannot function effectively with unprepared citizens. Even the U.S. is not an effective democracy, as amply demonstrated by widespread dismay concerning actions of federal officials after the economic meltdown of 2007, and that only a bare majority of eligible voters cast a ballot in national elections (invariably less than 50% in off-year Congressional elections). Had democracy functioned properly, public involvement would have precluded responses to the economic crises that were so much at odds with the wishes of the general public.

We have to recognize that democracy is not an inherent social propensity for humanity, as attested by the rarity of its institution, and far greater rarity of its success. The societal structure of primates, our nearest kin, and our own historical experience in social organization, indicate that hierarchy, autocracy and oligarchy have been much more the rule. The democratic experiments of ancient Greece and Rome reverted to autocracy and ultimate ruin when commitment to the challenging tenets of democracy slackened. The attainment of democracy has its price. Its values have to be worked at continuously to maintain its vitality, with inculcation of democratic values in youth the most significant part.

Yet aspiration for democracy appears to be widespread. Beatriz Magaloni (2007) studied the issue of transitions between autocracies and democracy during the period 1950 to 2000 (monarchy, military, single party, hegemonic party, democracy), concluding "the simulation yields good news for democrats, but not the dream of a democratic world." Only democratic and hegemonic party systems gained in frequency, with democracy transitions outpacing those of autocratic systems of all types. Democracies increased to slightly more than double the number at the beginning of the study period, many occurring at the time of the breakup of the former Soviet Union. Simulating the next 50 years using the transitions of the past decade (considering that the Cold War conditions that prevailed are no longer present), in 50 years time 77 percent of the regimes in the world would be democratic. Hegemonic party autocracies would be practically the only form of authoritarianism in 18 percent of the countries.

Children need to be oriented toward democracy because only informed self-governance inherently conduces to a secure future for our planet - for them as individuals, for society and for the rest of life. Intelligent and emotionally mature citizens, a prerequisite for a properly functioning democracy, make collective decisions from a perspective that encompasses the geographical and temporal panorama.

As nature is virtually synonymous with existence, humanity as a species apart from it is a dissonant concept that has somehow found its way into the rhetoric of politicians and religionists. Children need to be insulated from such destructive influences, or at least exposed to countermanding interactions and experiences that stress the identity of the individual with nature. One who so identifies will be unlikely to behave in ways that are disrespectful or destructive, thereby serving personal as well as societal interests.

The system of nurturing in the United States falls far short of what is required. Rather than create an environment for children that offers all of the essential elements indicated above, instead children are institutionalized each day in mind-addling classroom settings. Typically their natural inquisitiveness is stultified by the demand that they adhere to a lockstep force-feeding program and their identities are undermined by segregation from the daily societal rhythm. Is it any wonder that schools throughout the country are denizens of disoriented children and teachers? And yet, 'educators', their associations, unwitting parents and the political operatives who rely on their support, continually press for more of the same, demanding more edifices, higher compensation, and in general, more of a say in governance (to more securely assure their own aggrandizement?), too deeply positioned in the hole that we have created to even recognize the possibilities that lie just over the crest.

What the school system in the United States and the rest of the world needs is the wrecking ball. Children will develop their capacities to a much fuller extent, and maintain their identity with nature and society, if they are fully integrated into the social fabric from day one and from day to day. Children must never be shunted off to remote holding pens, and treated as if they are economic fodder. Certainly we have it within us to devise a system of nurturing that provides each child in the country, and in the world, the full panoply of elements required for healthy and productive citizenship.

A child living in deprivation is very likely to become a problem for society. Does it make sense to leave a child's environment to chance, particularly when there is a likelihood of inadequate support or even abuse? The mere begetting of children is not a license to treat one's offspring according to whim or to exploit them to satisfy self-oriented criteria. The stakes for society are too large to leave nurturing to chance. Our jails are already filled to overflowing with the products of poor parenting, and children around the world suffer unconscionable deprivation and abuse, so that some more secure guarantee of universally adequate nurturing is essential.

Child care

Do people who bear children and then abuse them (they cannot be called 'parents' in the true sense) have the right to control the lives of their offspring? Not only is it a miscarriage of justice to allow such people to willfully deprive any child of the necessities for solid upbringing, but an unwanted, maltreated and deprived child becomes a burden to society, with associated costs for the remainder of that young person's life.

Who is to be the nurturer of last resort? When individual caregivers fail, a society must be the default provider for the next generation. Standards are required that assure at least adequacy for each child in every area vital to her development and growth. People who are unable to provide for their children, or who are likely to raise them in substandard conditions have to forfeit their claim to direct the activities and fortunes of their offspring. On the other hand, procreation can no longer be considered a 'right', and some means must be found to prevent pregnancy in women and siring by men who are unfit to serve as parents. Although such interference in the reproductive process appears to be counter to the principles of freedom that prevail in the United States and many other countries, the severity of the problem of inadequate nurturing calls for draconian measures. Legislative bodies have to consider the balance between freedom and license regarding begetting of children.

At this writing 45 million Americans lack access to health care.[64] This is indicative of a mal-distribution of opportunity even in the country widely considered to be the wealthiest on Earth. It is reflective of the fact that many families, and particularly their children, are being deprived of adequate means to make the most of their lives.

Some attention has been paid to the plight of children by the United Nations. The Covenant on the Rights of the Child was promulgated by General Assembly resolution 44/25 in November 1989 and became international law on Sept. 2, 1990. The covenant outlaws exploitation and provides for their safety and well-being, specifically that:

- they grow up in safe and supportive conditions;
- they have access to high quality education and health care, and a good standard of living;
- governments agree to protect children from discrimination, sexual and commercial exploitation and violence;
- care is provided for orphans and young refugees.

The rights of children are defined (inadequate, but a start):

- To express opinion, especially concerning decisions that affect their lives;
- Freedom of thought, expression, conscience and religion;
- Private life and the right to play;
- To form their own clubs and organizations;
- Access to information, particularly from the state and the media;
- To make their own ideas and information known.

Another initiative was the formation of the Committee on the Rights of the Child, which began working in February 1991. There have been some positive developments, e.g. several countries have included articles in their constitutions that reflect the provisions of the Covenant. The World Health Organization (WHO) points to the need for data concerning the status of children around the world, but has not yet embarked upon a program of collection. However, WHO in 1999 acknowledged that child abuse had become a worldwide public health problem, and that about 40 million children suffer abuse each year. The organization asserts that they have evidence that it is possible to reduce the prevalence of child abuse when parents are provided training in parenting skills before and after birth in an environment supported by skilled personnel. Whether or not the impact of these initiatives has been significant is difficult to assess, but there is little evidence that the incidence of deprivation and abuse has improved worldwide.

Child abuse

At birth a human child is the most helpless offspring of any species on Earth. Without intensive protection and external management of virtually every area of its life support system, the child would certainly expire from lack of care, if not otherwise harmed or devoured by predators.

This extreme level of helplessness has been explained by retention of embryonic characteristics by juveniles (neotony). Because the human survival strategy is based upon intelligence and brain size, restrictions on the size of the pelvic opening in the birth canal required that human infants be born 'ahead of their time'.

For this reason, much of a child's brain development occurs after birth. Piaget[65] and other investigators of early childhood development have confirmed the significance of the immediate environment for youngsters, even during the prenatal stage. The conditions under which young persons are nurtured, the physical and social climate of the early years, are of greatest significance in the development of physical, intellectual and emotional characteristics. Regarding emotional health, people whose interests are closely aligned with those of the child best provide a supportive environment – caring parents, teachers, mentors and competent child care professionals. In the event of actual or imminent danger, these individuals' reactions would most likely serve the child's developmental needs.

Symptomatic of abuse are learning disorders, malnutrition, failure to thrive, conduct disorders, emotional retardation, and sexually transmitted diseases in very young children.[66] Andrea Sedlak and Diane Broadhurst (1966) explain abuse and neglect as a function of socio-economic status of the family, respectively 14 times and 44 times more common in poor families, findings that "cannot be plausibly explained on the basis of the higher visibility of lower income families to community professionals."[67]

In FFY (Federal fiscal year) 2008, 772,000 children were victims of maltreatment, 10.3 per 1,000 in the population. Children were subjected to neglect (71.1%), physical abuse (16.1%), sexual abuse (9.1%), psychological abuse (7.3%) and medical deprivation (2.2%).[68] An additional 9% of children were victims of abandonment, threats of harm or congenital drug addiction. Victimization rates varied by state from 1.5 to 29.1 per 1,000 children. Nearly 33 percent (32.6%) of all victims of maltreatment were younger than 4 years old.

At the beginning of the current century, almost two thousand children in the US die of abuse or neglect annually. Of survivors of abuse, about 20% suffer permanent injury. Children suffering from birth defects or other disorders are at higher risk. An estimated 1,356 children died from child abuse and neglect in 2000, *nearly four children every day*, a rate of 1.87 per 100,000. Of these fatalities, 80% of children were under 5 years and 40% under 1 year, second only to congenital anomalies as the cause of death in children of ages 1-4.[69]

In some cases those responsible for a child's welfare may not even be aware of abuse: children are particularly vulnerable to air, land and water pollution, which have been linked in numerous studies with some of the abuse symptoms. Community, commercial and industrial leaders are often insensitive to the cumulative buildup of pollutants in children's bodies.

The obvious forms of child abuse are denounced in most cultures, but are all too common: beatings and other physical maltreatment, abusive language and psychological oppression, sexual and labor exploitation. However, children are being increasingly abused and exploited in ways that have become acceptable in the industrialized countries and, through a kind of cultural imperialism, throughout the developing world.

A child is abused whenever its actions are directed by adults toward an objective that does not respond to the child's needs for developmental support and protection. Some of the most flagrant incidences of exploitation are perpetrated by media moguls subjecting youngsters to seemingly innocuous exposure to 'entertainment' and advertising media, where their helplessness is exploited by directing them to assume roles and to utter scripted materials that are, if anything, antithetical to their developmental needs. The resulting confusion and sense of betrayal appears to be of little concern to the perpetrators. It is one thing for children to take part in the school play, dances or games, coached and directed by teachers and parents who presumably care for them and would not place them in frightening or tense situations. It is quite another to be manipulated by commercially oriented media personnel, who generally regard the child actor as nothing more than an instrument of the trade.

Abuse and deprivation among children takes many other forms: they are physically and emotionally constrained to conform to the needs of their 'guardians'; neglected and left to fend for themselves; pressed into work, often in hazardous and stressful conditions with little or no compensation; widely malnourished; conscripted for military service and often manipulated into committing atrocious acts by sadistic overlords, sexually exploited by a wide array of pedophiles – rapacious offenders, members of the clergy, often relatives who demonically betray the child's trust. For insensitive or exploitative people around the world, children's vulnerabilities present too easy a target.

Dorothy Lewis, M.D., in a paper published in 1993[70], explained the relationship between abuse of children and subsequent antisocial behavior. One factor rarely discussed in associating behavior and early experience is the intrauterine environment. For example, minor viral infections, maternal anxiety and psychological stress during the pre-natal period, maternal alcoholism and other substances abuse by the mother affects fetal development and subsequent postnatal social and intellectual functioning. Other factors precipitating aggression and other antisocial behavior patterns, according to Dr. Lewis, include living under stress, isolation and neglect, exposure to aggressive adults, pain and physical abuse and the quality of early parenting - high rates of obesity, smoking, use of hallucinogens and other unhealthy practices leaves an inordinate number of child begetters in a state of health not conducive to proper child rearing.

But we do not need to be reminded by scientific investigators of the indelible effects on children of experiences of abuse. Think of a child locked up in a closet from birth for a number of years (there have been a number of instances of this kind) and deprived of most, if not all, of the elements required for development. Would it be any wonder that this child emerges from such maltreatment disoriented, angry, hostile and otherwise anti-social?

Child Hunger

Even in the United States of America, purportedly the wealthiest country on the globe, children go hungry. Deprivation of opportunity for children in the United States is endemic[71]:

- Nationwide, 18% of children, more than 12 million, live in families that are officially considered poor (13 million children), ranging from 7% in New Hampshire to 27% in Mississippi.

- Among ethnic groups, 35% of black children, 28% of Latino children, 29% of American Indian, 11% of Asian and 10% of white children live in poor families.

- 20% of children under age 6 (20%) and 16% of children age 6 or older live in poor families.

Hunger is one consequence of poverty. In 2008, 14.6 percent of households were food insecure at least some time during that year, an increase from 11.1 percent in 2007.[72] This is the highest recorded prevalence rate of food insecurity since 1995 when the first national food security survey was conducted.

In a study of childhood hunger in the United States, investigative journalist Loretta Schwartz-Nobel (2002) recounts horrific stories of areas in the United States where children forage for food in garbage cans. Deprivation of adequate nutrition in early childhood leaves an imprint that is virtually indelible, and which can only be ameliorated by extensive and long-term therapy.

"A young child's brain grows so rapidly that, by the age of two it has achieved 80% of its full development. If adequate nutrients are not available during this critical period, the brain's weight and size may be irreversibly compromised. The result may be a child who is mildly to moderately retarded for the rest of his or her life." Schwartz-Nobel reviews the consequences of advanced malnutrition: children's hands and feet lack warmth and color; muscles weaken and subcutaneous fat is depleted; in advanced cases the abdomen and extremities become swollen, the nervous system is stressed, mental faculties diminished, maintaining normal body temperature, blood pressure and pulse rate become difficult; injuries do not heal, intestinal bleeding occurs - the signs of advanced protein deficiency - kwashiorkor.

The extent of childhood hunger in America was covered in a report by the *All Things Considered* newscast of National Public Radio on March 10, 1998, which asserted that "hunger in America had reached a point where one in ten Americans regularly use a neighborhood food bank or soup kitchen in order to eat............ More than a third were families where at least one adult was working and 38% of the hungry were children." Globally, the UN Population Fund report for 2009 indicates that over 1 billion people worldwide suffer from malnutrition, about a third of them children.

Antisocial behavior and incarceration of youth

Social ostracism and economic deprivation that minorities have suffered is reflected in the rates of incarceration of youth and adults. Christopher Placek[73] reported the following national incarceration for American youth in the age group 10-17 (per 100,000): White – 5; African American – 44.1; Latino – 7.4; Native American – 9.2; Asian – 2.5. According to a US Department of Justice study on incarceration statistics, 64 percent of prison inmates belonged to racial or ethnic minorities in 2001. For males of all ages, imprisonment in 2001 was higher for black males (16.6%) and Hispanic males (7.7%) than for white males (2.6%), and higher also for black females (1.7%) and Hispanic females (0.7%) than white females (0.3%). A report from the nonprofit criminal justice research organization *National Council on*

Crime and Delinquency, released in Jan. 2007, found that Wisconsin led the country in the number of non-white youth committed to adult prisons (per 100,000 rounded): black 155; American Indian 110; Hispanic 51; white 8. The rate of incarceration in the US is higher than any other industrialized country – although only 5% of global population, 25% of global prisoners are in US detention facilities.

Is it any mystery that minority youths suffer greater rates of incarceration than whites? Even with minority parents who have every intention of raising their offspring to be responsible citizens, children who are deprived of opportunity or who are otherwise singled out for discrimination of one sort or another, as minorities have typically experienced, are more likely to exhibit antisocial behavior patterns that often end in brushes with the law.

A report by the organization *Fight Crime: Invest in Kids*[74] revealed that children who were given adequate nurturing in the early years were far less likely to exhibit antisocial behavior as adolescents and adults: "Powerful evidence from one study after another proves that quality education child care in the first years of life can greatly reduce the risk that today's babies and toddlers will become tomorrow's violent teens and adults" The report cites one study in which half of a group of at-risk three and four-year-olds were randomly assigned to a pre-kindergarten program. Twenty-two years later those who had been left out were five times more likely to have become chronic lawbreakers with five times more arrests. Children whose needs are neglected will inevitably vent their frustrations by resorting to dishonesty and violence against their peers, their caregivers and society in general.

Child health

Children suffer widespread abuse in another form, which leaves its lasting imprint on their bodies and mental states. The polluted environment to which all too many children are exposed is a significant factor in high rates of childhood physical and mental illness. In children's rapidly growing bodies, rates of ingestion compared with body weight is much greater than for healthy adults, which leaves them exceptionally vulnerable to the contaminants that are now so prevalent in the air they breathe, the water they drink, and the food that they consume. To add to this assault on their health, as a response to symptoms arising from the unwholesome conditions in which they live, and the incapacity or unwillingness of many modern day child begetters to provide the necessary quality and quantity of parenting, children are quickly shuttled off to medical establishments that thrive on the revenue source that they provide, and that uses them as guinea pigs (see below).

A report of the US Environmental Protection Agency[75] reveals that childhood illnesses have increased dramatically over the past few decades. The incidence of asthma has been growing steadily. Currently as many almost 14% of children in the US were, at some point in their lives, diagnosed with this disease. The incidence of cancer in children has been on a steady rise in past 3 decades, from about 120 to 175 cases per million children. Diagnosed mental retardation afflicts about 5 - 10 children per 1000, although the incidence of diagnosed childhood mental disorders of all types is much greater.

According to a report by the US Public Broadcasting Service (PBS)[76], there has been a 4000 % increase in diagnoses of bipolar disorder in children over past decade. Uncertainties within the medical establishment concerning diagnosis and treatment has led many practitioners to essentially experiment with medications because they have little knowledge about if, why and how they work. In recent years, there has been a dramatic increase in the number of children being diagnosed with serious psychiatric disorders and prescribed medications that are just beginning to be tested in children. Drugs that have been administered can cause serious side effects, and virtually nothing is known about their long-term impact. "It's really to some extent an experiment, trying medications in these children of this age," according to child psychiatrist Dr. Patrick Bacon. "It's a gamble. And I tell parents there's no way to know what's going to work." Child psychiatrist Dr. David Axelson states that "Very little is known about the effects of medications being used in the treatment of a complicated illness like bipolar. …So far, no antipsychotic drugs have been approved for treating children who have schizophrenia or bipolar illness. These drugs are used 'off-label', i.e. for purposes others than for what they were tested or approved by the FDA." Nonetheless, they are being used on children. In this report Dr. Kiki Chang explains how researchers are "at the forefront" in understanding how the medications work, but the field is not there yet.

Data from the EPA study suggest that childhood illness is attributable to the environment in which their growing bodies are exposed: About 65% of children are exposed to levels of ozone exceeding EPA standards, 15% to excessive particulate matter. Removal of lead as an anti-knock component in gasoline a few years ago, and improved emissions standards in many states have led to a significant decrease in childhood exposure to lead and carbon monoxide. About 11% of children are routinely exposed to cigarette smoke (2003 data). Serum cotinine, a marker for nicotine exposure, has reduced from about 2 to 1 micrograms per ml in the past 2 decades or so. About 2% of children in the US drink water with contaminants exceeding EPA standards - nitrate/nitrite, coliforms, lead and copper, disinfection byproducts, chemical and radionuclides. Detectible residues of organophosphate pesticides are found in approximately 20% of foods (grains, fruits, vegetables, drinks). 1-2% of children live within 1 mile of a hazardous waste site.

Although in its report on child health the EPA presents no data on exposure of children to PCB's, dioxins, furans or volatile organic substances, e.g. formaldehyde from insulation and carpeting, there is little doubt that these have significant effects. One study performed over a period of twenty years on about a thousand people of Seveso, Italy exposed to dioxin during an industrial accident in 1976[77] revealed an increase in incidence of all cancers. An excess of lymphohemopoietic neoplasm (malignant or non-malignant tumor originating in bone cells) was found in both genders. Hodgkin's disease (cancer originating in the white blood cells) risk was elevated in the first 10-year observation period, whereas the highest increase for non-Hodgkin's lymphoma (a type of cancer involving cells of the immune system) and myeloid leukemia occurred after 15 years. An overall increase in diabetes was reported, notably among women. Chronic circulatory and respiratory diseases were moderately increased, suggesting a link with accident-related stressors and chemical exposure. Results support evaluation of dioxin as carcinogenic to humans and corroborate the hypotheses of its association with other health outcomes, including cardiovascular- and endocrine-related effects.

Americans engage widely in unhealthful activities. According to a 2008 survey[78] of Americans 12 years of age or older, an estimated 20.1 million Americans were current substance abusers, including hallucinogens and non-medical prescription drugs. Slightly more than half of Americans use alcohol, and more than one fifth, 58.1 million people (23.3 percent) participated in binge drinking at least once in the 30 days prior to the survey, and 17.3 million were reported as heavy drinkers. An estimated 70.9 million Americans (28.4 percent of the population) were current (past month) users of a tobacco product. Approximately 70 million Americans, about a quarter of the population, are obese.[79] These practices must be reflected in future behaviors of impressionable children, who strive to emulate their role models.

From all indications, a number of conditions are adversely affecting the mental and physical health of children of the US and other industrialized countries:

- Exposure to substances resulting from environmental pollution for which the human body is intolerant, particularly significant for children with low body weight compared with adults;

- Under control of parents who are, themselves, suffering ill effects of pollution and widespread unhealthy life styles;

- Inclination of physically and mentally unhealthy parents to routinely seek treatment for real and imagined illnesses of their children from the medical establishment, rather than taking responsibility for providing a healthy environment, a tendency exacerbated by availability of publicly subsidized medical service plans such as Medicade and Medicare;

- Complicit medical practitioners, prone to treat symptoms that could easily be alleviated with proper parental care and involvement, and who prescribe drugs for children with little to no understanding of the impact mechanisms in the body or their consequences;

- A medical services system operated for profit and controlled largely by the insurance industry.

Hippocratic Oath notwithstanding, the medical establishment appears to be uninterested in keeping people healthy, its practitioners having invested huge amounts of time and money in gaining authorization to medicate people and to carry out surgical procedures.

How many times have you heard one of them tell you that you do not really need them, that if you go home and do the right things for your health, your body will take care of itself? After all, though there are useful analogies with machines, the body has a capacity that no automobile engine possesses - to heal itself. And yet, all too often medical practitioners act as if this capacity does not exist, and behave rather like auto mechanics, STP and wrench at the ready.

Child performers

One form of child abuse that is scarcely recognizable is subjecting children to the rigid control and confusing direction demanded by media, theatre and other public exposure. Children have been exploited in this way for their obvious appeal, in movies, plays, advertisements, and other forms of public display. If directed by one who is sensitive to the pitfalls, such experiences can be positive for children, but more often than not the experience is detrimental to the child performer's interests.

Children are increasingly recruited as media objects. Marketing and 'entertainment' professionals have discovered the latent predilection of potential clients to experience vicarious pleasure through identification with the powerful, as a potent mechanism for both titillating the passions and inspiring brand loyalty. Viewing a child in simulated subjugation strikes a responsive chord.

Media technology has progressed to the point where it should be possible in most cases to simulate the actions and utterances of children. In fact, many television and film presentations already have figured out how to do this, and the practice is already widespread. In some respects this is regrettable, as it does allow media to depict children in exploitative situations without employing real children. The solution resides in the level of awareness within the population. When adults are sufficiently repelled by such images, the practice will be curtailed either through legislative action or as market forces come to bear on the issue. There is no reason any longer, if ever there was, to directly involve children, or even images of children, in such productions.

The routine display by media of children in exploitative situations is of concern beyond the immediate consequences for the children involved. Such public displays tend to legitimate acceptability of preying on the helpless. It reinforces a cultural tendency to justify the exercise of advantage, regardless of the consequences to others. So much for the Golden Rule.

In the US these unwholesome practices are defended by some under the provision of the First Amendment of the Constitution. The equal protection clause, however, has greater relevance, as the ability of children to cope with exploiters is inherently inferior to that of adults. Equal protection implies that defenses from exploitation must be statutorily strengthened for children. The issue goes far beyond that of child labor laws, other forms of physical molestation, or corrupting the morals of a minor. The emotional health of the child has to be protected under any circumstances. Statutes can be promulgated that would prevent adults from influencing a child to perform any action or to make any utterance that is not related directly to the child's well being: criminalizing these practices would tend to keep the child out of harm's way. School and community activities in which the child's interests are the predominant theme would be encouraged. Harangues by autocratic and domineering sports directors and coaches would not. Certainly exploitation of children by media (and some misguided parental handmaidens) would be outlawed.

Some children led into performing or other public roles win lucrative contracts, awards or medals, usually shared with parents, guardians or agents. Others do not fare so well, and in addition to deprivation of their childhood, are forced to work excessively with attendant physical and mental stress. The needs of the child performer are not always aligned with those of her directors, who may be interested in gaining access to the child's earnings or driven by ambition. Child performers are exposed to dimensions of adult life with which they lack experience to cope, e.g. sex, alcohol and drugs. Involvement as public figures reduces the amount of time and opportunities for learning and character development, which for children may be irredeemable.

Child athletes typically develop eating disorders from demands to maintain size and weight. Malnutrition is problematic for young girls who develop menstruation and other problems of puberty, leading to fractures and osteoporosis. Child performers are subjected to pressures of exposure to audiences, which can be difficult even for seasoned adult performers

A case in point is the life of Judy Garland, child star of 'The Wizard of Oz' and many other theatrical 'successes'. Garland was thrust into the theatre by her vaudevillian parents and the tender age of 3, along with a sister. It was apparently the root of great antipathy that she eventually came to feel for her parents, from whom she became estranged, once characterizing her mother as "no good for anything except to create chaos and fear" and accusing her of treating Garland essentially as a cash cow from the earliest days of her career.[80]

To keep up with the frantic pace of making one film after another, Garland, her frequent child costar Mickey Rooney, and other young performers were constantly given amphetamines and barbiturates to take before bed so that they could keep up the frantic pace of production.[81] For Garland, this regular exposure to drugs led to addiction and a lifelong struggle, and contributed to her eventual death from an overdose of barbiturates, after reeling through five marriages. Despite her theatrical triumphs, Garland was plagued throughout her life with self-doubt and required constant reassurance that she was talented and attractive.[82] Garland's physical appearance was a source of consternation to the film moguls who sought to milk her talents to the utmost. During the filming of 'The Wizard of Oz', corseting and other devices were applied to alter her 16-year-old figure to the director's criteria. Her insecurity was exacerbated by insensitive treatment by her theatrical controllers, one of whom[83] referred to her as his "little hunchback."

Reality TV

The latest fad promoted by avaricious media moguls is 'Reality' television, which presents ostensibly ad-libbed situations with ordinary people performing rather than professionals. Children are frequent participants, placed in embarrassing and often dangerous situations that are a reflection of decreasing concern for children's welfare. It's clear that the quest for innovative programming runs wild as 'Reality' television programming exploits children for the aggrandizement of uncaring producers. Children's marketing appeal is too much of a lure for avaricious media functionaries, who will do anything to increase revenues and control costs. Children have great appeal, while at the same time not demanding much. They are malleable and vulnerable, qualities that endear them even more to money-grubbing producers.

Unthinking parents often sign away protections for their children, usually in violation of child labor laws, exposing them to danger. In one program a child reportedly burned her face and two children drank bleach from an unmarked bottle.[84]

Reality TV shows are "an opportunity for networks and producers to exploit kids' weaknesses, their frailties, their vulnerabilities, by putting them in unknown, shocking and often very embarrassing situations," says entertainment lawyer Robert Pafundi, who has represented reality-TV youths and child actors. "They're making the mistake of assuming that children are adults in little bodies and that they can handle all these things. And it simply isn't true."[85] One former child actor, Paul Petersen, is reportedly so concerned about the effects on children that he formed an organization 'A Minor Consideration' in 1990 to advocate legislation and other interventions to protect child actors, who are susceptible to great confusion in being directed to act according to script or circumstance rather than just being themselves. The American Academy of Child and Adolescent Psychiatry lobbied NBC to cancel the Reality show "Baby Borrowers" on the grounds that the program could cause the on-camera babies and toddlers distress and anxiety. The creator defends it as "an educational tool designed to prevent teen pregnancy - one that borrows from reality TV to keep folks engaged while it makes its point: Parenting isn't for the faint of heart and is best left to grown-ups. *What better way to educate, he says, than to entertain* (italics added)?"

Entertainment as education? Many academics apparently think so. Rather than focusing on opportunities for enlightenment, instead they treat the lecture room podium as a sound stage, titillating and mesmerizing their charges to serve their inflated egos.

What is wrong with Reality TV, you ask. It is simply this: any time a child is placed in a situation where she is directed to do something outside the context of her intellectual and other developmental needs, particularly by people with whom she is neither familiar nor comfortable, she is confused and troubled, if not needlessly exposed to danger. In fact, children should never be directed to do anything, much less by outsiders. What a child needs is proper nurturing, part of which is careful, delicate and scrupulous illumination of the nature and consequences of the situation in which she finds herself. This is best accomplished by caring people, mainly enlightened parents and others totally committed to the child's interests and welfare.

Reality TV with children is a bad idea that should be scrapped, along with the avaricious producers who cravenly exploit children, without concern for the consequences for the most precious of segment of any society's population.

Slave labor and prostitution

Employment of children in jobs that not only amount to slave labor but that also place children in situations where they suffer beatings, malnutrition, and, often, sexual exploitation is rampant across the globe. Children make up a significant part of the industrial work force in many countries. They are often employed under stressful and otherwise dangerous condition, and paid little to nothing. Many millions of children are producing furniture in Indonesia, soccer balls in Asia, and doing difficult and hazardous agricultural jobs throughout the world.

According to the United Nations Children's Fund (UNCF), as many as 1.2 million children per year are caught up in trafficking. Aside from being denied the opportunity for a normal family environment, trafficked children are used as sources of cheap or even slave labor and suffer violence in addition to sexual exploitation. According to UNCF, over 30% of the sex workers in Southeast Asia are between 12 and 17 years old.

In 2005 NBC News investigators from the Dateline television program found that in Cambodia impoverished families are selling their children, as young as 5 years old, for sex. In a country still reeling from the effects of the atrocities of the Khmer Rouge a couple of decades ago, sexual predators are able to gain control over these children for a pittance. Their exploiters, who operate sex-for-hire emporiums, sell virgins for premium prices because the demand is so great. A 14-year-old from a poor Vietnamese family while walking home from school one day was lured to work in a café that was really a brothel. The girl was forced to have sex with men, including many Americans. One pimp led stunned investigators to his 'stable' of prostitutes, some of whom were as young 8 years old. The same sort of thing is happening in other trafficking centers such as Bangkok and Amsterdam.

An article in the Cambodia Daily in December 2000 exposes the case of 57-year old American pedophile engaged in sexual encounters with a 14-year old. The Cambodian prosecutor publicly exonerates the child molester because he claims that the child is not a virgin and has previously operated as a prostitute. The fact that the child has been sucked out of the cesspool of grinding poverty, and manipulated by desperate or unfeeling family members and pimps for their survival or aggrandizement, as the case may be, is of little significance to the prosecutor. The assertion of willing participation by a 14-year old for this kind of activity is so patently absurd as to strain the imagination.

Aside from direct sale of children, a typical ploy for operators is to set up an agency ostensibly for supplying domestic workers for the relatively affluent. In many cases, desperate but well-meaning parents release their children in hopes of giving them an opportunity for gainful employment, for education or for providing adequate shelter. Typically the reality is that these young children become slaves who are forced to provide household services without compensation and often sex. A case in point is Adiza, a 10-year-old Togolese girl sent to work as a domestic by her aunt, who raised her after her parents separated. Adiza was sent to the home of a woman in Lome, Togo's capitol, who was only marginally better off economically. She was forced to work long hours without pay, beaten and denied schooling and adequate nutrition. She finally ran away and found her way to a shelter run by a Swiss charity.[86]

Poverty among children

At the present time nearly 45 million Americans live in poverty, defined as an individual earning $9,393 or less and $14,680 or less for a family of three.[87] This currently amounts to 10 percent of all families, 7.6 million. What is even more ominous is that the disparity in incomes between rich and poor is widening. According to Jared Bernstein, a labor economist with the Economic Policy Institute, "in the last few decades, pay for wealthier Americans has risen dramatically - fueled by growth in salaries, bonuses, stock options and other compensation, but wages for millions of lower-wage workers have dwindled. Many have lost their jobs altogether."[88] The wage gap in the U.S. will most likely continue to increase, according to Kent Hughes (2005), economist at the Woodrow Wilson Center in Washington DC. Hughes believes that competition from the foreign labor force, often willing to work for minimal compensation even in the skilled professions, will further pressure the collapse in wages for American workers.

The rate of child poverty in the United States is more than double that in most developed countries.[89] Children living in poverty have a few more strikes against them. According to J. Lawrence Aber, director of the National Center for Children in Poverty (NCCP), the current child poverty rate is about twice as high as it was in 1969. They typically have greater rates of school failure, illness and premature death. Poverty is also a function of ethnicity. In the year 2000 about twice as many African Americans and Latinos lived in poverty as compared with Whites and Asian Americans.[90]

U.S. Census Bureau data provides further evidence that economic growth does not necessarily translate into a better deal for children, as poverty among American youth has increased during the past three decades. Poverty among children is endemic in the western world and catastrophic everywhere: after the longest peacetime expansion in American history that ended in 2007, one in five American children (20.3%) lived in poverty, according to a study in 2001.[91] Sweden has the lowest rate of child poverty with 2.4%, but New York leads all states with 20.6% of its youngsters living below the poverty line. Deprivation suffered by children around the world is brought into stark relief with an understanding of the economic status of children in the United States, purportedly the richest country in the world.

Robert F. Drinan, S.J., a priest who was a member of the United States Congress, discussed the plight of children around the world in his study *Poverty in America, A Global Revolution for Children*.[92] He points out that almost a billion people entered the 21st century unable to read a book or sign their names. Father Drinan predicted that in the year 2000 over 130 million children would grow up without access to basic education. Girls constitute 73 percent of this number, which is linked to high rates of infant mortality. He points to the state of Kerala in southern India, where universal literacy results in the lowest rate of infant mortality in any developing country.

Progress in literacy rates continued up to the time that developing countries were confronted with payments on massive debt and were forced into restructuring by the International Monetary Fund in the 1980's. Currently almost 50 percent of children in the 47 least-developed countries have no access to primary education.

Children worldwide are plagued with sickness and malnutrition. "There are still nearly 11 million children who die every year of preventable causes."[93] Almost always they are the poorest and most marginalized. A more recent menace in sub-Saharan Africa is the prevalence of HIV - AIDS, with young people between 12 and 24 years of age constituting about 60 percent of infected individuals.

Child soldiers

"Approximately 250,000 children under the age of 18 are thought to be fighting in conflicts around the world, and hundreds of thousands more are members of armed forces who could be sent into combat at any time. Although most child soldiers are between 15 and 18 years old, significant recruitment starts at the age of 10 and the use of even younger children has been recorded."[94] This has led to efforts of international bodies to prevent the recruitment of children as participants. In May 2000 the General Assembly of the United Nations adopted the *Optional Protocol to the Convention on the Rights of the Child*, which had first been promulgated in the 1980's. The Convention affirms that children around the world require special protections and calls for improvements the status of children in conditions of peace and security. The Rome Statute of the International Criminal Court identifies conscription or enlisting children under the age of 15 years or using them to participate actively in hostilities in both international and non-international armed conflict as a war crime. In June 1999, the International Labor Organization Convention No. 182 approved a provision to prohibit forced or compulsory recruitment of children for use in armed conflict.

According to a report by the Coalition to Stop Recruitment of Child Soldiers, efforts to restrict or eliminate the use of children in armed conflict have not been particularly successful. "Armed groups in at least 24 countries located in every region of the world were known to have recruited children under 18 years of age, and many have used them in hostilities. Many have proved resistant to pressure and persuasion. Their widely diverse characters, aims and methods, and the varied environments in which they operate militate against generic solutions."[95] Myanmar is identified as the worst offender, with thousands of children used in the government's counter-insurgency campaign. Other countries that continue to press children into armed hostilities are Chad, Congo, Somalia, Sudan and Uganda. The report also states that children were used as human shields in some instances, for example by both Israeli forces[96] and the Palestinians[97] in their conflicts. In some instances children have been employed as spies, subjecting them to the risk of reprisal.[98]

Regrettably, the US military has apparently fought to prevent international agreement on a minimum of 18 years of age for conscription or recruitment[99] by inducements aimed at younger children, leaving high school students within their target population.

Debasing society's future

Children are a society's treasure. Failure to foster the physical and mental health of every young person, to provide the means for intellectual development and refinement of character, and to inculcate societal values, virtually dooms a society to decline and ultimately even to extinction. If democracy is cherished as a precious form of social organization, it has to be recognized that it cannot function for a population that is uninformed, intellectually deprived, and in a poor state of mental and physical health. Development of the greatest potential for every child has to become the first priority, certainly in the United States as a model for responsible leaders throughout the world. Achievement of a well-functioning democracy has its price, but the advantages to be gained by this expenditure in human capital are incalculable.

Chapter 5
RIGHTS ARE WRONG
IN DEMOCRACY

Societies that consider themselves enlightened and progressive take great pride in having granted their citizens 'rights' – legal guarantees concerning respect and support for citizens' aspirations, so long as they conform to social norms. While primitive societies tend to be autocratic, with little protection from arbitrary decisions of elites concerning the welfare of ordinary members, civilized society usually promulgates rules of behavior and legal standards that provide a greater degree of security for life, limb and property.

The second section of the Declaration of Independence of the United States of America, adopted by the Second Continental Congress on July 4, 1776, contains these words: "We hold these truths self-evident, that all men are created equal, that they are endowed by their Creator with certain inalienable *rights* (italics added), that among these are life, liberty and the pursuit of happiness"

Inalienable rights? What is inalienable is absolute, immutable, undeniable. As used in the Declaration of Independence, rights are fundamental perquisites that may not be abrogated. There are at least two problems with this statement: First, even if there is an interventionist Creator, it is not likely that she, he or it would be concerned with rights. Overwhelming evidence indicates that such a Creator would have to be considered anything but benevolent – too much bloodshed, other forms of violence and injustice inflicted even on its most devout followers (see Chapter 7). Even if a Creator does grant rights, there is little evidence that it carries much weight. In its earthly manifestations, rights promulgated for citizens of any state have proven to be anything but inalienable.[100]

Life? Citizens are routinely put to death by the state (with or without due process according to the particular system for doling out this type of punishment), either as retaliation for conviction for certain acts considered to be of capital offense or as a deterrent. *Liberty?* Millions of people are incarcerated and deprived of liberty, some for committing acts with only themselves as victims. *Pursuit of happiness?* In early 2010 there are officially approximately 15 million unemployed persons in the United States alone, many desperate to find a source of income. Millions more have abandoned the quest and are in a virtually permanent state of unhappiness. According to the United Nations Population Fund, over 1 billion people worldwide are hungry.

No, if there are any rights granted, it is by consent either of the governor or governed, depending on political structure. Obsequious political figures may claim a theological origin for rights, but only designated authorities in the political hierarchy can effectively grant them, and can as easily take them away or otherwise deny them on the grounds of expediency or security.

Granting 'rights' to subjects of political authority is a rather new social invention, probably derived initially from the Magna Carta, negotiated with King John in 1215 by English Barons who were interested in protecting some of their privileges. The document was amended from time to time, and the version of 1297 is still in effect in England and Wales. One of the main clauses is that of 'due process', whereby citizens are guaranteed a hearing by their peers for offenses charged by state authorities.

A 'Bill of Rights' was a condition for conferring the crown of England to William of Orange by the Westminster Convention of 1689, an 'Act Declaring the Rights and Liberties of the Subject, and Settling the Succession of the Crown'. By virtue of this act, William and his wife, Mary, were enjoined from enacting or suspending laws or levying taxes for their own aggrandizement without the consent of Parliament. Similarly, in an 'Act of Settlement' of 1701 the Hanoverian Princess

Sophia accepted the crown along with a 'Bill of Rights' containing a proviso that she and her heirs would be powerless to enact laws without the consent of Parliament.[101]

So, historically, the concept of rights derives from reaction to what were considered unjust laws and levying of taxes by royal prerogative. The mechanism of redress was to assign powers to a representative body of peers or citizens for approving royal initiatives.

In the U.S. the founding fathers in 1791 proposed and sent to the states during the First Congress the first ten amendments to the U.S. Constitution, a Bill of Rights that enunciated a series of liberties for individuals vis-à-vis constitutional authority. James Madison proposed the Bill of Rights as a concession to anti-Federalists, who threatened ratification of the Constitution, fearing the strong central government advocated by the Federalists. One early proponent was George Mason, a southern planter and delegate to the Federal Convention in 1787 charged with drafting the Constitution, who had previously proposed something similar for his home state of Virginia. Mason refused to sign the constitutional draft because it lacked a clear statement of individual rights.

The concept of officially specified rights resonated with libertarian national leaders in the face of virtually limitless opportunities for resource exploitation, which carried more weight than its functions as a constraint on authority or on the practice of selective granting of privileges, as in the Magna Carta.

The ninth Amendment asserts that the enumeration of certain (individual) rights in the Constitution "shall not be construed to deny or disparage others retained by the people." However, enthusiasm for the Constitution's 'inalienable rights' was tempered by caution even of Federalists who championed individual rights during the Constitutional Convention of 1789, but who, according to Morrison (1965) "had learned from experience that the natural rights philosophy, taken straight, would go to the nation's head and make it totter, or fall." There appeared to be at least a sense that 'rights' granted to citizens, or even those 'retained by the people', might be a polarizing influence, turning citizens inward to seek their own advantage even, if need be, at society's expense.

As these individual 'rights' have been so firmly entrenched in the American ethos, the concept has been extended accordingly, far beyond the original intent. The notion has surfaced in many contexts, such as 'human rights', 'civil rights', 'property rights', and ultimately to what makes society (i.e. the government) essentially the provider of last resort. Local governments in the United States and elsewhere, corporations and individual citizens, who have exceeded their ability to support their desired levels of expenditure or consumption, now routinely appeal to the federal government to bail them out.

Within the past century or so, and particularly since the publication of "Origin of Species" by Charles Darwin in 1859, it has become clear that humans descended from primitive organisms such as bacteria and archaea that formed initially during the Archeozoic Eon of 3.9 to 2.5 billion years ago. Only about five to seven million years ago, *H. sapiens* shared a common ancestor with the apes. During the past 4-5 million years several species of hominids (bipedal, large-brained primates), evolved and became extinct. Only Homo sapiens among these hominids stood the test of exposure to the changing environmental challenges. If the Creator was to invest humans with inalienable rights, it had to be a fairly complex endeavor, as the first human genes were propagating and replacing the then extant hominid stock. During the transition, the Creator would have had difficulty deciding if a particular individual or generation had been sufficiently transformed to qualify for inalienable rights (however, see comments of Pope John Paul II, Chapter 7, in which he reconciles the existence of soul in humans, while denying it for our primate ancestors and cousins, implicitly identifying the precise point at which his deity produced the genetic alteration separating humans from beasts).

It appears doubtful that 'rights' are writ large in the sky. This does not restrain massive numbers of Americans from assertions about their rights, whether or not constitutionally sanctioned. For example, many individuals assert their right to do with their property as they wish, regardless of consequences to their neighbors. The 'right' of control over one's offspring in a manner of one's choosing, regardless of the possibility of engendering - through negligence, incompetence or other deficiencies - insensitivity, abuse or (even worse) menaces to society, is stoutly defended. The 'right' to vitriolic, hate-mongering, or abusive speech is asserted to be under the protection of the First Amendment. The 'right' to drive an automobile in any condition of repair and at any level of control, particularly in the U.S., is widely thought to be inviolate (although about one third of states do conduct annual safety inspections). The 'right' of access to firearms is so firmly entrenched that efforts merely to keep guns out of the hands of incompetents and children are strenuously opposed by powerful lobbies - this despite, in the U.S. during 2006, 30,896 deaths from firearms: suicide 16,883; homicide 12,791; accident 642; legal intervention 360; undetermined 220.[102]

In early twenty first century United States, exercise of some 'rights' has resulted in catastrophe for the nation's youth. The mass media exercise their 'right' (if not obligation) to court the attention of children (and the legions of adults who are similarly vulnerable), adapting them through clever psychological devices to revel in violent solutions to every sort of problem. Couple this with the inviolable 'right' of citizens to bear arms, and you have a situation in which young people have taken to dealing with their "enemies" in the predominant mode of their socialization - to blow them away in a hail of gunfire in simulated, and sometimes all too real, assaults. The situation is exacerbated by actual access of youth to firearms, coupled with the culture of violence expressed in video games and internet web sites, such as those that provide instructions on how to construct pipe bombs and the like. There is little doubt that these media devices provide powerful influences for vulnerable youth, inciting them to violent responses, and reinforcing their anger from ordinary frustrations.

Is there any serious doubt about this connection? In the U.S., only homicide, as a cause of childhood deaths, has increased over the past three decades. About 1,800 juveniles were victims of homicide in 1999 - substantially higher than other developed countries. While murder of juveniles is rare in many areas of the country, overall, eight children die each day in the U.S. from gun-related incidents (homicides and accidental shootings).[103]

The 'rights' enumerated in the Constitution by the founding fathers were promulgated in an era when fear of autocratic rule predominated as a consequence of their experience with English monarchs. However, a very functional system of social organization and governance can more effectively be predicated on the concept of individual responsibility. Think what the consequences might be if all citizens are nurtured to internalize the virtues of social responsibility. Laws and regulations would be promulgated admonishing citizens to carry out their responsibilities rather than to exercise their rights. Most importantly, youngsters would be universally inculcated with the responsibilities of citizenship. If penalty, retribution or castigation were needed, they would result from failure to adhere to standards of responsibility rather than from violating others' 'rights'.

'Rights' set the individual against society. Citizens of societies in which they are inculcated with a sense of rights have to be inclined to think of themselves as alien to the social structure, employing this authority to extract self-aggrandizing perquisites that tend to enhance personal wealth, prestige and social advancement. Consequences for the society are far down on the list of concerns. Garrett Hardin explained the phenomenon as the 'tragedy' of the commons:

"Ruin is the destination toward which all men rush, each pursuing his own best interest in a society that believes in the freedom of the commons [in this context the socio-political framework]. Freedom in a commons brings ruin to all."[104] Hardin alludes to psychological denial that evolution, through natural selection, has created, allowing the individual to ignore the deleterious consequences of misuse of the commons. He suggests education as a way of avoiding this catastrophe, but that it must be applied relentlessly to have any significant effect.

Whence cometh rights but the commons, the socio-political structure shared by all citizens? And yes, the sense of responsibility required to circumvent the menace to which Hardin alludes, requires virtually constant reinforcement. Rather than being indoctrinated with a sense of rights, if inculcated instead with a sense of responsibility, the individual is drawn to society, with status dependent upon the degree of social contribution. Societies need more cohesive elements, not less, if they are to function successfully. Even though humans are, by nature, a socially oriented species, in the raw state it is a marriage of convenience, with individual goals and aspirations predominant.

Given the hierarchical nature of primate social organization and its obvious implications for human society, acceptance of civic responsibility by the individual citizen, the fundamental and essential characteristic of democracy, does not arise spontaneously. It requires that citizens throughout their life span be nurtured in an environment functionally democratic in every dimension, and thereby inculcating responsibility, so that they are thoroughly imbued with its principles and tenets.

Under the judicial system individuals would be held accountable for violations of their social responsibilities. Laws and regulations would be constructed so that the social implications of an illegal act or activity would be emphasized. Rather than defining robbery as "the felonious taking of property of another from his person, or in his immediate presence, against his will, by violence or intimidation" (Webster's Dictionary) it would be defined as an act in which the perpetrator irresponsibly deprived a fellow citizen of the possession and enjoyment of property to which he/she is entitled.

The 'Bill of Rights' instead would be a 'Bill of Responsibilities'. The following is one rewriting of the first ten amendments to the United States Constitution that reflect responsibilities, rather than rights, of citizens and governmental authorities (original and proposed modification):

Article I: Congress shall make no law respecting an establishment of religion, or prohibiting the free exercise thereof; or abridging the freedom of speech, or of the press; or the right of the people peaceably to assemble, and to petition the government for a redress of grievances.

Mod: The Congress shall be empowered to make laws that foster understanding on the part of citizens of their *responsibility* to respect the exercise of religion, the free expression of ideas by individuals and the media, the peaceable assembly of the people, and of their *responsibility* to petition the government to redress grievances of their fellow citizens.

Article II: A well-regulated militia, being necessary to the security of a free State, the right of the people to bear arms shall not be infringed.

Mod: The people shall be apprised of their *responsibility* to provide for the security of a free State, by participating, when called upon, in the activities of a well-regulated militia.

Article III: No soldier shall, in time of peace be quartered in any house, without the consent of the owner, nor in time of war, but in a manner prescribed by law.

Mod: It shall be the *responsibility* of the people, in time of peace and war, to provide for the quartering of soldiers, as prescribed by law.

Article IV: The right of the people to be secure in their persons, houses, papers, and effects, against unreasonable searches and seizures, shall not be violated, and no warrants shall issue, but upon probable cause, supported by oath or affirmation, and particularly describing the place to be searched, and the persons or things to be seized.

Mod: All citizens and governmental bodies shall be *responsible* for assuring that the people are secure in their persons, houses, papers, and effects, against unreasonable searches and seizures, and warrants shall be issued only upon probable cause, supported by oath or affirmation, and particularly describing the place to be searched, and the persons or things to be seized.

Article V: No person shall be held to answer for a capital, or otherwise infamous crime, unless on a presentment or indictment of a grand jury, except in cases arising in the land or naval forces, or in the militia, when in actual service in time of war or public danger; nor shall any person be subject for the same offense to be twice put in jeopardy of life or limb; nor shall be compelled in any criminal case to be a witness against himself, nor be deprived of life, liberty, or property, without due process of law; nor shall private property be taken for public use, without just compensation.

Mod: Citizens and government bodies shall have the *responsibility* to assure that no person be held to answer for a capital, or otherwise infamous crime, except on a presentment or indictment of a grand jury, unless such crimes arise while in the service of land or naval forces, or in the militia during time of war or public danger; and furthermore, to assure that no person for the same offense be twice put in jeopardy of life or limb; nor compelled in any criminal case to be a witness against himself, nor be deprived of life, liberty, or property, without due process of law; nor have private property taken for public use, without just compensation.

Article VI: In all criminal prosecutions, the accused shall enjoy the right to a speedy and public trial, by an impartial jury of the state and district wherein the crime shall have been committed, which district shall have been previously ascertained by law, and to be informed of the nature and cause of the accusation; to be confronted with the witnesses against him; to have compulsory process for obtaining witnesses in his favor, and to have the assistance of counsel for his defense.

Mod: In all criminal prosecutions, citizens and government bodies shall have the *responsibility* to assure a speedy and public trial for the accused, by an impartial jury of the state and district wherein the crime shall have been committed, which district shall have been previously ascertained by law, and to be informed of the nature and cause of the accusation; to be confronted with the witnesses against him; to have compulsory process for obtaining witnesses in his favor, and to have the assistance of counsel for his defense.

Article VII: In suits at common law, where the value in controversy shall exceed twenty dollars, the right of trial by jury shall be preserved, and no fact tried by a jury, shall be otherwise reexamined in any court of the United States, than according to the rules of the common law.

Mod: In suits at common law, where the value in controversy shall exceed twenty dollars, citizens and governing bodies shall have the *responsibility* to assure that the accused be tried by jury, and no fact tried by a jury, shall be otherwise reexamined in any court of the United States, than according to the rules of the common law.

Article VIII: Excessive bail shall not be required, nor excessive fines imposed, nor cruel and unusual punishments inflicted.

Mod: Citizens and governing bodies shall be *responsible* to assure that excessive bail not be required, nor excessive fines imposed, nor cruel and unusual punishments inflicted.

Article IX: The enumeration in the Constitution, of certain rights, shall not be construed to deny or disparage others retained by the people.

Mod: The enumeration in the Constitution, of certain *responsibilities*, shall not be construed to deny or disparage other *responsibilities* of the people.

Article X: The powers not delegated to the United States by the Constitution, nor prohibited by it to the states, are reserved to the states respectively, or to the people.

Mod: The *responsibilities* not delegated specifically to the United States by the Constitution, nor unassigned by it to the states, are reserved to the states respectively, or to the people.

The salubrious effect of these changes would be to encourage cooperation rather than alienation of citizens, who would no longer be set by their fundamental structural relationships in contraposition to society. This would tend to preclude situations in which individual citizens or groups press claims against society primarily to satisfy their own special interests at public expense. Stressing responsibilities brings people closer together, encouraging them toward identity with social goals and aspirations and more cooperative relationships, without sacrificing individual identity.

'Rights' – foundation of the 'tragedy of the commons'

Every perquisite protected by 'rights' sows the seeds of social disharmony, as so cogently explained by Garrett Hardin's analysis of the use of the commons. The extent to which civilized society grants rights to its citizens, rather than inculcating a sense of civic responsibility (rights' antithesis), is the measure of how far it is from achieving the salubrious environment and concomitant peace, justice and prosperity that are common aspirations of people everywhere. Society's granting of rights is, thereby, a threat to the future of life, as it promotes excessive demands on Earth's sustainable capacity and hastens the day of reckoning.

Chapter 6
SEXUAL REPRESSION AND THE PEEPING TOM

Humanity's transition from social organization based upon hunting and gathering to what is now known as civilization has greatly enhanced our potency as a cosmic threat. Acceptance of a greater degree of social organization is a Faustian bargain, conducive to aggressive behavior arising from frustration with a much more extensive and intrusive hierarchy and repression arising from mores, strictures and laws that are alien to our nature.

Marcus Hamilton, et. al. (2007) describes how hunter-gatherer societies were, and are, essentially egalitarian, and yet organized in a hierarchy of sorts, comprised of a nested series of discrete, yet flexible social units that occupy space and interact with exchanges of materials and information. These structures are apparently a means of dissipating social tension and maximizing information processing capacity.

During our formative stages of development, our large and active brain detected some ontogenetic advantage in more complex associations, but alas, did not see the entire picture. Why not sow crops instead of wasting a lot of time looking for them? Why not domesticate beasts instead of risking one's neck in a mad, coordinated dash through the brush as hunger pangs dictated? Why not agglomerate in communities rather than the rude and dispersed accommodations of our developmental experience? Why not accept a leader and a few underlings to manage things so that subsistence could be better assured?

Each new acquiescence to the gradual encroachment of civilization was accompanied by commensurate acceptance of concessions on limits to individual behavior, or liberty. In its most intrusive form, civilization involves hierarchy with defined social classes (potentates, nobles, chiefs, aristocrats, freemen, serfs, slaves), institutions, and rules embodied in mores, laws and statutes that constrain behavioral 'instincts' derived from our evolutionary history. Security provided by civilization is accompanied by the acceptance of a ruling class – leaders and their bureaucratic underlings - generally urbanites who are largely detached from the messy business of finding or producing goods and services.

Sigmund Freud (2005), in a compact but potent essay, analyzes the impacts of civilization on the human psyche and how the repressive elements of social organization promote aggression. Freud explains that impulses of the libido, creative energy directed toward personal (including sexual) objectives, are conflicted by civilization since 'love thy neighbor' and the Golden Rule are inimical to its fundamental aspirations. The social safety net provided by most civilizations reduces (in some cases eliminates) the need for the individual to invest time and energy in survival of offspring, and allows these impulses to be diverted to other purposes. At the same time, unfettered expression of the libido contravenes the requirement in polite society to maintain friendships, particularly with the potent instruments available to the individual to redress what are considered to be slights or offenses.

In some species aggressive acts are an important part of Darwinian strategy, but often limited to snorting and posturing. Computation of the most appropriate means of resolution - taking confrontation to the point of physical combat or not - depends upon signals related to possible outcomes. While this may not be equated to contemplation, it might be said that intuitive mechanisms, derived in the evolutionary process for the species, operate to decide on the appropriate course of action. If the mechanism is working properly the animal makes the right decision. But not all machines are equally proficient. Occasionally one goes awry with fateful consequences.

According to most paleoanthropologists, the monogamous pair bond derives from neotony of human infants (inordinate retention of infantile characteristics). The gestation period is insufficient to bring fetuses to anywhere near a state of self-sufficiency at birth, as is the case with most other animals. Nature then created devices that would ensure sufficient support for a period that would allow the faculties of the newborn to reach a state of readiness for survival in the environment. The mother and father became an 'item', primarily through the device of making the female sexually active, not only during estrus, but continually.

Civilization upset the applecart. Virtually every civilized society provides some sort of social safety net that somewhat relieves parents, particularly the male, from the natural demands of parenthood, thus permitting opportunities for other pursuits, one of which might involve free expression of libidinal impulses. However, this would be disruptive, as the monogamous love bond is one of civilization's pillars. Civilization then becomes antagonistic to sexuality. The libido, and particularly sexual expression, has to be repressed to avoid its potential for dissolving civilization's cement - cooperative, if not friendly, associations and collaborations among its citizens.

Although sex has become virtually a public sport in modern industrial societies, it is nevertheless repressed, with bizarre consequences. Rape, for example, is endemic in the United States. Somewhere in the country, a woman is raped every two minutes[105], about 300 thousand rapes of women per year. According to a study in 1992, one in six women and one in thirty-three men were raped at some time in their lives[106], although only 1 in 6 (16%) of rapes had ever been reported to police.[107]

Civilization, at least the American brand, has not been very successful, it seems, in repressing libidinal urges. While perpetrators fall into at least two categories, 'criminal' and 'psychiatric', the common theme seems to be one of releasing aggression rather than merely satisfying sexual appetite. According to research on the psychology of rape, the criminal rapist is viewed as a poorly educated male from lower socioeconomic levels, with a criminal record of offenses such as exhibitionism and fetishism, generally antisocial and subject to manipulation. The psychiatric rapist is of a higher socio-economic stratum suffering from feelings of inadequacy or other personal problems. A more general analysis places the root at a subculture of violence "whose values may be different from those of the dominant culture…these adolescents and young men may be demonstrating their toughness and masculinity in a more violent and antisocial manner."[108]

Violence has always been a part of the American way of life. The slaughter of Native Americans in the 18th and 19th centuries was perpetrated, according to Brown (2007)[109], with little regard by settlers of the west, and by the military contingents that cleared the way for their invasion, for the pain and suffering inflicted on the original occupants of the area. Now in the 21st century, violence has become so endemic that it cannot be avoided without completely shutting off communications from any media form, particularly television and electronic gadgetry, whose producers make a living on it. Young people appear to be mesmerized by flashy presentations in computer games and other forms of 'entertainment' that reek of gratuitous violence, in many instances with sexist overtones.

Violence was a way of life in the old South. According to one account, a code of honor prevailed during the antebellum period, when the south was primarily agricultural while the north became industrialized. Southerners engaged in herding were found to be more prone to violence than those engaged in farming: this hazardous undertaking apparently required its practitioners to be overly aggressive as a means of protecting their investments. Even children in the south were encouraged to engage in aggressive acts and roughhouse antics as a means of securing their identity, as reflected in their rigorous adherence to a code of honor – better to suffer pain of a thrashing rather than meekly accept the taunts of an oppressor.[110] Toqueville[111] commented on the greater military prowess of southerners as compared with northerners, with greater expertise in committing violent acts of aggression.

In some other societies, sexual taboos are taken so seriously that offenders risk being ostracized, incarcerated, maimed or even killed for offenses. Islamic law dictates corporal and capital punishment for offenses such as rape and adultery. Women's honor and modesty are to be protected, so immodest clothing is proscribed. Young men and women are encouraged to marry early, and many other proscriptions are intended to avoid rape and other crimes. The punishment for rape in Islam is the same as the punishment for zina (adultery or fornication), which is stoning if the perpetrator is married, and one hundred lashes and banishment for one year if he is not married.

Although not specifically mandated by religious tenets, cultural tradition often dictates isolation for Islamic women in the home, who are relegated to special areas forbidden to males. In many societies a woman may not leave the home unless accompanied by a male. Women are often permitted to be in public only when attired in the burqua, a form of dress that conceals everything but the eyes, even then covered with a mesh.

In some Islamic societies, females are subjected to genital mutilation and circumcision, although the practice is also prevalent in other religious and cultural environments, mainly in Africa and the Middle East. In its most extreme form the clitoris and both labia minora and majora are excised, with two sides of the vulva sewn across the vagina leaving only a small opening for passage of urine and menstrual blood.

When societies were still mainly rural and agricultural, the packing density of people allowed for sexual inclinations to be expressed privately and clandestinely in a variety of ways. Humans have probably always engaged in the same level of sexual acts, whether by dint of encounters with the same or opposite sex or through other outlets for sexual expression available in field and farm.

With the onset of urbanization and spatial density of humans much compressed, outlets for sexual expression in a natural and unhurried manner were reduced to the point of introducing sexual stresses that demanded relief. Sexually suggestive music, attire and behavior are very likely protests against the disappearance of trysting places that were so easily found in forest, field and farm. All of the hysterical mayhem of the 'entertainment' industry that has since followed is a phenomenon of sympathetic resonance, in which the pendulum has swung ever higher with increasing population density and other constraints on sexual expression imposed by civilization. Sexual repression in modern society is another wrong turn for humanity, with potentially devastating consequences.

There was a time when across the United States on any given day, a few articles could be found in the local press dealing with cases of the 'Peeping Tom'. These were primarily males who sought to indulge in vicarious sensual pleasures by peering in on the unknowing while they were either in states of undress or engaged in some kind of sexual endeavor. The voyeur was not only considered immoral, but was often subject to arrest and prosecution by virtue of having violated an ordinance or statute.

In that bygone era, voyeurs, if they were sufficiently discreet, would find plenty of opportunity for their lascivious satisfaction. With little concern for security, most Americans rarely took pains to secure their lodgings either from entry or observation. Humans are probably the sexiest creatures on this Earth. Lesser species generally engage in sexual activity, whether for pure procreation or for recreational, dominance or bonding purposes, only when conditions are ripe, for example when the female is in estrus. Human females, on the other hand, are sexually receptive almost always, even during lactation and menstruation. There is certainly no lack of sexual interest or constraint on human males outside of emotional or physical impediments, many of which incidentally, are related to their preoccupation with sex. So, the voyeur would have a better than even chance of success picking his targets at random.

Voyeurism is considered a psychosis, or serious mental disorder, in particular paraphilia, which involves sexual interest other than normal copulation. A characteristic of the disorder is that the perpetrator is motivated by an urge to surreptitiously observe others who are either naked, in a state of undress or engaged in sexual activity. In the voyeur, this is the primary mode of sexual arousal and expression. The voyeur is different from a person who simply enjoys nakedness or watching people have sex, since the arousal comes from the fact the other person is unaware they are being watched. Sigmund Freud (*Instincts and Their Vicissitudes* - 1915) and other psychoanalysts have identified the condition as an obsession to see other's genitals while hiding ones own, but with a desire to be noticed as observer. Related behaviors often include various antisocial disorders.

It is very unusual at the turn of the 21st century to encounter any public notice of the 'Peeping Tom' or voyeur, and it is interesting to speculate why this is true.

The public media, up to the 1960's, had to be content with occasional tentative forays into the forbidden land of sexual explicitness. Prior to the advent of television and its rapid acceptance as an entertainment and information medium after World War II, the local cinema was the primary source of family entertainment, supplemented by feature articles and comics in the local paper.

In films, sexual encounters were not so subtly hidden behind restrained physical contact and timely cuts. Sometimes sexual symbols were employed, such as the gushing fire hydrant. In this way, even films that were laden with sexual innuendo were rendered acceptable for even the most sensitive eyes and ears. All members of the family could attend without embarrassment or concern for moral corruption of the young.

When describing adulterous trysts, the print media alluded to 'indiscretions'. Sexually aggressive behavior was seldom identified explicitly. Rape was described as assault, violation, despoilment or some other oblique terminology.

A voyeur with the price of admission to a burlesque show, a kind of bawdy theatrical presentation featuring risqué skits and provocative choreographies, could somewhat satisfy his lustful proclivities, but usually liberties that could be publicly exhibited during such performances were constrained by local religious and civic authorities. Under these conditions, the serious voyeur had no choice but to scuttle among the bushes on a moonless night.

As television began to capture the attention of the masses during the 1950's, diminishing the market for traditional entertainment and information, the industry sought to differentiate its product as a means of survival. Dismantling the inhibitions and proscriptions on sexually explicit exposition was a process of acclimatization. Legitimating public sex was easily, albeit programmatically, absorbed by viewers chafing at Victorian constraints, but generally reluctant to be the 'first one in the water'.

Media moguls who suddenly found a use for the US constitution that was certainly not envisioned by the founding fathers systematically demolished social and legal barriers to what was previously considered anathema to the social warp and weft. Incremental escalations in the degree of explicitness were skillfully orchestrated. Whenever challenged, producers claimed to be merely following the evolving mores of an enlightened social transformation. Their role was not to overturn cultural norms but they certainly had a responsibility to respond to what their audiences demanded.

It's safe to assume that large numbers of people have some voyeuristic tendencies, even if they are usually below the clinical threshold. The primary clinical factor is the requirement that the subject be unaware, i.e. surreptitious viewing of nakedness or sex, but commercial media operators have cashed in on the widely incipient affliction by cleverly simulating the condition in darkened theatres or dimmed dens in the modern home. An object of observation in a film or TV show is inherently unaware, even though the presentation is designed specifically to exploit widespread voyeuristic inclinations.

There appears to have been a direct correlation between the penetration of these new players in the entertainment and information market and the ostensible disappearance of the voyeur. The reason is very simple. Opportunities for sexual titillation have been so successfully disseminated that voyeurism has replaced baseball as the national pastime, and is now no longer noteworthy. In other words, we have become virtually a nation of voyeurs, with little distinction between the average upstanding citizen and one who, short decades ago, would have been locked up and prosecuted for criminal behavior.

An observer from Mars, unaware of the sexual potency in the dominant species on Earth, would attribute our ubiquitous preoccupation as observers of sex – in provocative street dress of both males and females, in posters and advertisements for everything from soda pop to military aircraft, in 'entertainment' media directed toward all age segments including young children, in both amateur and professional sports activities – to a vital part of the social fabric conferring great benefits.

Sex in its proper time and place

The truth is something quite different. Our obsession with sex in vicarious forms that make up such a large part of our daily intercourse is symptomatic of mass psychosis. But should we be chastised for our illness? Oh, that it were otherwise! Its existence is certainly not a cause for optimism. Untreated, it will surely be a contributor to the ultimate catastrophe. Why? Rational thinking, oriented to the welfare of future generations, is necessary to change behavioral patterns that might avert such an outcome for life on Earth. The powerful force of the sex drive, as any human trait, if channeled into such bizarre behaviors, is antithetical to this possibility.

Chapter 7
SPIRIT, RELIGION AND POLITICS

The Hubble space telescope has provided a powerful source for insight into the significance of life on this tiny planet relegated to a remote corner of the vast Milky Way, just another one of billions of galaxies floating in space. It would be a boon if every human being would not only view the images produced by this impressive instrument, but would also contemplate their significance. We might then humbly ask if our existence from the cosmic perspective is something special, designed and fabricated by a celestial superpower, perhaps even in its image. If so, why are we relegated to such a remote speck of terrestrial matter? If we were really wonders on a cosmic scale, why would we not have a more prominent place in the heavens, perhaps beings acclimated to thriving on a supernova or quasar?

These questions arise because we are sentient beings. We humans suffer an incurable malady that will surely be our undoing. It is called 'consciousness', a blessing that is really a curse in disguise. It may also be a precursor of our dark and mysterious unconscious, although the order of development may never be known. Consciousness leads to questions that are unanswerable, with attendant frustration and self-flagellation, one form of which is religion. It has been said that god did not invent man, but rather that man invented god, many times over if its ubiquitous presence among human societies is any indication.

The inexorable élan of sentient beings derives directly from the life force.[112] Left to one's own inclinations, the life force serves to link the individual to all matter and energy that comprise one's observable environment, and through the mind's eye, what may lie beyond. Élan[113] inherently beats in the breast of every human, as well as every other living thing, except that in humans and perhaps some of the more intelligent animals with varying degrees of consciousness, there is a *sense* of identity with nature. In humans, this sense is not only intrinsic, but also potent, inherently at one with nature and 'respectful' of its form and essence.

A divergence of the élan from its identity with nature arises when, particularly in human society, questions concerning the unobservable or logically imponderable are answered with images conjured up by aggressive opportunists, seeking advantage by co-opting the energy and allegiance of more passive individuals. One of the more common forms of this subterfuge involves assertions of their authority to intervene with a supernatural force, the claim of communication with, and the capacity to negotiate favorable terms for proselytes in both conditions of life on Earth, as well as a life beyond conventional existence. There are both psychological and physical perquisites for interveners in this process. Successful perpetrators of this kind of chimera undoubtedly feel fulfilled emotionally, physically protected by a cohort of loyal acolytes, and uplifted by extended spheres of influence. In more extreme circumstances, these allegiances are exploited to the point of gaining or expanding political and/or territorial hegemony.

Appropriation of the élan by such interveners (hereinafter, religious operative or RO) is what we call 'religion', one of the more corrosive influences on human behavior. To achieve their ends, the élan must be corralled with at least two lassos: first, collective acquiescence to the dominion of one or more ROs, abetted by the natural tendency of sheep to maintain their membership in the herd; and second, for the sake of improving their effectiveness at proselytizing and maintaining subordination of their subjects, organization into some sort of hierarchy with the ROs at the top of the heap, a structure so efficacious that it has been successfully emulated by commercial and industrial enterprises throughout the world.

In the primeval state human hunter-gatherers had little need for hierarchical organization, which likely first rose to prominence in a 'religious' context, as shamans and other types of pioneering ROs introduced a structure that would serve as the pattern for diffusion throughout the world. It is likely that religious hierarchy was the model for what we now call 'politics', the art of gaining allegiance of the multitudes in the earthly ambit. The main difference, then, between politics and religion is the manner of gathering and retaining the flock: religion's appeal relating primarily to supernatural phenomena and politics to what earthly life has in store. For religion, personal salvation is usually the carrot (rarely is there a collective appeal) and condemnation to eternal hell the stick, whereas in politics collective appeal gains some traction from social instincts that were part of the fabric of our ancient cooperative lifestyle. There are benefits to be gained or costs incurred in material and security terms, the magnitude depending on one's level of acquiescence to dominion of interveners. Generally, the political operative (PO, counterpart of the RO) ostensibly centers the appeal on something outside herself, a cause, objective or goal selected for its acceptability by sufficient numbers of the target audience to make it worthwhile, who can be convinced of its prospects for security and prosperity. The subliminal appeal is to the indispensability of the PO to shepherd the flock to the verdant pasture. The efficacy of hierarchy obtains, so that populations are organized into wards, towns and cities, provinces and nation states, which are mutually compatible with, and reinforced by, parallel organization and emergence of commerce and industry.

The unholy connection between religion and politics has a long history (Diamond 1999). By the late Medieval and Renaissance periods of the 13th century and beyond, feudal and tribal organizations that previously predominated in most of Europe and Asia came under the control of nation states and empires, which sponsored "..official religions that contributed to state cohesion, being invoked to legitimize the political leadership and to sanction wars against other people." Their RO collaborators amply provided divine inspiration for the territorial ambitions of medieval POs, truly a marriage made in heaven.

While élan directs the unfettered individual, ROs foster belief in a superhuman power to be obeyed and worshipped as the creator and ruler of the universe, in accordance with rules promulgated through divine edict, or at least guidance. The dogma, canons and hierarchies of ROs constitute a system of worship and obeisance. Their counterparts are the system of rules, statutes and laws, and political organizations of civil society, set up to be appropriated by POs through a variety of mechanisms such as heredity, coups d'état, conquest, election.

Now that it's clear that politics is indistinguishable in its essence from religion, we might just as well concentrate on one or the other. Religion is the more interesting domain.

Consciousness

As the *sine qua non* of religion, examination of the origins and characteristics of consciousness will shed some light on the RO phenomenon and what is behind their successful endeavors.

The descent of humans from much more primitive forms of life is well established, so there seems little reason to suppose that one of humanity's essential qualities, consciousness, arose in any way other than the process of human evolution. Consciousness is apparently non-existent to shadowy in the simplest life forms from which all more complex forms, including man, derive, so it must be an acquired characteristic that evolved by natural selection, in a manner similar to the somewhat earlier acquisition of the ear, nose, finger or toe. In early stages of the hominid line, certainly the level of consciousness that we currently experience did not exist. At some phase in the evolution of modern humans it developed gradually as a consequence of its selective advantage.

This assertion is not universally shared. Some paleontologists, for example Dr. Ian Tattersall[114], are uncomfortable with the idea that human consciousness arose through the process of natural selection. He does not invoke divine intervention, but rails against 'strict Darwinians' who explain all phenomena in natural terms. Does rational analysis suggest any other mechanism that we can even speculate about? Is it possible, for example, that a creator implanted consciousness in latent form in a more primitive human ancestor? This would deny the entire premise upon which the foundation of evolution is constructed, random accumulation of (what we now know to be) genetic mutations that confer selective advantage.

We apparently experience instantaneous sensations, for example, banging one's head against a pole, but is this consciousness? Any organism needs a survival strategy, some instinctive way of dealing with crises. An amoeba must 'sense' that it's corpus is being crushed or otherwise harmed, and automatically deploys whatever defense mechanisms it can muster.

How can consciousness be defined? It is a subject contemplated by philosophers over millennia, but inevitably involves displacement of sensory impressions over time and space:

Robin Allott (2000): "..evolutionary epistemology proposes that the natural selection of brain processes has provided us with practical concepts of time and space to allow us to manage reality. The momentariness of everything and thus of ourselves means that we are in constant changing patterns, changing aggregations of material." The continuous process of metabolizing and being impacted by external stimuli means that we are not the same person from one instant to the next. The present moment is fleeing - it has "melted in our grasp."

Consciousness, then, might be defined as the displacement of awareness in time and space, the translation of observation from the here-and-now to the there-and-then. Does consciousness have meaning at an instant? As many philosophers who have pondered the question have concluded, change is inherent in animate being. Strip away the time domain and change is necessarily precluded as well. Limited only to the present, awareness seems to be divorced from consciousness, as it cannot relate to change, to *what was* compared with *what is* or what *will be*. According to Immanuel Kant (1996): "Time and space are necessary forms under which sensation and perception are accommodated in our minds, in our brains; we can have no knowledge of the ding(en) an sich (the thing itself)."

Popper (1998) alludes to change as an inherent characteristic of being: "Human experience does not perceive real life as simply a uniform progression along some imaginary line extended in space, but rather a continuous flow. The real world is one of continuous becoming or process. This discreteness is not real. So-called discrete elements are only apparent when we have a need to pluck them from our continuing experience. We may appear to ourselves as things but we find that we are processes." James (1890) describes the continuous alteration in conformation of the brain as differential elements of experience are processed: "Whilst we think, our brain changes, and, like the aurora borealis, its whole internal equilibrium shifts with every pulse of change ... from one relative state of equilibrium to another, like the gyrations of a kaleidoscope."

Some philosophical schools, e.g. the Sautrantika of Buddhism (also known as the 'Holders of Discourse') assert that all events and phenomena exist only at the present moment, that past and future are mental constructs.[115] But even if this is true, the notion of consciousness is virtually impossible to conceive in a timeless framework.

With the river as his model Siddhartha[116] concludes that the flow of time does not exist, that all of past, present and future are indistinguishable: " ... the river is everywhere at the same time, at the source and at the mouth, at the waterfall, at the ferry, at the current, in the ocean and in the mountains, everywhere, and that the present only exists for it, not the shadow of the past, nor the shadow of the future."

On the other hand, some Buddhist schools explain time in relative terms: "...it (the Madhyamika-Prasangika school) generally explains time in terms of relativity, as an abstract entity developed by the mind on the basis of an imputation, the continuity of an event or phenomenon. This philosophical view ascribes, therefore, an abstract concept whose function is dependent on the continuum of phenomena. From this point on, to try to explain time as an autonomous entity, independent from an existing object, proves impossible. That time is a relative phenomenon and can claim no independent status is quite clear."[117]

One can conceive how consciousness arose. Anyone who has ever been lost in the woods, with no available references, can begin to comprehend the onset of consciousness in our distant forebears. The senses scan the environment for information: visual clues from the type and condition of grass and foliage, sounds and smells emanating from the presence and movement of other creatures. It is one thing to know that a predator or prey is about, and quite another to project, on the basis of sensory information, its past or future. It is only a small step from this kind of consciousness to self-awareness, as the observer takes its place in the array of physical entities that comprise its environment.

Self-consciousness is not unique to *H. sapiens*. It is a characteristic that we share at least with some of our primate cousins, the chimpanzees and apes.[118] Studies of language capabilities of primates have indicated a high degree of self-awareness by our nearest relatives. As there was a stage in our evolutionary tree where consciousness was absent, that we are presently aware of self indicates that this characteristic evolved much as any physical attribute. There is nothing very special about its origins, except its profound influence on the environment of Earth and its consequences for our fellow inhabitants of the planet.

Human self-consciousness must have arisen during the transition from primitive primate ancestor to sapient homo. Exactly at which state the first stirrings of consciousness appeared is uncertain, but it almost certainly arose as an evolutionary response to a selective opportunity.

Acknowledgement of the evolutionary origins of consciousness could have salubrious effects for the future of life. Greater awareness of self as an outgrowth of natural forces can only serve as social cement, a unifying and binding link for all of humanity. A sense in the individual of a closer relationship with fellow humans promotes altruism and cooperation, which are essential ingredients for a new approach to our relationship to the commons – the planet that we share.

Whence religion?

Familiar questions have rattled about in the mind of man since the dawn of self-consciousness:

Who are we? Is humanity unique as an intelligent being?

Consciousness inevitably leads to the issue of identity – what is the significance of being human. Clearly humanity has dominion over all of life on Earth, on the strength of intelligence more than any other characteristic. The individual may be, and usually is, in awe and bewilderment of the vastness, order and beauty of the heavens, the creation of life from seed, the power and occasional fury of nature, the cycle of life and death. There is also unease about the future after death, the disposition of the élan that apparently resides in every living thing.

As we humans progressed toward greater comprehension of our surroundings, we observed that some things we could do, e.g. make tools, hunt and domesticate other animals, find alternative foods, then cultivate crops. But there remained many things that we could not do or create, leading to the conclusion that some superior force was necessary to explain what was beyond our capacity or control. Even today, in an era of global communications, intricate knowledge of cosmic events and phenomena, fabrication and replacement of body parts, speculations about our origins and uniqueness continue: are we a select form of life, commissioned to this role by a higher power, the creator of the cosmos? Are there other, more intelligent forms of life, as yet unidentified either because we have not found them or are incapable of understanding what they have to say?

Our uniqueness as an intelligent form of life has been the subject of speculative scientific investigations. One organization, SETI (Search for Extraterrestrial Intelligence), based in California, USA, conducts a program to find other intelligent life in the cosmos. They search for electromagnetic signals from outer space, justified, according to their mission statement, by expanding knowledge about the natural origin of life on Earth and discovery of planets with environments conducive to originating life, even though its form may differ from the carbon/oxygen base upon which earthly life is based. Rather than anticipating interactions of one sort or another with alien life forms through scientific exploration, our propensity toward mysticism prompts many to imagine that they have observed unidentified flying objects and expect that they carry alien creatures seeking opportune conditions to invade the planet.

What are we? Are we made in the image of a god or a flawed creation?

According to the Old Testament of the Bible, Genesis 1:27, "So God created man in his own image, in the image of God he created him; male and female he created them." To what extent the likeness prevails is unstated. Moses (if he was indeed, the conveyor to humanity of the word of God) may have understood the likeness to apply only to physical attributes, but there are other possibilities. In fact, the assertion gains some credibility when other attributes of humanity are taken into account. Rather than ethical and moral behavior - universal brotherhood, truthfulness, kindness, generosity, compassion - instead humanity often displays characteristics of Jehovah as described in scriptures: jealousy, venality, violence, deception.

There is little doubt that there is a serious flaw in our constitution, if for no reason other than our propensity to despoil our home planet and to consign to extinction so many of our fellow travelers on Earth, cousin species that have shared with us eons of evolutionary history. No other species is so heedless, if not overtly contemptuous, of its own living environment. If humans were purposefully created, it would appear that either we were the product of the creator's sadistic streak, or left to our own devices we gravitated toward depravity.

Another indication of our fall from grace is our inclination for violence. For example, according to data of the World Health Organization, more than 1.6 million people worldwide lose their lives from suicide, homicide and armed conflict, one of the leading causes of death for people aged 15-44 years worldwide, accounting for 14% of deaths among males and 7% of deaths among females. In addition to death by violence, many more are injured from violent acts, and thereby suffer from a range of physical and mental health problems. In the United States alone there are about 50,000 deaths annually attributable to violence. About 1 million annual fatalities globally are attributable to another type of aggressiveness – motor vehicle collisions.

Aside from fatalities, aggressiveness of humans toward their fellow men, and particularly women, (see Chapter 6 for more thorough discussion) is rampant. Rape is an all too familiar form of aggression against women, with about one in six experiencing this kind of outrage at some point in their lives. In the United States a rape occurs about every two minutes.

Why are we? Is there a purpose, or end, to life? Does it have any meaning?

ROs make a lot of hay promoting the idea that life has purpose, which they generally propose is in serving their particular gods, often proscribing worship of any alternative. In the more benign versions, service to a god takes on a number of earthly forms: individual and collective worship in which the virtues of the benevolent deity are expressed, often in cadence; prayer for one's self, one's soul and for one's fellow men, even occasionally for other life forms; following prescriptions for acceptable behavior, often merging with, or serving as the framework of, cultural norms such as marital constraints, dietary choices, times for work and play. Some ROs have parlayed fealty of their 'subjects' to gain political hegemony, sometimes to the point of inciting them to commit mayhem and even murder. Islamic jihadists, at the instigation of Muslim clerics, and backed by the government of Sudan, declared holy war against the largely non-Muslim south in 1989, although conflict erupted over a decade earlier.[119] An estimated 2 million people have died, in what then Sec. of State Colin Powell identified in September 2004 as genocide and "the worst humanitarian crisis of the 21st century." The real issue is control of the oil deposits of the south.

Guidelines prescribed by the deity, as transcribed by ROs, are sometimes conducive to peaceful relations among men and respect for all forms of life. In other cases gods have been known to sow the seeds of hatred, particularly against those who fail to heed its strictures.

If there is a purpose to life, it is rooted in the life force, the propensity to survive and to propagate, that seems to be embedded in every living entity. However, ROs have been able to appropriate this force, often in a system that conflates ordinary life with an afterlife, treating them as if the latter is a hyperbolic extension of the former. An eternity of pleasure or pain, enhanced by orders of magnitude as compared with ordinary experience, will depend on assessment of one's fealty to the deity and its earthbound and celestial subalterns. The life force thereby transcends its earthly constraint and seeks expression in the amplified domain of the afterlife. For example, Islamic suicide bombers carry out their missions in the expectation that extraordinary perquisites, including unlimited access to a harem of virgins, will be at their beck and call for eternity.

How did we get here? Was there a creator, or first cause that initiated a process that made us what we are? Or, is there no 'isn't'?

A recent poll revealed that 40% of American citizens believe that heaven and earth, humans and all other forms of life were created in their present state within the last 10,000 years, in accordance with the six-day program specified in Genesis, the first book of the Old Testament. Creationists, as these literal interpreters are currently identified, propose the existence of a Grand Designer, who decided to utilize its powers to give us the planets, the heavens and all other forms of matter, animate and inanimate. They often attack the principle of evolution on what they see as purposeful design embedded in biological organisms, asking rhetorically, for example, if there is any use for half an eye.[120]

The cycle of birth and death of living things is a convenient framework for ROs to postulate a creator of heaven and earth. But if this inherent bias derived from ordinary human experience can somehow be put aside, it is possible to speculate that the cosmos is eternal, i.e. there was no beginning, nor will there be an end. Even though cosmologists estimate that the universe appeared in a 'Big Bang' about 15 billion years ago, this is not inconsistent with the idea that matter and energy exist eternally, that the cataclysmic event was merely another cycle in a progression without a creative event in past or future. It is, in fact, axiomatic in the domain of science that matter/energy can neither be created nor destroyed.

The billiard ball concept of cause and effect has been shown to be a macroscopic illusion. At the level of atomic sub-particles of which billiard balls, and all of matter, are comprised, events are unpredictable. A property of nature is that a physical system cannot be described completely, the result of quantum indeterminacy[121], but rather can only be described in terms of probability. Important physical systems, such as the human brain, can be affected by quantum indeterminacy.

Physicist Richard Feynman developed the idea of the Feynman Diagram, which illustrates the relationship of two subatomic particles over time as the exchange of a third particle. These diagrams show particles traversing time and space in both the forward and backward direction. As antimatter, particles are 'allowed' to travel backward in time, so cause and effect as commonly conceived are called into question. Whether or not this applies to the everyday world has been a subject of debate, most analysts concluding that departures from our common conception of time sequence is precluded. For example, it should not be possible, and a violation of quantum mechanical principles, for you to travel back in time and murder you grandmother.

Many people who identify as 'scientists'[122] see no inconsistency between what science has revealed about the cosmos and the existence of a superior creative force, some to the extent that they identify as members of one or another organized religious denomination. Others dismiss the idea of religion while maintaining their spirituality, inspired and enhanced by their greater knowledge of the intricate workings of nature, and profoundly awed by proportions of the cosmos, its majesty and its fascinating rules of behavior. However, there is not complete agreement concerning the extent to which the superior force, once having lain down the rules, either stood back to observe the results or engaged in their enforcement.

The efforts of scientists are mainly concerned with discovering these rules of nature and how they are expressed in interactions between matter and energy (physical sciences), or between individuals and societies (social sciences). These studies reveal increasingly greater detail and complexity of natural processes, but at the end of the day they are still left with the imponderable question of how the apparently immutable rules of nature were framed and set into motion. When they encounter the unanswerable, they are inclined, as are most human beings, to attribute what is intellectually inaccessible to a superpower operating beyond the realm of ordinary life. This leads many of them to a kind of deist or spiritualist philosophy. It leads others to more traditional forms of religious belief. For example, 40 percent of U.S. scientists believe in a God with whom they can interact through prayer.[123]

Victor Stenger (2008), who identifies as a physicist, has studied the attributes that are typically associated with the existence of a god from the scientific point of view. If a god exists, it should be reflected in characteristics of the natural universe. If such reflections are absent, then it is difficult to postulate the existence of a god. The author concludes that the facts do not support the existence of the kind of god that is commonly perceived. All of the attributes of the universe derive from natural forces, leading to his conclusion that a god does not exist.

Few scientists have not embraced the principles of evolution, as expounded by Charles Darwin in *Origin of Species* published in 1859, but according to a Gallup poll in 2001, 45% of Americans failed to accept evolution as the process leading to the existence of modern humans. Scientists, who generally look upon biblical accounts as allegorical, almost universally reject a literal interpretation of Genesis, in which God is purported to have created the universe and all of its life forms in 6 days.

Einstein asserted that "Science without religion is lame, religion without science is blind."[124] For him there are at least two 'religious' tiers, one reserved for the scientifically minded, for whom a god exists that does not intervene in the ordinary affairs of humankind, but who set the clockwork in motion. Another is the spiritual vehicle for the ordinary human, a god who not only lays out the rules, but engages in shepherding adherents, meting out rewards and punishments depending on one's compliance with its guidelines:

"You will hardly find one among the profounder sort of scientific minds without a peculiar religious feeling of his own. But it is different from the religion of the naive man...For the latter God is a being from whose care one hopes to benefit and whose punishment one fears; a sublimation of a feeling similar to that of a child for its father, a being to whom one stands to some extent in a personal relation, however deeply it may be tinged with awe".[125]

Einstein firmly believed in the principle of universal causation, which put him at odds with many members of the scientific community. Morality he considered a human affair, having nothing to do with divinity. Scientists, he suggested, were religious in the sense of awe at the harmony and order in the universe, a revelation of superior intelligence of which ordinary affairs are an insignificant reflection. So long as the scientist could keep himself from "the shackles of selfish desire", his religiosity is the guiding principle of his life's work.

When did we appear? Four thousand years ago as envisioned by some biblical scholars, or are we of ancient origin?

Fundamentalist Christians and Jews have calculated the origin of the cosmos at about 4000 years, based upon generational chronology as described in the holy Bible. Genesis contains a detailed description of the sequence of events during 'Creation Week', the seven days in which heaven and earth came into being. According to one account[126], 1656 years elapsed between Creation Week and the great flood, in which Noah preserved all life forms by bringing a mating pair of each onto his ark. Literal interpreters calculate their time line from Creation Week to the present based upon the chronology of biblical figures. However, other analysts take the position that the chronology is correct, but incomplete, i.e. only a skeleton of the actual sequence of begetting, or perhaps a biblical year is a compression of an eon or so. The chronology described, in this view, ignores generations, which if included, would exactly conform to the scientifically determined existence of life on Earth.

According to Hebrew scholar William Henry Green (1890): "The result of our investigations thus far is sufficient to show that it is precarious to assume that any biblical genealogy is designed to be strictly continuous, unless it can be subjected to some external tests which prove it to be so. And it is to be observed that the Scriptures furnish no collateral information whatever respecting the period covered by the genealogies now in question."[127]

The writer laments the absence of a continuous genealogical record between creation and the Flood (during which the master mariner Noah preserved posterity), and from the Flood to Abraham, and the absence of other data that might have provided a basis for testing for completeness the genealogies described in Genesis.

The general scientific consensus is a universe of an age in the order of 13-14 billion years. Radiometric dating indicate that Earth has existed for 4.54 billion years, the first life forms appear at about 3.5 billion years, the split with our primate cousins about 5-7 million years, about 2.5 million years for the homo line, and modern humans approximately 200 thousand years, only about 4 thousandths percent – a minute fraction - of Earth's life span.

It is fairly clear that our planet got along quite well without us for almost its entire existence. And yet in this blink of an eye humans have managed to create havoc on this once beautiful orb, with excessive presence and all of its consequences – war and mayhem, disfiguration, contamination, destruction of countless species who shared our evolutionary experience.

Why are the just often punished and evildoers rewarded?

Innocent children, who have not yet had the opportunity to commit what might be called 'evil deeds', incomprehensibly have been injured, abused and murdered. In Iraq, for example, during and after the invasion of US military forces in 2003, many young children were maimed and killed while attending school. There are countless examples of children, clearly too young to be held accountable for moral transgressions, meeting agony and horrible death. As one example,[128] in 1998 a five-year old child fell into a well while out with his mother. The child cried for several hours and then nothing more was heard. The boy's body was recovered after thirty hours of rescue operations.

On the other hand, many individuals who committed heinous crimes against humanity lived out their lives in comfort. Many Nazi war criminals of WWII, which ended in 1945, continued to enjoy the good life over 60 years after their incredibly horrible deeds were committed.

It seems incongruous that an omniscient deity, of the interventionist type that is usually the object of worship and adoration, would create humans to make them miserable, or to leave innocents to the mercy of predators, such as pedophiles who occasionally stalk children on the streets or who abuse them in the sanctity of their houses of worship.

President John Kennedy once reiterated what is virtually an adage, the observation that 'life isn't fair'. "It's very hard to assure equality [justice] . . . Some men are killed in war, others are wounded, and some never leave the country."

That performers of altruistic deeds are punished, and perpetrators of acts of destruction and mayhem rewarded, is well established. Under these circumstances, is it not a virtual certainty that if a creator exists, it is either detached from earthly phenomena, or downright sadistic? Is it unfair to suggest that if there were a creator who promoted justice, that justice would prevail on Earth?

The Old Testament is replete with sadistic acts of Jehovah, the god of the Israelites. For starters, God creates Adam and Eve in the Garden of Eden, along with the tree of knowledge. They are enjoined from eating its fruits, and yet are imbued with traits that cause their expulsion. Cain and Abel experience god-created sibling rivalry, resulting in the murder of one by the other. God decrees that children must pay for the sins of their fathers (contrary to the principles of the US constitution concerning cruel and unjust punishment, purportedly inspired by this very god) - Exodus 20:5 and 4:7.

God informs Moses about the dire fate of the Egyptians if Pharaoh does not release the Israelites from slavery, then diabolically tells Moses that he will cause Pharaoh to refuse to free the Israelites, virtually assuring a bad ending (Exodus 12:29). As punishment for his own induced imprisonment of the Israelites by the Egyptians, God decides to kill all of their first-born, a model for genocide to be perpetrated by his earthly creations. Neither is Jehovah above condoning murder by his followers against those who stand in the way of their hegemony. Although one of the Ten Commandments collected by Moses on Mt.

Sinai proscribes murder, he is directed to "save alive nothing that breatheth: but thou shalt utterly destroy them; namely the Hittites and the Amorites, the Canaanites and the Perrizites, the Hivites and the Jebusites, as the Lord, thy God, hath commanded thee" (Deuteronomy 20:16-17),

In the New Testament slavery and oppression is condoned by Jesus and his apostles in the gospels and in the letters of St. Paul:

Jesus (Luke 12:45-48): "The lord [owner] of that servant will come in a day when he looketh not for him, and at an hour when he is not aware, and will cut him in sunder, and will appoint him his portion with the unbelievers. And that servant, which knew his lord's will, and prepared not himself, neither did according to his will, shall be beaten with many stripes. But he that knew not, and did commit things worthy of stripes, shall be beaten with few stripes. For unto whomsoever much is given, of him shall be much required: and to whom men have committed much, of him they will ask the more."

While in Prison, the Apostle Paul met a runaway slave, Onesimus, the property of a Christian. Rather than providing sanctuary, in a letter he agrees to return Onesimus to his master, Philemon:

"Therefore though I have all boldness in Christ to command you that which is appropriate, yet for love's sake I rather beg, being such a one as Paul, the aged, but also a prisoner of Jesus Christ. I beg you for my child, whom I have become the father of in my chains, Onesimus, who once was useless to you, but now is useful to you and to me. I am sending him back. Therefore receive him, that is, my own heart, whom I desired to keep with me, that on your behalf he might serve me in my chains for the Good News. But I was willing to do nothing without your consent, that your goodness would not be as of necessity, but of free will. For perhaps he was therefore separated from you for a while, that you would have him forever, no longer as a slave, but more than a slave, a beloved brother, especially to me, but how much rather to you, both in the flesh and in the Lord."

Although there are mitigating sentiments concerning the fate of Onesimus, the act perpetrated by Paul is proscribed in Deuteronomy 23:15-16:

"Thou shalt not deliver unto his master the servant which is escaped from his master unto thee…He shall dwell with thee, even among you, in that place which he shall choose in one of thy gates, where it liketh him best: thou shalt not oppress him."

Apologists have ascribed Paul's action to other motives suggested in the letter, one that Onesimus remain with him as a disciple, no longer a slave to Philemon; another is that Paul is returning Onesimus to Philemon after he (Philemon) had proffered his slave as a servant in Paul's mission.

Judeo-Christian scriptures allude to god's creation of evil. The King James Version (KJV) of Isaiah 45:7: "I form the light, and create darkness: I make peace, and create evil: I the Lord do all these things." Amos 3:6 confirms this contribution to the spice of life: "Shall a trumpet be blown in the city, and the people not be afraid? shall there be evil in a city, and the LORD hath not done it?" The Hebrew 'rah' has been interpreted in a number of ways in the Bible, so the KJV interpretation as 'evil' is not necessarily accurate. Some claim that evil is not a thing to be created in any case, on grounds that one can neither "see, touch, feel, smell or hear" it. However, neither can intelligence - a characteristic attributed by believers to the creativeness of the superpower - be detected from any of these sensory impressions. But there is really no controversy: if evil exists (say, extreme anti-social behavior), it was surely created by god, who created everything. Skeptics have good reason to reject the existence of a benevolent creator, since such a god would neither create evil, so prevalent on Earth, nor a universe in which evil exists.

Need more be said? ROs sometimes cleverly fabricate their gods with characteristics that are imponderable in the context of civil society, the better to confuse and, thereby, conquer and bind souls to their nefarious objectives.

Features of religion

What is religion, anyway?

Many peoples around the world have conceived relationships between humans and supernatural forces, perhaps since the dawn of human history. Even Neanderthals, whose final days on Earth occurred about 20 thousand years ago, appear to have embraced the concept of afterlife, a central feature of most religious systems. Artifacts found at the earliest burial sites yet discovered, of our now extinct cousins, indicate a concern for the fate of the deceased. Some sites contain remains of groups, perhaps with the intention of keeping families united even after death. Gravesites also contained tools, food and other items, which suggest that they may have considered death as a kind of extended sleep or perhaps a period of transition to the next life. Bodies were adorned with plants and pigments, and carefully arranged in the fetal state, as if they were being prepared for rebirth. One in Shanidar, Iraq, contained a number of plants currently used for medicinal purposes.

Before trying to set down the essential features of religion, it is useful to understand what it is not. Individuals and groups have devised frameworks for evincing social harmony, for producing and dispensing goods and services required for sustenance, and for assuring justice based on respect and support for the aspirations of others, without the need for a supernatural force to set the rules and mete out rewards and punishments based upon degree of compliance with its tenets. Secular humanism, for example, predicated on a kind of operational, ethical morality from a naturalistic perspective, lacks some of the main features of what might be identified as religion.

So, what might be essential features of religion, indispensable elements in the relationship of its adherents to the supernatural?

- First, the existence of a superpower, who:
  - Creates heaven and earth, and all animate and inanimate components;
  - Sets immutable laws of nature;
  - Defines the relationship between humanity and nature (e.g. dominion over other creatures of Earth);
  - Defines rules governing acceptable human interactions, i.e. a set of principles, guidelines or commandments;
  - Dispenses perquisites for adherence to the above, and exacts penalties for transgressions.
- Acceptance on *faith*, rather than reason of the superpower's existence, edicts and powers of intervention;
- A collective endeavor of humans;
- An ecclesiastical hierarchy of POs (political operatives)

who intervene in the relationship between the individual and the superpower.

The superpower, god, or divine being, is necessary to justify existence of what is perceived by the senses. In the framework of human experience, anything that exists must at some point not have existed. Since there is no ready explanation for all that sensory impressions tell us is out there, postulation of a supernatural creator is rather easily accepted.

That nature operates under rules or laws is confirmed by everyday natural phenomena: apples always fall from trees; water seeks a level; lightning only strikes from heavy cloud cover; the moon incessantly goes through its twenty-eight day cycle; the sun always rises in the east. Those who investigate the rules of nature in great detail are usually even more greatly impressed with order in the universe, even though some of the rules are obscure and seemingly undecipherable. Does Heisenberg's uncertainty principle mean that there is fundamental unpredictability in natural phenomena, at least at the subatomic level, or is this just a matter of our incapacity to penetrate to deeper levels of understanding, as Einstein suggested? Alluding to the vast difference in behavior of subatomic phenomena as compared with everyday experience, Neils Bohr, a leading quantum theorist of the 20th century, stated "Those who are not shocked when they first come across quantum mechanics cannot possibly have understood it".[129]

How does humankind relate to other creatures and material substances? Judeo-Christian scripture assigns to man dominion over all other forms of life. However, a Buddhist precept unifies all things, as elaborated in the Four Noble Truths and the Eightfold Path, prescriptions for attaining cessation of suffering. These are guidelines for relating to the everyday world, leading to liberation from attachments and delusions.

The Judeo-Christian Bible, the Islamic Koran, the Analects of Confucius and the Mahayana (Buddhist) Sutras are now widely considered to be scriptures prescribing behavioral relationships between humans and their deity, and in some cases defining benefits of acquiescence and penalties for transgression. Although the Bible and Koran are overtly in the religious tradition, the Analects and the Sutras are examples of essentially philosophical treatises dealing with life on Earth that were co-opted by ROs, followers or disciples of Confucius and the Buddha, and gradually converted over millennia into essentially religious dogma functioning similarly to theological canon in the Western religious tradition.[130]

For example, the sutras of the Mahayana, which have a decidedly religious connotation, are claimed to be original teachings, while Theravadas assert that these are later compositions not taught by the Buddha. Perceptions of Siddhartha Gautama, the Buddha, more akin to philosophy than religion, contain no reference to intervention of a divine being. As his teachings spread throughout India, then China and much of the rest of the world, ROs, apparently with a variety of motivations, attributed divine qualities to the Buddha, forming the Mahayana and Theravada schools. Mahayana, the Great Vehicle, stresses inclusiveness and a devotional structure that is antithetical to Theravada's doctrinal approach. Mahayana Buddhists universally reject personal salvation, an effort reserved only for Theravada elite. Theravadas tend to seek salvation individually, whereas a Mahayana congregation often has responsibility to inculcate spiritual values in its members. Mahayana adheres to the principle of the Buddha-nature, with innate potential in every individual, whereas Theravadas look upon the human state as an obstacle in the way of enlightenment. These divisions are analogous to the dichotomy that prevails in most political arenas, one segment more populist and liberal, the other more conservative - traditional and elitist.

Ensoulment

One of the major selling points of ROs is that they have the power to affect the disposition of the immortal soul, a non-material entity that purportedly lives on after the physical body in which it resides in life is no longer around. The idea of the soul or eternal spirit apart from the body has ancient Greek origins,[131] was likely invented many times in the course of human history, but the original conception was modified considerably by Hebrew and Christian theologians.

Strange as it may seem, considering the general acceptance of the immortal soul among Christians and Jews, that the soul lives on after death, there is little in theological scripture to support it. The Old Testament Hebrew uses the term *nephesh*, which is translated into the

Greek *psuche* in the New Testament. In almost all instances, there is little reason to believe that the writers of the old and new testaments connected these terms with immortality.

Soul has various shades of meaning in the Old Testament[132], which may be summarized as follows[133]: living being, life, self, person, desire, appetite, emotion and passion. *Nephesh* can only denote the individual life with a material organization or body. The terms are mentioned numerous times in the Old and New Testaments, with few allusions to immortality, one in Matthew 10:28: "…fear not them which kill the body but are not able to kill the soul: but rather fear Him which is able to *destroy* (italic added) both soul and body in Gehenna."

Only the deity can kill the soul in this view, a quite different interpretation of its vulnerability than what is contained in most of the rest of Christian and Jewish scripture in which the 'psuche' is killed or otherwise destroyed as a result of human intervention. As a general rule, biblical scholars admit that *soul* is throughout a great part of the Bible simply the equivalent of 'life' embodied in a living creature. "In the earlier usage of the Old Testament it has no reference to the later philosophical meaning as the animating principle, and still less to the idea of an 'immaterial nature' which will survive the body."[134]

Another reference to the immortal soul, according to Luke 23:42: a thief crucified along with Jesus asks to be allowed into the kingdom of heaven, "Jesus, Lord, remember me when Thou comest into Thy kingdom." The dying Jesus answers: "Today shalt thou be with me in Paradise." Although his body would die, his soul would follow Jesus immediately into the domain of eternal peace and security.

Aside from the few biblical references, one of the principle exponents of immortality is St. Augustine[135], who infused Christian theology with the soul's immaterial and spiritual qualities:

"For if the mind dies wholly when life abandons it, that very life which deserts it is understood much better as mind, as now mind is not something deserted by life, but the very life itself which deserted. For whatever dead thing is said to be abandoned by life, is understood to be deserted by the soul. Moreover, this life which deserts the things which die is itself the mind, and it does not abandon itself; hence the mind does not die." Who could dispute this impeccable logic?

In the Homeric epic poetry of the 9th century BCE, *psuche* denotes the entity that lives on in the underworld after death. However, its continued existence had to be linked to the 'owner', along with personality traits and other characteristic activities and behaviors. Homer does not attribute any activity of the *living* person to its soul, so the soul represents more the life essence rather than the controller of ethical character. Moreover, the existence of the soul is restricted to human beings, and not to animate life in general, so that in the underworld there is no vestige of non-human animal life.

In Greek literature of the sixth and fifth centuries BCE the concept of soul was extended to all living things. Soul became the distinguishing feature between life and death, the soul departing after demise of the corpus, and, in the later part of this period, associated with emotional feelings. Ajax explains his imminent suicide in an ancient Greek tragedy of unknown authorship: "Nothing bites the soul of a man more than dishonor".[136] Oedipus' soul, the font of boldness and courage, laments the misery of his city and its inhabitants (Sophocles, 5th century BCE). Ignorant as they were of modern understanding of origins of the universe and evolutionary history of humankind, we can't blame early Greek philosophers and Christian theologians for postulating the existence of soul in their speculative flights into the unknown.

That life traversed the span from pre-Cambrian forms, through the Paleozoic era, when proto-mammals made their appearance, through the Mesozoic, when higher forms of proto-mammals were prey to the dinosaurs, and into the Cenozoic in which hominids and finally *H. sapiens* made an appearance, begs the question concerning the precise stage in which the soul was acquired.

Only five to seven million years ago *H. sapiens* and other present-day primates shared common ancestry. If soul exists as a presence associated with the individual, may it be assumed that once having been granted by the Grand Designer to a species (presumably to all of its members), the bequest would never thereafter be rescinded, and therefore is passed along from one generation to the next, even as speciation occurs? If so, unless present-day apes have souls also, at some time during this span, from the split to the present, the hominid line acquired a soul, i.e. was blessed (or cursed) by the phenomenon of ensoulment. Several species of hominids that existed in the interval since the ape-hominid split have been identified from the fossil record, from *Ardipithicus ramidus* to the *Australopithecines* and the various species of homo including *H. habilus*, *H. erectus*, *H. neanderthalensis*, and *H. sapiens*.

It is interesting to speculate on what characteristics would qualify a species for 'souldom'. Here it is assumed that soul is granted at the level of species. It is beyond the human ken to contemplate the soul as a perquisite to be dispensed discriminately, i.e. for some members but not others. Presumably the soul is present from infancy, if not conception, perhaps even waiting in the wings to suffuse the body as it exits from the womb. Fairness dictates that no helpless and unworldly fledgling should be denied a soul for the sins of its parents, nor for disqualifying thoughts or acts for which it does not yet have the wherewithal to contemplate consequences.

Matt Ridley (1999) describes the Papal interpretation of ensoulment process: "Pope John Paul II, in his message to the Pontifical Academy of Sciences on October 22, 1996, argued that between ancestral apes and modern human beings there was an 'ontological discontinuity' – a point at which God injected a human soul into an animal lineage. Thus can the Church be reconciled to evolutionary theory. Perhaps the ontological leap came at the moment when two ape chromosomes were fused, and the genes for the soul lie near the middle of chromosome 2." [Humans have 23 chromosomes and apes have 24. It is postulated that two large ape chromosomes fused at the transition from the common ancestor to humans].

The Pope's neat reconciliation notwithstanding, does *H. sapiens* qualify?

From our narrow perspective as only one of millions of extant species, and dwelling on this side of the Great Divide between earthly and super-terrestrial existence, we might venture to identify the behavioral repertoire of qualifying species: *altruism*; *fairness*; *compassion*, *loyalty*; to these would be added *monogamy*, or at least *family values* (in deference to the superior vision of the Moral Majority), *belief in an afterlife*, and indubitably, *belief in god*. One troubling aspect of this list of qualifying characteristics is that they are not universally shared among all species-mates in the case of humans. Does this merely imply that compliant souls will go to heaven and transgressors to hell, or, more pointedly, that the soul is expunged from those who do not live up to standards?

Although pre-Neanderthal and Cro Magnon cultural patterns are difficult to discern from the archeological and fossil evidence, there is some indication that Neanderthals, and certainly Cro-Magnons, were concerned for their fellows and even believed in an afterlife, as evidenced by the survival of individuals with what appear to be disabling injuries and by burial arrangements that indicate a concern for future perambulations of the deceased.

Carl Sagan (1997), astronomer and author, who popularized astronomy in a public television series during the 1980's, puzzled over the possibility of destroying the soul by aborting a human fetus: "The attempt to find an ethically sound and unambiguous judgment on when, if ever, abortion is permissible has deep historical roots. Often, especially in Christian tradition, such attempts were connected with the question of when the soul enters the body - a matter not readily amenable to scientific investigation and an issue of controversy even among learned theologians. Ensoulment has been asserted to occur in the sperm before conception, at conception, at the time of "quickening" (when the mother is first able to feel the fetus stirring within her), and at birth. Or even later."

Resolution of this question may differ for other species if ensoulment (infusion of a body with soul) is available to them, particularly the many hominids that have gone extinct during the past 5-7 million years, and our current primate cousins, the monkeys and apes. If so, it may well be that other primate fetuses, which mature much more rapidly than their human counterparts, acquire their souls at an earlier stage of their development.

ROs promote the idea of the eternal soul as a mechanism for binding adherents to their doctrines and purposes, one of which is to generate more adherents: are there any known ROs who promote reproductive restraint? They exert leverage by promising salvation and threatening damnation to the immortal essence. In this way, acquiescence to this mythical concept is detrimental to the future of life, fostering expansion of the human population beyond Earth's sustainable capacity, and thus posing a dangerous threat to all other forms of life.

Inconsistencies and lies

What may shake the faith of believers in Judeo-Christian theological precepts are inconsistencies, some bordering on outright deception, in Hebrew and Christian texts. Bart D. Ehrman, professor of religious studies at University of North Carolina, has extensively analyzed inconsistencies in the Christian gospels and related texts. He laments the fact that there is such a gulf between public perceptions of scriptures and what has been learned from historical-critical analysis, even though there are thousands of scholars engaged in this type of biblical study.

"Yet such views of the bible are virtually unknown by the population at large .... Many pastors who have learned this material in seminary have, for a variety of reasons, not shared it with their parishioners once they take up positions in the church.........before long, as students see more and more of the evidence, many of them find that the inerrancy and truthfulness of the Bible begins to waver. There is simply too much evidence, and to reconcile all of the hundreds of differences among the biblical sources requires so much speculation and fancy speculative footwork that eventually it gets to be too much for them."

Ehrman shows that New Testament writers have differing views on Jesus' origins, philosophy and actions. Parts of the New Testament that were attributed to apostles were actually written by others who may not even have been contemporaries – only 8 of the 27 books were attributed to the actual authors. Many fundamental doctrines of Christianity do not have their origins in the gospels, but are much later additions, e.g. Jesus' divinity, his messianic role, and the concepts of heaven and hell; the Trinity of Father, Son and Holy Ghost is nowhere found in the Bible; the popular story of Jesus' birth, death and resurrection is actually a composite of four different descriptions in the gospels. The gospel of Matthew and the letters of the Apostle Paul are diametrically opposed regarding early Christian observance of Jewish law.

Theological scholars generally agree that the four gospels of the New Testament (Christian Bible) were written in the first century AD, although there are disputes among them concerning their timing and authorship. Whether or not any of the Gospel writers were witnesses to the events surrounding the life and death of Jesus is uncertain. Matthew was possibly a disciple, but almost certainly Mark and Luke were not, and learned of the events from others. Mark was a disciple of Peter, who undoubtedly was the source of his information. The gospel of John is written from the perspective of one who actually witnessed the events of Jesus' life.

Although there are significant differences in the Gospels, it is likely that information available to each of the writers differed. Some scholars believe that early Greek versions were, in some cases, translations from even earlier documents written in Hebrew and/or Aramaic, particularly the Gospel of Matthew. Some passages are identical in two or more of the Gospels, for example, Matthew 10:26-33 and Luke 12:2-9, even though they were ostensibly independently written, leading some scholars to believe that both of these writers used Mark as their source, or perhaps some other as yet undiscovered source document identified as Q for 'quelle' ('source' in German).

Another reason for differences in the Gospels is that the authors had differing agendas. For example, Matthew sought to proselytize his Jewish brethren, while Luke, almost certainly a gentile, moved the tenets of Christianity further from the traditional Jewish law that prevailed as the code of conduct for transitional Jewish Christians.

The point is that differences in the Gospels are to be expected, considering their variegated authorship and their differing perspectives and purposes. However, evangelical Christians take the word of the Bible literally, and it they who need to be apprised of these inconsistencies. It is one thing to view an incident from differing perspectives, but this would not ordinarily lead to the kinds of contradictions in accounts of the same incident, particularly if a god was behind the hands and pens of the writers.

Stephan Huller (2009) makes the case that the standard bearer of Christianity, Jesus, may not be the Jewish Messiah. He extensively supports the notion that the true Messiah was Saint Mark, who was designated Messiah as a young boy and who was the author of much of the canonical texts that comprises the present day New Testament. He bases his analysis on the existence of the throne of St. Mark, which was a miniature seat that could accommodate only a small person, and which is replete with symbols that have been analyzed by scholars to reveal that it was constructed for the messiah Mark, who was designated as a young boy by his Jewish contemporaries.

According to recent evidence, the first five books of the Old Testament, the Hebrew Torah, were written in the period after the life of Solomon, perhaps around 600 BCE, certainly not during the life of Moses, who lived many centuries earlier. The Dead Sea Scrolls, which contain fragments of the Torah, date from no earlier than 1 or 2 centuries BCE. Writings of the ancient prophets were apparently preserved over centuries and compiled by unknown authors. To claim that the Torah is the word of Jehovah does not appear to bear scrutiny.

As confirmation of the earthly origins of the Torah (five books of Moses, or Pentateuch), researchers have found many inconsistencies, indicating that its origins are anything but godly. Only a few are listed below, just to provide the flavor[137]:

Man was created after the plants. Gen.1:12, 26.
Man was created before the plants. Gen.2:5-9.

The birds were created out of the water. Gen.1:20.
The birds were created out of the land. Gen.2:19.

The animals were created before man. Gen.1:24-26.
The animals were created after man. Gen.2:19.

So, what's wrong with religion?

Let me count the ways[138]:

- Prescribes faith, rather than inquiry and reason, as the primary means of problem-solving (thrives on ignorance);

- Answerable to no system of earthly laws, but rather a law unto itself;

- Justifies unequal distribution of life's perquisites, on the grounds that accounts will be squared in an afterlife – misery, servitude and even slavery have been condoned;

- Promotes human population increase in the face of a global glut and unsustainable growth;

- Acquiesces, and is often complicit, in unequal administration of justice (castigates non-believers and sanctifies miscreant behavior of adherents, regardless of their contributions to society)

- Subverts the exercise of functional ethics (e.g. Golden Rule) in relations between people; distracts people from doing the right things on Earth;

- Injects an intermediary between the élan and nature; thereby diminishing spirituality;

- Promises what it can't deliver (eternal salvation) and threatens what it cannot impose (eternal damnation);

- Sets up competition among adherents of alternative deities, sometimes with violent or otherwise tragic consequences;

- Promises everlasting blessings for deeds in god's name, while justifying harming and maiming others with allegiance to another god or no god.

ROs thrive on human number. Without souls as subjects for fulfilling their roles as intermediaries with the superpower, they would have to find other, less fortuitous opportunities for self-aggrandizement. The Catholic Church, for example, promotes population growth in the face of vastly excessive human population. A papal encyclical, Humanae Vitae of 1968, lays out the Church's position on birth control: The sexual act must "retain its intrinsic relationship to the procreation of human life." Direct interruption of the "generative process already begun" is proscribed. Abortion of a fetus, for any reason whatsoever, is forbidden, as is any means of contraception other than natural family planning methods, e.g. abstaining from intercourse during the fertile part of the woman's menstrual cycle, as this is a "a faculty provided by nature."

One of the unfortunate consequences of this doctrine on the use of contraception as a means of birth control is the spread of HIV/AIDS in Africa. As church influence spreads, so does the stricture on the use of condoms, which currently is the only way to safely protect transmission of the virus from one sex partner to the other. The church position that abstinence is the way to prevent pregnancy and HIV/AIDS is a chimera, as sexual encounter is a phenomenon whose ubiquitous occurrence will not be diminished by papal edict.

Most adherents to one religion or another would be shocked, upon examining its scriptures, to learn that their gods are deceitful, vengeful and violent. "It was only when I undertook to read the Bible through from the beginning to end that I perceived that its depiction of the Lord God – whom I had always viewed as the very embodiment of perfection – was actually that of a monstrous, vengeful tyrant, far exceeding in bloodthirstiness and insane savagery the depredations of Hitler, Stalin, Pol Pot, Attila the Hun or any other mass murderer or ancient or modern history."[139]

It is a misreading of American history to state that religion underpinned the founding of the United States. The founding fathers primarily identified as deists, believers in a supreme being, but disdainful of organized religion. In a letter to Benjamin Rush, after being vilified as an infidel by the clergy of Philadelphia, Thomas Jefferson (2009) voiced his attitude toward the church:

"It is by the exercise of our reason that we are enabled to contemplate God in His works, and imitate Him in His ways. When we see His care and goodness extended over all His creatures, it teaches us our duty toward each other, while it calls forth our gratitude to Him. It is by forgetting God in His works, *and running after the books of pretended revelation, that man has wandered from the straight path of duty and happiness, and become by turns the victim of doubt and the dupe of delusion* (italics added)."

Thomas Paine, journalist and publisher in 1776 of Common Sense, which was highly influential in coalescing opposition to British dominance and promoting independence of the American colonies from England, similarly had nothing but contempt for organized religion: "Except in the first article in the Christian creed, that of believing in God, there is not an article in it but fills the mind with doubt as to the truth of it, the instant man begins to think. Now every article in a creed that is necessary to the happiness and salvation of man, ought to be as evident to the reason and comprehension of man as the first article is, for God has not given us reason for the purpose of confounding us, but that we should use it for our own happiness and His glory."[140]

Paine identified a litany of appalling acts of the deity worshipped by Christians and Jews as described in the holy Bible: "Whenever we read the obscene stories, the voluptuous debaucheries, the cruel and tortuous executions, the unrelenting vindictiveness with which more than half the Bible is filled, it would be more consistent that we call it the word of a demon than the word of God. It is a history of wickedness that has served to corrupt and brutalize mankind; and, for my part, I sincerely detest it, as I detest everything that is cruel."

" Priests and conjurors" he asserted, "are of the same trade… All national institutions of churches, whether Jewish, Christian or

Turkish, appear to me no other than human inventions, set up to terrify and enslave mankind, and monopolize power and profit...Of all the tyrannies that affect mankind, tyranny in religion is the worst; every other species of tyranny is limited to the world we live in; but this attempts to stride beyond the grave, and seeks to pursue us into eternity."[141]

John Adams, second president of the United States, similarly had little use for organized religion. Although he identified as a Unitarian, it appears from his writings that he did not believe in an interventionist god. He agreed that conventional religion was needed by some people as a means of stimulating ethical behavior, but his views are probably closer to Jefferson and Paine as deists, rather than consistent with tenets of any organized religious denomination. He castigates the Catholic Church more than any other, but his primary objective, one that he adamantly propounded, was to keep the affairs of state free of religion. His essential views on religion, and particularly the relationship of religion and state, is summed up as follows (Adrienne Koch, 1980):

"The United States of America have exhibited, perhaps, the first example of governments erected on the simple principles of nature; and if men are now sufficiently enlightened to disabuse themselves of artifice, imposture, hypocrisy, and superstition, they will consider this event as an era in their history... It will never be pretended that any persons employed in that service had interviews with the gods, or were in any degree under the influence of Heaven, more than those at work upon ships or houses, or laboring in merchandise or agriculture; it will forever be acknowledged that these governments were contrived merely by the use of reason and the senses."

In his searing condemnation of religion, Christopher Hitchens (2009) points out the failure of an omniscient and benevolent god to bring to humanity what it most covets - health, peace and prosperity: "If Jesus could heal a blind person he happened to meet, why not heal the blind?....With all this continual prayer, why no result?" His objections to religious faith: "that it wholly misrepresents the origin of man and the cosmos, that because of this error it manages to combine the maximum of servility with the maximum of solipsism[142], that it is both the cause and the result of dangerous sexual repression, and that it is ultimately grounded on wishful thinking"

Scottish biologist Richard Dawkins (2008), a fervent critic of creationism, who has written extensively on natural origins of all animate and inanimate matter in the universe, similarly regards religion as a dangerous invention: "Had my chaplain (who was awed by the majesty of nature) been aware of (Darwin's *Origin of Species*) he would certainly have identified with it and, instead of the priesthood, might have been led to Darwin's view that all was 'produced by laws acting around us'".[143] In a more recent work[144] Dawkins takes on the creationists in an exhaustive review of the evidence for evolution. He cites the extensive hominid fossil record with many 'missing links' that clearly show the transition to modern humans from primitive primate ancestors dating from up to four million years ago. He also reviews genetic confirmation of evolution, and examples of evolution taking place virtually before the eyes of experimenters using organisms such as bacteria and fish species with relatively short life cycles. In his painstaking expositions on evolutionary processes, Dawkins is reminiscent of his great mentor, Charles Darwin, the originator of our modern concept of natural selection.

In his monumental work, Origin of Species, published in 1859, Darwin brightly illuminates the temporal panorama of life's natural origins: "Thus, from the war of nature, from famine and death, the most exalted object which we are capable of conceiving, namely, the production of the higher animals, follows. There is grandeur in this view of life, with its several powers, having been originally breathed into a few forms or into one; and that, whilst this planet has gone cycling on according to the fixed law of gravity, from so simple a beginning endless forms most beautiful and most wonderful have been, and are being, evolved."

Dr. Charles Kimball (2003), professor of comparative religion in the Department of Religion and the Divinity School at Wake Forest University, discusses five warning signs of religious corruption: claims to absolute truth, blind obedience, establishing the 'ideal' time, the end justifies any means, and declaring holy war.

Is truth derived by any means absolute? Study of the laws controlling phenomena in the physical universe indicate that there are no absolutes, and certainly not in the domain of religion, which is a human invention. However, ROs and their indoctrinated acolytes tend to believe that their version of truth supersedes that of all others, and that holders of opposing views are not only wrong, but often deserve condemnation or even persecution.

Believers are often led to obey the strictures and canons of their ROs without question, leaving their rational faculties behind in the process. Fundamentalist ROs exploit devotion of their followers to the point of self-destruction in the process of doing violence to non-believers, in exchange for eternal rewards and other perquisites of blind obedience.

Extremist ROs often lead their followers to believe that a supernatural phenomenon, such as the second coming of Christ, Armageddon, the end of times, are imminent, sometimes with bizarre consequences. According to the Contender Ministries [145]: "It is increasingly obvious that the time of our Lord's coming is drawing near. Prophecy is being fulfilled daily, and at a faster pace than ever before. Whether you believe in a pre-tribulation rapture, or believe Christians will be witness to the full tribulation, wrath, and final judgments, matters not." Imminence of the end of times, or the establishment of god's kingdom on Earth, has been used as a pretext for political action to impose religious law, e.g. the Taliban takeover of the government in Afghanistan in 1996.

Religious fervor is often the basis for justifying any means to achieve an end. Fanatical Jewish and Islamic ROs in the Middle East successfully exhort their followers to commit acts of violence and murder, including suicide bombings, to further their agendas. Since the Crusades of the 11th to 13th centuries CE, intended to restore Christianity to the Holy Land, mass killings of Muslims and other non-Christians in Holy Land were the rule. It was common practice to behead captive enemies and impale them on pikes as gory testament to the sanctity of the Crusaders' mission. According to the Gesta Francorum (anonymous chronicle of the capture of Jerusalem), "... [our men] were killing and slaying even to the Temple of Solomon, where the slaughter was so great that our men waded in blood up to their ankles..." Raymond of Aguilers, a chronicler of the First Crusade (1096-1099): "It was a just and marvelous judgment of God, that this place [the temple of Solomon] should be filled with the blood of the unbelievers." On the Second Crusade (1147-1149), St. Bernard of Clairvaux pronounced: "The Christian glories in the death of a pagan, because thereby Christ himself is glorified."[146]

The Taliban, mainly militant Pashtun who comprise about 40

percent of Afghanistan's population and who are the predominant ethnic group in southern provinces bordering Pakistan, have attacked many girls' schools in both countries. For example, in Feb 2010 Taliban militants used explosives to destroy a girls' school in northwest Pakistan. In May 2009, 90 schoolgirls were hospitalized as a result of a gas attack on a school in Kapisa province, northeast of the Afghan capital. Other desciples spread god's word by throwing acid in the faces of school girls. The Taliban's justification is that education for girls violates Islamic principles and that strict isolation of women is a Pashtun cultural tradition. On September 11th, 2001 disciples of al Qaeda, an extremist organization of Islamic fundamentalists, hijacked four commercial jetliners and crashed them into the World Trade Center (WTC) in New York City and the Pentagon in Washington, D.C. killing over 3000 workers and service personnel. Justification for the attack is contained in a statement of the leaders of al Qaeda, their justification in part a *quid pro quo* regarding the Crusades of 8 or 9 centuries ago. A rambling al Queda document provides further rationale for the attack, admonishing followers to struggle against non-believers in the 'religion of truth'. "Prayers and peace be upon the unique leader of the warriors (mujahedeen), Muhammad ibn Abdullah who said to unbelievers, 'I have come to you with slaughter.' May the most excellent prayers and perfect greetings be upon him, his family, and his friends."[147]

The document lauds the motivations and performance of the perpetrators of the WTC attack, attributing their martyrdom to sacrifice for the religion of Allah and for "defending Muslims whom American hands had mistreated by various types of torture and forms of domination and subjugation in every place." In 2004 information began to emerge about mistreatment of detainees (alleged terrorists) in prisons maintained by U.S. military forces at Bagram in Afghanistan, Abu Ghraib in Iraq and at the detention facility at Guantanamo, Cuba.

Holy war is the instrument of scoundrels, extremist ROs who seek to mobilize vulnerable segments of their co-religionists in pursuit of essentially political ends. The appeal is ostensibly predicated on carrying out theological mandates, but the prescribed actions are all too earthy.

'Just' wars, inspired by RO/PO cabals, have been undertaken on similarly shaky pretexts. One of George W. Bush's principle constituencies in his successful bid for the US presidency in 2000 was the religious right, evangelical Christians in the tradition of politically conservative preachers such as Pat Robertson and Jerry Falwell. "Eighty-four percent of them voted for Bush, providing nearly one-third of his total."[148] After the attacks on the World Trade Center and Pentagon on September 11, 2001, Bush, with British cooperation under Prime Minister Tony Blair, launched the invasion of Afghanistan - "Operation Enduring Freedom" - purportedly as a struggle against the Taliban, which had taken control of the country, and their al Qaeda (self-pronounced perpetrators of the September 11 attacks) supporters, who were reportedly operating training camps for terrorists to launch further attacks in North America and Europe. The intervention eventually evolved into a counterinsurgency, whose target remains cloudy in 2010 as the military intervention continues - the longest war in US history.[149]

In his State of the Union message of January, 2002 President Bush identified the world *center of depravity*, the 'axis of evil' - Iraq and Iran, with North Korea thrown in to demonstrate equanimity. Subsequently, on March 20, 2003, Bush and Blair ignited the incendiary mixture of oil and religion by heading a multinational force in "Operation Iraqi Freedom". From the time of the invasion, justification metamorphosed according to political expediency: first the intent was to deny the government of Saddam Hussein non-existent weapons of mass destruction; subsequently, Iraqi insurgents became terrorists who posed a threat of further attacks on the US; by 2006 military leaders began to identify the conflict as a civil war between Sunni and Shia Islamic factions. In 2007 Iran became the culprit, a fomenter of terrorism.

As a result of Bush's pursuit of the unified agenda of the religious and political right, in the U.S. presidential election of 2004, evangelical Christians were highly aggressive and organized: "The White House struggled to stay abreast of the Christian right and consulted with the movement's leaders in weekly conference calls. But in many respects, Christian activists led the charge that GOP operatives followed and capitalized upon."[150] These actions resonate with evangelical Christians, whose aim has been to dominate and even to convert Islamic people, including Afghanis, to Christianity.[151]

Not to be outdone, President Barack Obama, apparently to wrest allegiance of the Christian right (now respected for their political clout) from his Republican adversaries, after his election in 2008 expanded military intervention in Afghanistan by calling for the insertion of more troops, in effect continuing the misguided policies of the Bush administration (in fact, this was a central feature of his campaign platform).

Exuberance for one's god extends even to protecting its name, as something owned by adherents of a particular faith. To many Muslims the name of the one god Allah belongs exclusively to them. They believe that liturgical use of the name by Christian clerics could confuse Muslim worshipers, even while Arabic and Malaysian language Bibles describe Jesus as the "son of Allah". Continuation of this practice by Malaysian Christians set off an uproar of in Kuala Lampur, during which a number of churches and convents were firebombed and defaced. The attacks were in response to a Malaysian court ruling voiding a government ban on the use of the name Allah as the Christian God. According to news reports[152], Muslims were concerned that by invoking the name that Islam had assigned to the one god, who by Abrahamic tradition must be shared by Christians, Jews and Muslims, Christians sought to pave the way for conversion of Islamists to Christianity. This begs a question: what was the motive of the unique deity in creating monotheistic rivals? Was it merely mischief or downright pandemonium that *it*[153] intended?

Simply stated, this is the problem: once invented, god can promise things that the rational intellect knows are not possible from nature, so people succumb to mystical predilections and are thus distracted from doing the right things. Religious practices, taken in conjunction, constitute one of the most dangerous behaviors of the human repertoire, responsible for inordinate expansion of the human population, far beyond the capacity of Earth's sustainable, renewable resources and thus exploitative of natural capital. They are like placebos, which allow the 'disease' to continue exacting its toll - empty promises of eternal salvation in exchange for following the agendas of religious operatives rather than focusing on fostering a decent life on Earth for all its inhabitants.

To believe or not to believe – that is the question

What are the risks in believing or disbelieving in one god or another? Assume an interventionist god whose existence or non-existence is equally probable, and who will wreak vengeance on those who have the temerity to deny its existence. Aside from the problem of selecting the right god of the rather significant array of possibilities, four scenarios have to be considered: god does or does not exist, coupled either with one's belief or disbelief:

> God exists, and one either
> believes, with eternal bliss visited upon one's soul, or
> doesn't believe, in which case eternal damnation, or
> God doesn't exist, and one either
> believes, with neutral consequences, or
> doesn't believe, with neutral consequences.

Earthly cost of belief is small, perhaps some disdain on the part of those familiars who consider any sort of religiosity to be gauche, but there is always the possibility to have public and private faces that differ in this regard. Similarly, cost of disbelief is usually small, except if one considers a public career, in which case the result could be political suicide. However, earthly effects are transitory, while approbation or condemnation by a deity carries eternal consequences. It appears that the wisest choice is to believe, as the result can only be neutral to fortuitous, while to disbelieve carries the chance of consignment to everlasting hell.

Even so, some simply cannot bring themselves to the point of belief in organized religion, regardless of the consequences, Sam Harris (2008), for example[154]: "The fact that my public and continuous rejection of Christianity does not worry me in the least should suggest to you just how inadequate I believe your reasons for being a Christian are."

In the course of the 200,000 year history of modern humans, and perhaps in earlier ancestral populations, growing consciousness stimulated wonder at the majesty of the cosmos, leading to questions concerning the meaning of life – how and why we are here. For Descartes "Cogito, ergo sum" (I think, therefore, I am) - consciousness (thinking) invokes a sense of self, and introspection, but that still doesn't explain the source. Some are merely awed by the majesty of the cosmos and inspired to a kind of spirituality, an identity with all that is observable or contemplated, and elevated to an even more profound reverence with the proliferation of information concerning the magnitude and order of the universe. For others, with no answer in sight, the agile human brain invokes a super-force as creator of the heavens, earth and its inhabitants. Still others, alert to the life force that drives all organisms to seek survival and growth, see opportunity in using their capacities to influence others by conjuring up versions of the superpower and preying on the vulnerable with carrot and stick to join a movement.

Evangelicals of every stripe have mesmerized their flocks with flowing oratory, often thereby confiscating real property for their self-aggrandizement. Evangelism not only is good for business, it is good business. Evangelicals have amassed great wealth by exploiting human vulnerabilities, often leading private lives that are antithetical to their professed standards of spiritualism and purity. One TV evangelist profits handsomely from her long-standing ministry, consisting of TV and radio programs that reach millions of people in about 70 countries[155]. The evangelist and her husband receive millions in compensation, and perquisites befitting the pop stars that they have become.

In one of the ironies concerning religion, a member of the Catholic clergy accused the Disney entertainment enterprise of exploiting children by encouraging them to consume products marketed by the company. Christopher Jamison, Abbot of Worth in West Sussex, UK, condemns the corporation for "exploiting spirituality" to sell its products and of turning Disneyland into a modern day pilgrimage site.[156] He cites some films produced by Disney, e.g. *Sleeping Beauty* and *101 Dalmatians*, that he claims encourage consumerism among young children. While ostensibly presenting a moral message, the underlying purpose is to implant materialistic sentiments in children, thereby enhancing commercial opportunities. The Abbot credits Disney films with showing good triumphing over evil, but that this is only a ruse to influence children to demand Disney products from their families. He laments the practices of Disney as "a classic example" of how consumerism is promoted as a route to happiness, an alternative to traditional moral behavior.

Religion's threat to posterity

The negative side of religion resides in the propensity of vulnerable people to accept and to become devotees and mindless acolytes of purveyors of mythical supernatural concepts about superpowers, who promise eternal perquisites in the life after death and threaten eternal damnation if their dictates, with supernatural overtones, are not followed. Religion has been a corrosive and even cancerous force, a form of tyranny that is antithetical to development of rational faculties needed to solve the multitude of problems facing mankind. There are functional justifications for ethical and even moral behavior that are more productively evoked by appeal to the intellect - religion is unnecessary in a species with cooperation as an essential component of its inherent operational strategy. The myths and superstitions promoted by ROs will fade into history if and when mankind realizes that our intrinsic spirituality and rationality can more effectively bring about universal aspirations for a healthful environment in a social climate of peace, justice and prosperity.

Chapter 8
A ROAD NOT TAKEN

Although there are severe penalties for attempting to take down a sacred cow, one human activity that should evoke displeasure, if not condemnation, for its consequences is the manner in which knowledge is pursued under the aegis of *science*[157]. The transition over the past two millennia, from its foundation in natural philosophy to what we now know as the scientific method, has not been fortuitous for the continuation of life on Earth. A 'road not taken' is the one that would have retained a philosophical underpinning.

Yes, there have been incredible strides in understanding nature - extending the human life span by a few decades is one example of the achievements of medical science. In the 1950's medical researchers Jonas Salk and Albert Sabin developed vaccines for polio, eliminating a scourge that particularly targeted young children. But in general the cost of scientific innovation has been horrendous for our planet. One only has to figuratively stand in outer space and regard our once magnificent orb crumbling under the onslaught of human 'progress'.

Advances in technology, and the pursuit and acquisition of scientific knowledge, upon which they are largely dependent, are considered widely to be defining characteristics of modern humanity. The word 'science' has been adopted in most languages, even if a word for 'knowledge' already existed. 'Scientific' has emerged to mean a special kind of knowledge, derived from application of the 'scientific method'.

The march of science cannot be arrested – it is too indelibly ingrained in the human psyche – but something is amiss, and needs a course correction. The leading edge in the pursuit of knowledge would more assuredly be advantageous to the future of life in the hands of people whose perspective encompasses the broad consequences of their investigations. A more philosophical foundation is required, in some respects a reversal of the trend that has resulted in a virtual barrier between philosophy and science, even though they are in some respects like mother and daughter. Scientists would be unlikely to engage in research on more effective poison gases, for example, were the framework of their inquiries fundamentally philosophical.

Philosophy and science

All living species, including humans, acquire and apply information. Charles Darwin shed much light on the impetus for the pursuit of knowledge in humans and all other species as an indispensible element in the evolutionary development process. This must derive from the life force (essentially the libido of Freud and Jung), which engenders the 'quest' for a successful strategy – a plan for survival and replication. Characteristics of species are adaptations to the exigencies of nature – the giraffe's neck, the cheetah's fleetness, the human's cerebral cortex. Nature, in turn, provides austere feedback to inevitable modification brought about by genetic mutation and sexual reproduction, vital elements in the process of natural selection. Our propensity and capacity to use information to alter the environment to suit our aspirations is the distinguishing feature of human existence acquired in this process, part of our fundamental strategic conformation – the most cerebral of all – that has proved to be one of the most successful, along with those of cockroaches and rats.

Prior to the onset of civilization, humanity was too close to the brink to consider the nature of learning, i.e. epistemology – what is knowledge, and *how and why* it is acquired. As agricultural and industrial revolutions changed the landscape so that resources could be managed rather than simply mined or gathered, knowledge about the manner of collecting information and its consequences, took on a new level of significance.

In its earliest form, the pursuit of knowledge focused on the heavens and earthly matter, as there were utilitarian consequences. Celestial cycles and positioning were linked over time with seasons and climatic variations that were determinants of the food supply. The mystical side of human nature extended the relevance of celestial alignments to the social domain, which gave more impetus to the search for meaning in the heavens.

What grew out of this inquisitiveness came to be known as philosophy (from Greek *philosophos*)[158]: thought; the search for (and love of) wisdom or knowledge; logical analysis of principles for the conduct of life; inquiry into the nature of the universe; and comprised of study of ethics, aesthetics, logic, epistemology, metaphysics. Definitions of the term 'philosophy' often focus on its intellectual and speculative nature, but observation or empiricism has to be a part of any pursuit of knowledge. For one thing, mind-matter duality may be only an illusion (see Chapter 2): even thought itself, the cybernetic process of ideation, has a material quality. But of even greater significance is the inexorable connection of an entire organism such as 'man' to its external, material environment.

How does the pursuit of knowledge differ in the philosophical vs. scientific context? *Science* is derived from the Latin word *scientia* – knowledge, discernment. *Philosophy*, as noted above, has a very similar meaning. Historically, two forces were responsible for the birth of philosophy's child - science. Proliferation of knowledge, not only about the nature of matter but extending into the social domain, resulted in a trend toward specialization. Secondly, complexities of civilization demanded a more utilitarian approach to knowledge, attuned to the needs of increasingly organized, politicized, militarized and forward-looking (planning) society. While philosophy allowed for flights of intellect, science demanded more rigorous empiricism – acquisition of systematized knowledge derived from observation, study and experimentation.

In the West most notably during the two millennia from the age of ancient Greece to Galileo, but in the East thousands of years earlier, momentous advances in knowledge and its applications were achieved as an outgrowth of human inquisitiveness. Gradually, knowledge under the banner of science took on the aspect of a commodity, to be exploited in the mercantile arena, by monopolists in universities, and by governments - primarily to support their military adventures.

What is the contemporary relationship between science and philosophy? It is simply this: aside from its insistence on more stringent empiricism and mathematical rigor, science has narrowed its field of view and has come to mean learning about some aspect of nature without implicitly referencing its wider social, political and ecological implications – something like knowledge in a partial vacuum – partial only because there is the unavoidable umbilical to a society that science feeds upon. For example, while sociology is now considered a legitimate field of scientific inquiry, behavioral phenomena and relationships, and not necessarily their wider socio-economic implications, are usually in focus. Some subdivisions of social science are inherently tied to the human environment, but tend toward a narrow, utilitarian orientation, e.g. political science (study of government and political processes, institutions, and behavior). Philosophy, in contrast, as open-ended inquiry, implicitly takes in the existential panorama.

To put this in more concrete terms: most scientific inquiry is like climbing Everest, not only because it's there, but also because it is a fundable challenge. But there is something wrong with this - climbers leave behind a residue – tracks and trash and other detritus that mark the mountain and change it forever, usually not considered when knowledge is pursued in the scientific mode. The broader vista of philosophy evokes concern about these things.

The unfortunate bifurcation

As human consciousness evolved in the transition from ancestral forms, the heavens and the nature of matter became the focus of intellectual scrutiny. Knowledge was undoubtedly pursued inevitably for utilitarian reasons[159], as virtually endless cycles of stars, sun, moon and planets traversing the skies were progressively linked empirically to fundamental issues of survival - to factors essential to food security – drought, inundation, extremes of heat and cold. The pace and content of acquired knowledge was part and parcel of cultural development, among humans such a powerful adjunct to genetic evolution.

The word *science* is simply the Latin word for knowledge: *scientia*.

Until the 1840's what we now call science was natural philosophy, so that even Isaac Newton's great book on motion and gravity, published in 1687, was titled *Philosophiæ Naturalis Principia Mathematica* (The Mathematical Principles of Natural Philosophy) Newton was, to himself and his contemporaries, a 'philosopher'. In fact, "..although Newton may have provided physics with its paradigm [his laws of physics], he himself worked largely within its pre-paradigmatic context, and the latter, according to Thomas Kuhn (1996)[160], is typically characterized by extensive epistemological debates and controversies over the "foundations" or "first principles" of the science"[161]

The transition from philosophy, or natural philosophy, to science was certainly not an orderly process. The methods of some who identified as natural philosophers differed from those of later investigators such as Robert Boyle (known mainly for his work on temperature, pressure and volume relationships in gases), Francis Bacon (experimental and inductive scientific truth), and Galileo (kinematics and observational astronomy), who based assertions about their discoveries on experimentation and replication. Most natural philosophers instead employed a speculative, intellectual approach in developing their concepts about the natural world. Eventually science became largely divorced from epistemology, and natural philosophy in general, relying more on observation and experimentation to authenticate their speculations.

The history of western civilization is commonly divided into periods predicated on advancement of culture, measured by the level, reliability and application of knowledge. Although intellectual innovation occurred in many parts of the world prior to the ancient Greeks, philosophical history usually begins from that era. None of the pillars of Greek philosophy, while engaging in the quest for knowledge and recording their ideas for posterity, very likely thought of themselves as scientists, and in fact probably never heard of science as it is currently understood. The term *scientist*, as epithet for a seeker of knowledge via the scientific method, was not in common use until the 19th century (attributed to William Whewell, 1794 – 1866, Anglican priest, philosopher, theologian and historian). Through prior centuries intellectual supermen sought knowledge without the benefit of modern scientific methodology, discovering ideas and principles, some of which involved empirical information, mainly through the intellect, without benefit of the instruments and mathematical tools available to modern day science.

How did the unfortunate split from a philosophic to a scientific foundation for the pursuit of knowledge come to pass? Let us review the process of transition from open-ended inquiry into the secrets of nature, to what has turned out to be a decidedly utilitarian process:

Socrates (4-5th century BCE) never wrote anything, and is known only through his student, Plato. His path to understanding focused on pursuit of truth rather than acquisition of knowledge *per se*. Plato, through dialogues with his master, gazed intently on human society, identifying reality in ideas and forms examined through the intellect. Plato's student, Aristotle saw reality more in physical terms, understood through observation. In the 3rd century BCE, Aristotle conceived a model in which celestial bodies were attached to 55 concentric spheres that rotated at different velocities (angular velocity constant for a given sphere), to explain motions of the sun, moon and planets relative to the centrally positioned Earth. Aristotle was much concerned with the nature of physical reality, but wrote also on topics that we now identify as biology, morals and politics. Although a brilliant student, when his master died he was not appointed to head Plato's academy, probably because their philosophical outlooks differed so significantly. Even then, the knowledge arena was a battleground – a tradition that has mushroomed into open warfare in the laboratories of academia and industry.

Ptolemy (Claudius Ptolemaeus) was a Roman citizen of Greek ancestry, who in the second century CE produced several works based upon his celestial studies. His observations were systematic and extensive, but would hardly qualify for contemporary scientific approbation. He produced the Almagest, a treatise on astronomy that explained celestial motions in geometric terms. He presented his astronomical models in convenient tables, which could be used to compute the future or past position of the planets. Through the Middle Ages it was regarded as the authoritative text on astronomy, with its author becoming an almost mythical figure. In his Planetary Hypothesis, Ptolemy improved on the Aristotelian model with a concept that explained planetary motions in terms of epicycles (circles rotating on the circumference of a circle).

Religious factions were drawn to astronomy to support theological concepts. For example, the timing of Ramadan, the Islamic period of reflection and fasting, is linked to the lunar cycle. The Qur'an, counterpart of the Judeo-Christian Bible as the principle guide for the practice of Islam, alludes to celestial significance: "And it is He who ordained the stars for you that you may be guided thereby in the darkness of the land and the sea."[162] From the 7th century CE Arabic astronomers assimilated and expanded upon the work of the ancient Greeks. Many navigational stars have Arabic names, from Acamar (end of the river) to Zubeneschamali (the northern claw) and Zubenelgenubi (the southern claw).

The Ptolemaic view of the cosmos reigned until the 16th century CE, when Nicolai *Copernicus* developed his heliocentric view of the universe, upending the idea that the Earth was the center of the Solar System. His model provided an explanation of obvious deficiencies in the Ptolemaic model, such as varying brightness of the planets and the fact that some planets exhibited inconsistent retrograde motions. Copernicus retained the idea of circular obits for the planets (now known to be elliptical) so there were still some anomalies that could not be explained by his model. He was motivated to undertake his study because " (he) began to grow disgusted that no more consistent scheme of the movements of the mechanism of the universe, set up for our benefit by that best and most law abiding Architect of all things, was agreed upon by philosophers who otherwise investigate so carefully the most minute details of this world."[163] Copernicus was a reluctant revolutionary, fearful of retribution from ecclesiastical authorities, who clung to the geocentric model apparently to avoid upsetting their smoothly running applecart, so his ideas were not published until his death and were not widely disseminated until a century later. In his preface he expressed the wish to "contribute something to the ecclesiastical state whose chief office Your Holiness (Pope Paul III) now occupies."[164]

If the 'scientific revolution' as a point in epistemological history is to be defined, perhaps it is with Copernicus, whose work encompassed – even if in rudimentary form – the essentials of the classical scientific method: observation and description of phenomena; formulation of an explanatory (and falsifiable) hypothesis; prediction of other phenomena based on the hypothesis; experimentation to test predictions of the hypothesis, and if eminently successful, elevation to the status of a theory or law of nature. On the other hand, designating astronomy as a scientific discipline at that point in time is somewhat misleading, as is considering Copernicus as scientist rather than philosopher – for an inquisitive mind there were not very many games in town, i.e. few alternatives to astronomy. The utilitarian character of science that emerged after the industrial revolution was as yet nowhere in sight.

During its thousand years from about 500 BCE, intellectual pillars of the ancient Roman Empire were mainly concerned with war, expansion and political intrigue, so little attention was paid to philosophical matters other than essentially absorbing and building on the learning of the Greeks, although there were instances of literary brilliance in the works of Cicero, Marcus Aurelius, Plutarch, Seneca and many others. Religion followed the pattern of the Greek pantheon, although monotheistic Christianity arose as an outgrowth of ancient theologies, including that of the Hebrews.

The Middle Ages (including the 'Dark Ages' of the early centuries CE when invading tribal groups swarmed over much of Europe) are widely considered a period of cultural stagnation lasting until the mid 15th century, when Johannes Gutenberg's invention of the printing press with movable type served as the catalyst for the European Renaissance – a period of renewed interest in classical knowledge of the ancient Greeks and Romans, artistic advances (aesthetics and perspective of Michaelangelo, Rafael, da Vinci) and educational reform (classics, philosophy, humanities).

Study of astronomical phenomena and characteristics of matter has undergone an operational metamorphosis since the 17th century, when science began to be applied to secure information about anything, not only the natural world. In the early part of the century Johannes Kepler advanced on the Copernican model of planetary motions, doing away with the need for epicycles by formulating mathematical expressions to explain the positions of the planets in terms of elliptical orbits. Although astronomy and physics were already recognized as distinct scientific disciplines, what ignorance had torn asunder, Kepler unified by dealing with astronomy as a form of celestial physics.[165] Just as it was clear that a more thorough understanding of cosmic phenomena demanded integration of what were formerly distinct disciplines, so it is with modern-day science, where proliferation of disciplines and compartmentalization of knowledge are impediments to systematic analysis of natural phenomena, a situation that does not bode well for the future of life on Earth.

It can be argued that modern science originated with Galileo Galilei (1564-1642), since he added mathematical refinement to the astronomy of Kepler and applied mathematical rigor to other areas of knowledge. For example, by rolling balls down an incline, he was able to show that, contrary to Aristotelian observation, all objects fell essentially at the same rate, not dependent on the weight of each. In fact, he determined the acceleration constant, and explained why movement at constant velocity is not sensed, but only acceleration (change in velocity over time). His employment of optics developed in the Netherlands provided views of the heavens previously unknown, with planets as disks rather than points and moons of Jupiter. All of this was upsetting to the Church, but validated the ideas of Copernicus. Galileo eventually fell into the displeasure of the church and was compelled to recant by the Inquisition. But in his last moments he is reported to have said, "and yet it (the Earth) moves".

Isaac Newton, a giant in the pantheon of intellectual superstars, was born in the year Galileo died, 1642. Newton's laws of motion were fundamental principles of physics until Einstein's relativity superseded his concept of absolute space and time. In July 1687 Newton published *Principia*, in which he revealed his three laws of motion: a body with no applied force continues its motion; acceleration related to the force applied to a mass, action and reaction between two bodies in contact. He also developed the law of universal gravitation, and through his new models, explained Kepler's laws of planetary motion. Despite Einstein's refinements, Newton's laws of motion still constitute the foundation of much of modern engineering and technology.

Did Newton consider himself a 'scientist'? The title of his major work indicates otherwise, that he was merely pursuing truth in nature. Furthermore, he states rather forcefully his philosophical approach in a letter to Robert Hooke (15 February 1676)[166]:

"Hitherto I have not been able to discover the cause of those properties of gravity from the phenomena, and I frame no hypothesis; for whatever is not deduced from the phenomena is to be called an hypothesis; and hypotheses, whether metaphysical or physical, whether of occult qualities or mechanical, have no place in experimental philosophy. *In this philosophy particular propositions are inferred from the*

phenomena, and afterward rendered general by deduction [italics added]."
A statement attributed to him by Sir David Brewster[167] provides further
confirmation that he was of a philosophical, rather than a scientific
bent:

"I do not know what I may appear to the world, but to myself
I seem to have been only like a boy playing on the sea-shore, and
diverting myself in now and then finding a smoother pebble or a
prettier shell than ordinary, whilst the great ocean of truth lay all
undiscovered before me."

However, even in Newton's time the pursuit of secure knowledge
about anything, not only the natural world, began to be identified as
'science'. By the 18th century the Enlightenment, characterized in the
Western world by advancements in cultural life, set the stage for the
industrial revolution, with technology feeding on the proliferation
in scientific knowledge. In the 19th century, *philosophy* began to
distance itself from *natural philosophy*, which in some quarters was
transposed into a form of inquiry relying on empiricism with well-
defined mathematical precision - increasingly the term *natural science*
was applied.

During the 19th and early 20th centuries improved measuring
instruments allowed researchers - Lavoisier, Rutherford, De Broglie,
Faraday, Boltzmann, Kirchhoff, Planck, Bohr and many others - to
probe more deeply into the structure of matter, at the atomic and then
subatomic levels. Large telescopes allowed the study of astronomical
phenomena with greater precision.

Science up to the 19th century focused mainly on natural science.
Gradually during this timeframe, researchers in various areas or
disciplines took up places in the universities of Europe and later North
America, forming departments specializing in narrow areas of interest.
Barriers between the disciplines were further fortified with the practice
of conferring degrees within disciplines, and then filling the ranks of
academic posts only with members of a particular 'club'.

By the 20th century science had come into its own, the respectable
way to pursue knowledge via the scientific method. In fact, it has
become commonplace for knowledge gained by any other means to
be attacked by both scientists and lay people alike as 'unscientific' and
unworthy of consideration. Legislative bodies, regulatory agencies and

the press have similarly denigrated any conclusions, predictions or forecasts not 'scientifically' supported.

What are now social sciences were not recognized as disciplines until the 20th century. The study of social phenomena began to employ techniques that mimicked the physical and biological sciences, leading to specializations in sociology, psychology and even economics.

The result finally was a virtual compartmentalization of acquisition and application of knowledge, which has been the cause of much degradation of Earth and its inhabitants. Scientific knowledge and its offshoot, technology, have revolutionized culture, leading to unprecedented accumulation of wealth by a minority, subordination of the interests of vast numbers of humans by an industrial and commercial behemoth, and hazards to life on Earth in the form of environmental pollution, grinding poverty and ignorance among the masses. These developments have led to hostility among social classes, ethnic groups and nations, with attendant rise of terrorism, proliferation of weapons of mass destruction and the propensity to use them. In the hands of humanity, applications of scientific knowledge and technology, as awesome as they may be, have managed to vastly increase insecurity rather than serve to uplift the quality of life on Earth.

Despite the predominant transition toward compartmentalization and application of the 'scientific method' from ancient Greece to the Enlightenment, two post Enlightenment intellectual luminaries illustrate the uplifting effects for humanity of a more wholesome approach to the accumulation and applications of knowledge:

Darwin

Although the idea of evolution was not new at the time, Charles Darwin (1809-1882) revolutionized the entire framework for the existence of life on Earth with his explanation of speciation, with natural selection as the essential mechanism.[168]

Darwin attended Cambridge University, not a particularly good student, but his passionate interest in insects attracted the attention of one of his respected teachers of botany, John Stevens Henslow, who arranged for him to serve as naturalist on a five-year round-the-world voyage of the Beagle. Darwin spent most of these years investigating and amassing voluminous data about the geology and zoology of South America, the Galapagos Islands and the Pacific islands.

After his return to England, he learned that many of the species that he studied in the Galapagos were unique to the islands, but similar to species found on the mainland of South America, about 600 miles away. This led to speculations about the origin of species, which was anathema to ecclesiastical authorities, which clung to the Biblical explanation of creation. Also weighing on him were his own religious upbringing and his devout and devoted wife.

He was not the first to suggest that species could be transmuted. In fact, he was familiar with the evolutionary speculations of his own grandfather Erasmus Darwin, a physician and also a respected naturalist, poet and philosopher, and by the French zoologist Jean-Baptiste Lamarck. After his return from the Beagle voyage, over many years he conducted exhaustive experiments in horticulture and animal husbandry. To supplement his own experiments, he communicated with many other naturalists and geologists, and with horticulturalists and animal breeders who were improving their species by successively selecting for desirable traits.

From Thomas Malthus' Essay on the Principle of Population (1798), which explained how unrestrained growth in human population would overextend the capacity for food production, Darwin realized that a large proportion of organisms do not reach reproductive age. Otherwise, population of every species would expand indefinitely, which was obviously at odds with experience: species populations eventually reach a stable level in a given area. He extended this idea to speculation that favorable variations within species would provide the wherewithal for some to survive to reproductive age and others to perish before they were able to beget offspring. This process he called 'natural selection', as compared with selective breeding in domesticated animals and plants, which ultimately leads to new breeds (even to the point of speciation) over a number of generations.

Darwin's monumental work, *Origin of Species*, was finally published in 1859, over two decades after completing the Beagle voyage and after having first prepared the outline of his theory in 1842. He was prompted finally to introduce his ideas into the public arena because he learned that Alfred Russell Wallace had arrived at an almost identical explanation for evolution of species. He deliberately and painstakingly explained that species are not immutable, using examples from nature and from horticulture and animal husbandry. Then he showed how differential survival rates in isolated populations would favor propagation of some traits and extinction of others, leading to speciation, such that viable sexual reproduction with parallel populations would no longer be possible. Darwin provided a view of the panorama of life with all species related through branching over the eons since life first appeared on Earth.

Although Darwin, on occasion, connected his efforts with the scientific milieu of his day, he would not pass scientific muster according to today's standards. First and foremost, Darwin was drawn to what we might now identify as zoology like a moth to candlelight. He considered himself a naturalist, one interested in probing into the nature of nature, and focused on characteristics of species inhabiting Earth. Most significantly, his major contribution to human understanding, The *Origin*, which profoundly altered the conception of man's relation to nature, was written in a style that any layperson could read cover to cover without flinching. *He communicated with anyone who happened to be interested in his findings*, and not a select group of scientific specialists for whom a barrier existed between knowledge and its consequences. The last paragraph of *Origin* sums up his worldview and its universal relevance:

"Thus, from the war of nature, from famine and death, the most exalted object which we are capable of conceiving, namely, the production of the higher animals, directly follows. There is grandeur in this view of life, with its several powers, having been originally breathed into a few forms or into one; and that, whilst this planet has gone cycling on according to the fixed law of gravity, from so simple a beginning endless forms most beautiful and most wonderful have been, and are being, evolved."

Although he tantalized readers by alluding to human origins, it was only in a later work, the Descent of Man, that he proposed evolution of human life from simpler forms and a common ancestor with living species, in particular the other primates.

"Man with all his noble qualities, with sympathy which feels for the most debased, with benevolence which extends not only to other men but to the humblest living creature, with his god-like intellect which has penetrated into the movements and constitution of the solar system - with all these exalted powers - man still bears in his bodily frame the indelible stamp of his lowly origin."[169]

Einstein

Albert Einstein, who was born in the latter part of this period, and whose intellectual acuity was one of the greatest (arguably *the* greatest) in human history, continually alluded to the essential philosophical framework for scientific inquiry, suggesting that to ignore the philosophical underpinnings of scientific endeavor is to diminish its quality.[170]

That the breadth of his vista extended far beyond what is knowable about the physical universe is revealed in his response to assertions about the absence of causality in subatomic phenomena as described by quantum mechanics, which his own work on photons (packets of light energy) helped to advance: "Quantum mechanics is certainly imposing. But an inner voice tells me that it is not yet the real thing. The theory says a lot, but does not really bring us any closer to the secret of the 'old one'. I, at any rate, am convinced that He does not throw dice."[171]

As a young man Einstein had found it difficult to breach the barriers to academia within the university system of his native Germany, spending years as a patent investigator in Switzerland before finally landing an academic post. While at the patent office he wrote four papers, on the structure of light (which eventually earned a Nobel Prize), on Brownian motion, and two related to his later proposal on special relativity.

That this work involved little contact with the scientific community illustrates that Einstein was by no means a traditional scientist. His method of inquiry involved mainly intellectual exercises (thought experiments) in which he posed questions about physical phenomena and then tried to answer them by building explanations upon existing knowledge and mathematical structures.

Although it's clear that Einstein identified as scientist, he insists that a philosophical underpinning is essential for a secure path to understanding. However, in the midst of the tempest of intellectual ferment that prevailed during his most creative years concerning the nature of matter and energy, he was reluctant to deny to those at the leading edge - the 'point men' - the opportunity to choose its direction. In an article published in 1936, he acknowledges that the scientist, although perhaps a "poor philosopher", nevertheless might more appropriately identify questions about the implications and direction of the pursuit of knowledge, particularly at a time when the very foundations of physics were being shaken: "...the physicist cannot simply surrender to the philosopher the critical contemplation of the theoretical foundations; for, he himself knows best, and feels more surely where the shoe pinches. In looking for a new foundation, he must try to make clear in his own mind just how far the concepts which he uses are justified, and are necessities."[172]

In a 1916 memorial note for Ernst Mach[173], physicist and philosopher with whom Einstein maintained a close correspondence, he expressed concern for the lack of interest on the part of many of his colleagues in epistemology (the nature, sources and limits of knowledge or truth), pointing out that those students whom he considered most able had a "vigorous interest" in the subject, who ".. happily began discussions about the goals and methods of science, and ... showed unequivocally, through their tenacity in defending their views, that the subject seemed important to them. Indeed, one should not be surprised at this."

Only those concerned with the methods and larger consequences of their investigations and acquisition of knowledge gained Einstein's respect. Even though they follow the rites that characterize scientific research, nevertheless they must think as philosophers, always conscious of the wider implications of knowledge. There is no such thing as 'knowledge for its own sake': its repercussions spread like ripples from a stone dropped into a pond.

In a letter of 1944 to Einstein, young physicist Robert Thornton, who was beginning his tenure at the University of Puerto Rico, asked for his thoughts on introducing "as much of the philosophy of science as possible" into the modern physics course that he was to teach the following spring. Einstein replied:

"I fully agree with you about the significance and educational value of methodology as well as history and philosophy of science. So many people today - and *even professional scientists - seem to me like somebody who has seen thousands of trees but has never seen a forest.* A knowledge of the historic and philosophical background gives that kind of independence from *prejudices of his generation* from which *most scientists are suffering. This independence created by philosophical insight is - in my opinion - the mark of distinction between a mere artisan or specialist and a real seeker after truth* [italics added]"[174].

To Einstein, knowledge outside the philosophical context is dangerous. Professional scientists see the trees within their disciplines, but fail to see the forest of which the trees are both a part and a consequence. What are these 'prejudices of his generation' from which most scientists suffer? They are the pressures exerted on them as a consequence of the strategic human plan, as manifested in this narrow context: (1) attain status and recognition; (2) accommodate to peer review of research papers and grant applications with "conformity, cronyism and plagiarism"; (3) select research topics following interests of those who pay the bills; (4) adopt the politically correct or advantageous point of view; (5) present a (deceptive) iconoclastic and skeptical image to the outside world.[175]

Yet, Einstein reveals the tension that he senses between philosophy and science, centering on epistemology, a fundamental feature of philosophy. The scientist, isolated from the philosophical domain in which inquiry would have greater relevance, employs an epistemological system only to the extent that it satisfies the need for structure in her line of investigation.

"The reciprocal relationship of epistemology and science is of noteworthy kind. They are dependent upon each other. Epistemology without contact with science becomes an empty scheme. *Science without epistemology is - insofar as it is thinkable at all - primitive and muddled* (italics added).[176]

The tension erupts into rebellion, as the scientist ignores constraints that might be imposed by conducting investigations in the broader epistemological context:

"However, no sooner has the epistemologist, who is seeking a clear system, fought his way through to such a system, than he is inclined to interpret the thought-content of science in the sense of his system and to reject whatever does not fit into his system. The scientist, however, cannot afford to carry his striving for epistemological systematic that far. He accepts gratefully the epistemological conceptual analysis; but the external conditions, which are set for him by the facts of experience, do not permit him to let himself be too much restricted in the construction of his conceptual world by the adherence to an epistemological system [thus ignoring its relevance to a higher order of knowledge]. He therefore must appear to the systematic epistemologist as a type of unscrupulous opportunist [using whatever type of epistemology seems to be useful in a particular circumstance]…"[177]

However, in this way the scientist constructs her world in a kind of vacuum, maintaining the philosophical connection only to the extent that it is convenient. The deleterious consequences of this isolation from the wider domain of knowledge have become all too apparent in devastation of the environment of Planet Earth and premature human ventures into the heavens.

Einstein was instrumental in furthering the development of the atomic bomb, its design based on his discovery of the relationship between energy and matter of the theory of special relativity. In August 1939 physicist Leo Szilard wrote a letter to President Roosevelt, signed by Einstein, urging President Roosevelt to undertake a development program, expressing concern that Germany might be working on the bomb. This was followed up in 1940 with another letter, once again written by Szilard and signed by Einstein, to the Briggs Committee that was appointed to study uranium chain reactions, but which Szilard and others feared was proceeding too cautiously. The bomb was ultimately constructed under the Manhattan Project, and two of them were dropped on Japanese cities in 1945, bringing and end to World War II.

After the war he became a leader of the World Government Movement, which sought to outlaw production and use of nuclear weapons. "I know not with what weapons World War III will be fought, but World War IV will be fought with sticks and stones."[178] In July 1955, Einstein and Bertrand Russell jointly issued the Russell-Einstein Manifesto, which stated: "In view of the fact that in any future world war nuclear weapons will certainly be employed, and that such weapons threaten the continued existence of mankind, we urge the Governments of the world to realize, and to acknowledge publicly, that their purpose cannot be furthered by a world war, and we urge them, consequently, to find peaceful means for the settlement of all matters of dispute between them."

Einstein deeply regretted his role in creating the bomb, as expressed in November 1954, five months before his death: "I made one great mistake in my life… when I signed the letter to President Roosevelt recommending that atom bombs be made; but there was some justification - the danger that the Germans would make them." [179]

Compartmentalization and division

The transition from natural philosophy to science has resulted in a virtual compartmentalization of acquisition and application of knowledge, the cause of much degradation of Earth and lives of its inhabitants. Scientific knowledge and its offshoot, technology, have revolutionized culture, leading to unprecedented accumulation of wealth by a minority, subordination of the interests of vast numbers of humans by an industrial and commercial behemoth, and hazards to life on Earth in the form of environmental pollution, grinding poverty and ignorance among the masses. These developments have led to hostility among social classes, ethnic groups and nations, with attendant rise of terrorism, proliferation of weapons of mass destruction and the propensity to use them. In the hands of humanity, applications of scientific knowledge and technology, as awesome as they may be, have managed to vastly increase insecurity rather than serve to uplift the quality of life on Earth.

The general public is not very well equipped to exercise control on the scientific juggernaut. The system has fortified itself by projecting a divine aura in the public mind. The concerns of lay people are like the flea on the back of the scientific elephant. Public positions lack potency because the arcane dimensions of scientific achievement are obscured in the argot of the insiders club, with very little attempt to translate the nature of the development and its consequences to lay language.

Another indication of the absence of holistic thinking within the 'scientific community' that is needed to keep our planet intact is the plethora of 'specializations'. The proliferation of academic disciplines seems an inexorable phenomenon, like a tree sprouting limitless branches.[180] Each specialization has a way of dividing, like mitosis in cell division, into an array of subcategories, which in turn are candidates for a repeat of the process, ad infinitum. Just taking into account what are currently considered respectable 'scientific' disciplines, are the following[181]: (1) Natural sciences: Space Science, Earth Science, Life Science, Chemistry, Physics; (2) Formal sciences: Mathematics, Computer; (3) Social sciences: Anthropology, Archaeology, Area studies,

Economics, Ethnic Studies, Gender and Sexuality Studies, Geography, Political Science, Psychology, Sociology; (4) Professional and Applied sciences: Agriculture and forestry, Business, Education, Engineering, Family and consumer science, Health sciences, Journalism, media and communication, Law, Library and museum studies, Military sciences , Personal service professions, Public affairs, Social work.

As an example of the branching into subcategories related to just one of the above areas of knowledge – Life Science as a sub-category of Natural Science: Aerobiology, Anatomy (Comparative anatomy, Human anatomy), Animal communications, Biochemistry, Bioinformatics, Biology, Biophysics, Botany, Ethnobotany, Cell biology, Chronobiology, Cryobiology, Ecology (Human ecology, Landscape ecology), Endocrinology, Entomology, Evolutionary biology, Genetics, Human biology (Human anatomy), Limnology, Linnaean taxonomy, Marine biology, Microbiology, Molecular biology, Mycology, Neuroscience, Paleobiology (Paleontology), Parasitology, Pathology, Phycology, Physiology (Human physiology), Systematics (Taxonomy), Virology (Molecular virology, Epidemial virology), Xenobiology, Zoology (Cryptozoology, Entomology, Ethology, Herpetology, Ichthyology, Oology, Ornithology, Primatology, Zootomy).

There are further subdivisions at the next level for some of these. An aspirant to a scientific career has a multitude of areas in which to learn more and more about less and less. The consequences for Planet Earth are profound. An old adage is that 'a little knowledge is dangerous'. While a particular researcher may spend her entire life diligently investigating and discovering, its external significance seems to be of little concern, except in regard to maintaining the approbation of those responsible for sustenance.

Consequences of compartmentalization

There is a spectrum of possible approaches to the pursuit of knowledge – from the unstructured to the highly focused, which we might now call 'applied science'. There are philosophers, philosopher-scientists of all gradations, and scientists.

When knowledge is pursued in a narrow context, such as at Peenemunde (V2 rockets), at Los Alamos (atomic bomb) and in most contemporary laboratories of universities and industry, the outcome is almost always disastrous for humans and for life in general. Scientists responsible for knowledge leading to wondrous miniature electronics, for example – lap top computers, cell phones, games, cameras - did not seem to be concerned that they were unleashing a flood of enormous waste, much of which is toxic. The launchers of spacecraft do not seem to be concerned that their creations will eventually come down to earth, contaminating the air, land and waters and even perhaps dropping in on quiet neighborhoods. The ton of solid waste per capita per annum collecting in landfills in the United States and other industrialized countries is mute (and odiferous) testimony to the insensitivity of the scientific community responsible for much of its creation.

The narrower the context in which knowledge is pursued, the more likely it is that it will turn out badly. This is not hypothetical. Just consider what a few hundred years of science have wrought on Earth: means of melting snow caps, endangering and driving to extinction many species, the capacity to destroy all of life by pushing a few buttons, billions without adequate food and water, mountains of waste – radioactive, solid, liquid and gaseous. This is a consequence of the 'Von Braun syndrome' within the domain of scientific inquiry and its aftermath – what a beautiful rocket launch, and who cares where it comes down? – replicated in countless numbers of academic, industrial and government laboratories around the world.

Knowledge is a double-edged sword, with potential to elicit a sense of security or terror. Knowing where the tiger is lying in the bush is comforting because defenses can be organized to meet the threat, but fear inducing owing to uncertainty that defenses are adequate.

In contemporary life, the scientific method is considered not only the secure path to knowledge, but also the most reliable foundation for deciding what to do about critical issues of the day. For lay people, the scientific method is considered a precise method of proof, even though scientists acknowledge the tentativeness of any conclusion and that nothing can be really 'proven' owing to inherent uncertainties in phenomena and measurements. The lay public is mesmerized by the authority of scientifically justified pronouncements, usually too intimidated by the arrogance (dismissal of other paths to knowledge) and arcane jargon emanating from the scientific community to protest.

The problem is not that the scientific method itself is flawed, but the narrow context in which it is usually applied leaves much to be desired. When issues are examined within the compartmentalized system that prevails in most research institutions, the results are tainted because they normally ignore conditions outside the rigid confines of the discipline. When this is clearly preposterous, scientists collaborate or even cross boundaries, albeit with trepidation – fear of reprisal or at least condemnation from their disciplinary rivals.

The science of chemistry has provided humanity with many thousands of synthesized substances employed in agriculture, industry and medicine. These materials are unknown in nature, many of them resistant or impervious to biological degradation so that they persist in the environment indefinitely, accumulating in the land, air and waterways. While they ostensibly produce beneficial effects such as increased food production, useful products and health improvements, the build-up of these substances in the environment is a time bomb. According to the World Health Organization[182], 47,000 people die per annum from direct exposure to toxic chemicals, but the actual toll is far greater and will increase as the environment becomes even more heavily laden with these toxic and persistent substances.

There is a reverence on the part of the general public and within the scientific community for facts and relationships derived from scientific investigation. The scientific method is regarded as indispensible for secure knowledge about how nature can be 'harnessed' to fulfill human aspirations. Science is even regarded as the instrument for resolving problems created by science – e.g. environmental pollution can only by alleviated by applying more science and technology. Rather than return to a more panoramic, philosophical vantage point, conventional scientific/technological solutions are prescribed - for example, the solution to carbon-emitting coal plants is to apply technology to clean up the emissions rather that to return to the basic issue about whether or not the attendant strip mining is in our long-term interests.

Space exploration – a special case

During the 20th century, technology had reached the point of shooting rockets into space, largely as a consequence of missile and rocket developments undertaken by Germany during WWII as a means of pounding Britain into submission with aerial assaults that maimed about 9 thousand Londoners (a third fatalities). Interest in outer space was stimulated in the United States by the launch of an unmanned satellite, Sputnik, by the Russians on Oct. 4, 1957. President Dwight Eisenhower in 1958 created the National Aeronautics and Space Administration (NASA), which became the central institution for scientific space exploration. Then on April 12, 1961 the Russians placed their first cosmonaut, Yuri Gagarin, into Earth orbit.

After developing a number of unmanned programs involving communications and weather forecasting systems, NASA, in conjunction with parallel military organizations, became involved in the use of satellites for intelligence gathering and other military purposes such as anti-missile defense systems. Not to be outdone by space accomplishments of the Soviet Union, shortly after John Kennedy was elected president of the U.S. in 1960, he set a goal of landing men on the moon before the end of that decade. NASA began with a series of suborbital and orbital flights of John Glenn, and finally in 1969 with the Apollo program, Alan Sheppard was the first of three astronauts to set foot on the lunar surface.

Did landing people on the moon have any practical significance? According to one study, it was identified as a 'societal bubble', a collective excess of enthusiasm based on "public and/or political expectations of positive outcomes…".[183] Support by the public was almost unanimous in the heat of the 'Cold War' with the Soviet Union. Those directly associated with the program were exhilarated by the challenge. "…… political and social factors weaved a network of reinforcing feedbacks that led to widespread over-enthusiasm and extraordinary commitment by those involved in the project as well as by politicians and by the public at large."[184] The Apollo program is one of the most egregious examples of misguided public policy, a project undertaken with no substantial societal purpose except an almost infantile compulsion to flaunt technological prowess.

Once the pointlessness of the moon mission became clear even to man-in-space advocates, NASA then began to concentrate on manned space stations, for what reason is not clear except that like Mt. Everest, it was something to climb. But as we have learned, just because something can be done is not sufficient justification for doing it.

In January 2010, facing massive budget deficits, President Barack Obama announced his intention to change the direction of the space program to rely on privately financed rocket launches.[185] There was also fear that the Constellation Program, initiated by previous president George W. Bush to return to the moon and maybe even Mars, might go by the wayside. One of the major concerns was that the jobs of 1,500 Huntsville contractor employees and 700 employees at Marshall Space Flight Center working on the program would be lost.[186]

On its own web site, the National *Aeronautics* and *Space* Administration outlines benefits derived from its space program, described in terms of improvements on the ground rather than in space[187]: home appliances, (more interesting?) museums, accurate thermometers for medical applications, crops and livestock on the farm, sunglasses and facial cosmetics, firefighting and rescue equipment, unspecified benefits for the sports world, virtual reality, airport safety, a safer and more beautiful Earth! (emphasis added). In addition, miniaturized integrated circuits, satellite technology, GPS navigation systems, bone-density measurements, miniaturized heart pumps, water filtration, wireless light switches, remediation solutions for sites contaminated by chemicals, the development of sensors on reconnaissance robots used in Afghanistan and Iraq to deal with improvised explosive devices.

But most, if not all, of these 'benefits' that NASA identifies have little to do with space exploration, developments that would have been achieved through the normal process of research and development in universities and industries.

There is little doubt that the national space program has been instrumental in achieving incredible technological breakthroughs. Space exploration has provided benefits that could substantially increase the hope for the future of life. Global communications systems using space satellites (television, internet, voice messaging) have provided information to people, even in the remotest corners, about a much wider range of life's options than would ordinarily be available. Awesome images of celestial bodies and stellar phenomena have been produced by the Hubble telescope, which should also provide humanity with a little needed humility, and with proper redundancies, would not require human maintenance. Weather systems have allowed farmers and ranchers to make better decisions.

Placing humans in space is another matter. The Apollo program was undertaken primarily for geopolitical reasons, as attested by the fact that no further space missions of that kind were undertaken in the next 4 decades.

Is space exploration worth the cost? The debate about the relative merits of exploring space with humans and robots is as old as the space program itself. One ardent supporter of space exploration, G. Scott Hubbard[188], cites enthusiasm of Werner Von Braun [father of the V2 rocket developed at Peenemunde, Germany during WWII that killed thousands of British citizens], a moving force behind the Apollo Program that sent humans to the moon and the architect of the mighty Saturn V rocket, who "believed passionately in the value of human exploitation [of space] – especially when it meant beating the hated Soviet Empire".

He points out that James Van Allen, discoverer of the belt of charged particles girdling the Earth and held in place by its magnetic field, was an "ardent and vocal [supporter of] robotic exploration".

Hubbard advances five arguments concerning the utility of space exploration and the roles of humans and robots, in roughly ascending order of advocate support:

(1) It will eventually allow us to establish a human civilization on another world (e.g. Mars) as a hedge against the type of catastrophe that wiped out the dinosaurs.

The likelihood of this kind of natural catastrophe is so remote as to be almost ludicrous as justification for a man-in-space program. More likely it is that such a catastrophe would be man-made, e.g. a conflagration involving nuclear warfare.

(2) We explore space and create important new technologies to advance our economy. It is true that, for every dollar we spend on the space program, the U.S. economy receives about $8 of economic benefit. Space exploration can also serve as a stimulus for children to enter the fields of science and engineering.

While the technology developed in the space program is impressive, these inventions and initiatives did not need the space program as a platform. The economic benefits purportedly derived from the program would most likely have been greater if they were not accompanied by wasteful expenditures on putting people into space.

(3) Space exploration in an international context offers a peaceful cooperative venue that is a valuable alternative to nation state hostilities. One can look at the International Space Station and marvel that the former Soviet Union and the U.S. are now active partners. International cooperation is also a way to reduce costs.

This implies that the choice is either international hostility between former Cold War opponents or meetings in a space station. While such catalysts for international cooperation are useful, they are by no means indispensible for political leaders - Presidents and Prime Ministers, Departments of State - and institutions such as the United Nations, to resolve international disputes.

(4) National prestige requires that the U.S. continue to be a leader in space, and that includes human exploration. History tells us that great civilizations dare not abandon exploration.

Are there better ways to enhance national prestige? How about taking the lead in calling on international leaders to deal with crises on the ground - excessive population growth that is sure to increase the havoc already created by a human population perhaps three times the number that can be comfortably accommodated? Eliminating world poverty by making more equitable distribution of the world's wealth a top priority? Are there more useful avenues for exploration, e.g. how to live together on Earth in peace, with justice and prosperity?

(5) Exploration of space will provide humanity with an answer to the most fundamental questions: Are we alone? Are there other forms of life beside those on Earth?

Do we need man in space to answer this question? What do humans in space have to do with finding out if there are other forms of life out there, unless the idea is to send an embryonic contingent to the infinities of space without hope of return? And what is the purpose of this type of information? Is it the equivalent of the infantile ego trip that causes Alpha types to match their machismo against potential rivals? The likelihood of significant intercourse between humans and other forms of life on celestial bodies is not only remote, but also pointless and foolhardy.

Hubbard offers these additional observations:

"Personally, I think humans will be better at unstructured environment exploration than any existing robot for a very long time... There are those who say that exploration with humans is simply too expensive for the return we receive."

Not only is exploration with humans too expensive, but chimerical. Will excess human population be exported to some distant planet? And if you think that a human nucleus will be sent out for some good purpose to occupy other parts of the cosmos, after seeing what humans have wrought on the one planet that we already occupy, is this something that should be replicated elsewhere? Humans are in no condition to populate the rest of the cosmos: One only has to view the condition of the one planet on which we enjoy hegemony to realize that it would be a disaster. Before humans evolve to a state where wisdom is a universal trait, it can only be anticipated that ventures into the reaches of space will result in the same kind of havoc and destruction that our species has wrought on Earth. To answer in the affirmative you have to be either the proverbial madman or economist.

"However, I cannot imagine any U.S. President announcing that we are abandoning space exploration with humans and leaving it to the Chinese, Russians, Indians, Japanese or any other group. I can imagine the U.S. engaging in much more expansive international cooperation. Humans will be exploring space. The challenge is to be sure that they accomplish meaningful exploration."

Heaven help us!!!

Environmentalism

Planet Earth auto-assembled from cosmic material about 4 billion years ago. Living things first appeared about a billion years later. During the enormous span of time before humans appeared, nature spawned hundreds of millions of species of flora and fauna, each finding its niche for a time in a dynamic network of interactions and habitats, with most eventually succumbing to inhospitable changes in their domains. Natural and catastrophic extinctions leave Earth at present with an estimated 50 million species.

The first inkling of humanity appeared in Africa about 2.5 billion years ago. Then through a veritable avalanche of speciation, at least three or four ancestors (and possibly many more) lived concurrently, and perhaps even as neighbors – each occupying a slightly different niche that enabled them to coexist in relative harmony. The advent of humanity as we know it occurred approximately 200 thousand years ago, which is about 0.0025% - .005% of the total span of Earth's history. To put this in perspective, if all of Earth's history were compressed into a 24-hour day, modern humans would be around for about the last 4 – 8 seconds.

According to Judeo-Christian tradition man is above nature, granted hegemony by Yahweh over flora and fauna of Earth, free to exploit, consume and even propagate without constraint. As a consequence of our special place in the panoply of life we are supposedly exempt from natural exigencies, widely believed to receive our marching orders from inner prodding of soul, altruism, morality. Distinguishing outward traits - self-consciousness, cognitive and analytical powers, speech, manual dexterity, bipedalism – ostensibly confer upon humanity a unique relationship with nature, at once its master and super-benefactor. Our singular role in this regard is fortified with self-proclaimed sanctity of divine manifest destiny.

Most of us do not ordinarily contemplate the possibilities for the future of humankind, scarcely considering the prospects for the next generation much less posterity or the possibility of extinction[189]. Widespread inaction in the face of momentous degradation in the condition of our planet while it was happening attests to this indifference. Wrangling over the costs and benefits of limiting greenhouse gases, the lack of alarm about a burgeoning human population growing by a Germany or Egypt each year, general unconcern for the trash defacing and befouling even the most isolated landscapes and positively inundating urban centers in virtually every country of the world, accepting the stench of human effluvia pervading waterways and rendering most fresh water sources unfit for consumption as an acceptable consequence of 'progress', indifference to grinding poverty as the lot of over a billion wretched human souls and its murderous consequences, to the loss of natural habitat and near-extinction of wondrous creatures and plants in formerly pristine settings , to the accelerating diminution of Earth's forest cover and desertification of heavily populated areas. This is the path of those who either weigh more heavily the immediate stimulus to general material prosperity arising from consumption of our planet's natural capital or who seek to exploit natural resources for their personal aggrandizement without regard to the consequences for present and future generations of flora and fauna.

No, it is not necessary to insist on 'scientific' evidence to acknowledge the adverse consequences of human hegemony over Earth. Anyone who observes how humans have debased the planet, particularly in the centuries since the industrial 'revolution' (one hardly needs to make any effort to do so) does not need certification to statistical standards that something is desperately wrong. We do not need to count the number of bricks in the ton that is falling on us to know that the building is collapsing.

Yet, that is precisely what is demanded. Those who claim that the house is falling, and do not think it necessary to count the bricks, or cannot because they've been smashed beyond recognition or because they are falling so fast that our counting resources are inadequate, are labeled with the pejorative 'environmentalist' by fierce advocates of the status quo – generally those who feed on the carrion and their political collaborators. The same badge is pasted on a few sensitized scientists who attempt to reconnect their severed umbilical by counting the bricks and making their results known, even when current and impending environmental catastrophes are infinitely more self-evident than the premise that "all men are created equal". Public acquiescence to stigmatizing the messenger is abetted by widespread ignorance and economic desperation.

There is a way to counter this ploy. The folly of those concerned with adverse consequences of environmental degradation of flora and fauna of our planet, and for future generations of humans and other living beings upon whom our health and well-being depend, is to play into the hands of the myopic and ill-willed by loudly and proudly proclaiming affiliation with an environmental movement.

'Environmentalists' display their colors by behaving much like scientists: they identify as 'environmentalists'. The problem is that this identification sets up a barrier between advocates of a more sustainable and wholesome relationship with nature and those whose present state of awareness leaves them unconcerned or even hostile. It would be far more productive to direct attention to specific issues, and to the rational connection between pollution and the magnitude and distribution of its costs. This is not environmentalism, but sanity.

Those who label others as environmentalists identify themselves as anti-environmentalists (the label is never 'partial environmentalist' – an individual is either in or out of the group). If it is sane and rational to be concerned with the quality of one's habitat, upon the quality of the physical, social and economic features of the surroundings upon which health and well-being depend, then those who are unconcerned would have to be insane and irrational. So the proper duality is the sane and the anti-environmentalist. In other words, those in the class of anti-environmentalists are the insane, and should be treated as such.

What is the proper way to deal with the insane? Formerly they were institutionalized, both for their own protection and for what was perceived as the general good of society. Currently the practice is to 'mainstream', and this is only fair and just. After all, the insane did not really choose insanity, but were victims of adversity in nature or nurture, or both. Mainstreaming involves the process of arranging suitable environments in which the insane can function with relative immunity from further emotional and bodily harm, and in which the ability to harm others is precluded.

Anti-environmentalists must be afforded the same consideration. The only way to do this effectively is to protect them from environmental degradation. As they are irrational, arguments based upon the ordinary analytical process would be to no avail. Their participation in this effort must be co-opted with ploys that would appeal to the irrational. Attractive symbols are needed to which the irrational respond.

One potentially fruitful area for investigation is professional sports, which thrives on the loyalty of individuals who identify easily with symbols. One is an inveterate Yankee (baseball) fan or devotee of the Chicago Bulls (basketball) not because there is any tangible benefit to be derived, but because this identification responds to fundamental instincts that are beyond what is normally considered rational in the modern world. In fact, loyalty is often strong if the relative proficiency of the team is low, underscoring the irrationality of such an affinity.

The sane (non anti-environmentalists) would sponsor one or more of the national professional sports leagues, with team names such as 'Podunk Polluters'. Anti-environmentalists, much more numerous than the sane, would thereby be enticed to render support through attendance and purchases of appropriately trademarked paraphernalia. As the sane would be directors and economic beneficiaries, and the anti-environmentalists their loyal supporters, much economic power would accrue to the sane, who would presumably utilize the accumulated resources for the benefit of the environment. Thus, both sane and anti-environmentalists would profit, even though the latter would have little idea, and care less, why. They would continue to berate 'environmentalists', but their loyalty to the symbol would be much stronger than distaste for their perceived adversaries, so that the quality of the environment would continue to improve, to the everlasting benefit of both sane and anti-environmentalist.

In a more practical vein, the interests of those concerned with the impact of human activity on Earth's natural environment would be better served by rejecting the label 'environmentalist' altogether. For one thing, it presents too easy a target for those who would accept despoliation of our planet in exchange for short-term economic and political gain. It allows them to define the environmentally concerned as irrational preservationists rather than perceptive and rational conservers of our natural heritage. Furthermore, the label erects a barrier behind which anti-environmentalists can too easily lure masses of people who are not currently concerned on account of ignorance or economic desperation.

So, what's wrong with science as we know it?

During the past four centuries, applications of scientific discoveries have radically altered the human landscape. The nature of civilization has been transformed in step with technology, an indispensable component of social organization. Information technology has been at the forefront, infused into virtually every aspect of private and public life, at home, at work, at play and at war. Transportation technology has extended the domain of humankind into the heavens, vastly increased global trade, and radically changed settlements patterns. Agricultural technology has altered the process of food production, with genetically modified organisms and innovative techniques of cultivation and animal husbandry. Medical science and technology have provided immunities from many viral and parasitic threats, substitutes for defective body parts, and much more effective and yet less intrusive methods of diagnosis and treatment, leading to longer average life spans for populations in developed economies. This is only a sample of the wonders derived from increased scientific knowledge and its technological consequences.

Despite its potential to achieve the best of worlds – peace, prosperity and justice for all - the pursuit of knowledge via the scientific method, and its applications - has produced quite different outcomes. We see instead, Planet Earth beset with problems: excessive human population; inordinate extinction of species; military confrontation and terrorism. Why point the finger at science? Isn't it the rapaciousness of humankind that is responsible for these excesses? The truth is that science, in its current conformation, has created these problems by foisting on a worshipping and unwitting populace, technology that is inconsistent with the common aspirations of people around the world - solutions that fail to take into account realities on the ground. The mountains of solid waste accumulating all over the world, liquid and gaseous effluents being dumped into oceans, lakes and rivers, noxious gases released into the atmosphere, food and water scarcity, economic volatility (with bust becoming more the norm than boom) – all of these attest to the insensitivity of scientists and their technologist collaborators in setting into motion a production and consumption chain that ignores sustainability. The pernicious system of creating scientists, their methods of pursuing knowledge, and their resultant myopia concerning consequences of their discoveries, is responsible.

The practice of science today covers the entire spectrum from pure inquiry to what might be called 'applied science', which is virtually indistinguishable from engineering and technology. Very few scientists are engaged in pure research. The reason is that priorities of sponsoring institutions, through the research grant process, determine the priorities of the scientific community. Research topics are most commonly selected to answer questions of the funding institutions. Scientists operate in academia, in industry and in government, most undertaking research projects as directed by those who pay the bills. In 2006, private interests funded 65 percent of research and development (R&D) in the United States.[190]

Anyone who has had direct contact with the academic science mill, either as grist or grinder, can potentially comprehend the destructive nature of the system. Although the pursuit of knowledge is an organic imperative for humans, within this institution the force takes on bizarre dimensions as otherwise competent and discerning people are lured in mainly by the promise of prestige, security and compensation. The most significant flaws, and perils, in the contemporary scientific mode are its divorce from philosophy and compartmentalization, which are really part of the same phenomenon. In the 18th century poet Alexander Pope cogently expresses the hazard:

"A little learning is a dangerous thing; drink deep, or taste not the Pierian Spring: there shallow draughts intoxicate the brain, and drinking largely sobers us again."[191]

The academic establishment that has been commissioned to produce scientists by common consent in most parts of the world is structured so that destructive outcomes are virtually assured. Rather than allow a few talented people to pursue their natural intellectual inclinations in freedom and collegiality, what actually happens is that large numbers of acolytes are recruited by special interests, who are then subject to political and intellectual subordination:[192] Students and researchers are favored whose natural inquisitiveness is diverted to issues selected under external pressures and who adopt dutifully the point of view of their superiors (professors), a form of 'ideological discipline'.

Rather than allowing for an easy collegiality between mentors and their charges, instead faculty professors serve as judge and jury, administering qualifying examinations and certifying the validity and contributions of research.

"Any students who instead follow their own interests by only studying things that intrigue them personally are risking their professional future." Rather than permit students to remain immersed in a wide array of issues confronting life on Earth, they are forced into a narrow channel of inquiry, fitted with blinders according to the priorities and exigencies of their sponsors. Through the qualifications and examination wringer, students are forced to "accept alienating work in a hierarchical system." The compromise is not erased from the student's consciousness, and in fact is a source of discomfort. "Although the professional has sidelined his original goals, he usually retains some memory of them. Any such memory inevitably points to the compromises he has made and therefore can be an unrecognized source of unease in the professional's life."[193]

Need more be said about the need to restructure our system of learning and research? One who identifies as scientist under current conditions admits to knowing more and more about less and less, to narrowness in perspective that ignores concern for the consequences of her activity on the welfare of the community. It is one thing to study a narrowly delimited area (the spearhead of inquiry requires this kind of concentration), but to spend one's entire professional life without venturing to the field at right or left is conducive to a kind of myopia - a dangerous condition for one whose conclusions influence the course of human events.

The 'ivory tower' continues to create highly focused functionaries rather than enlightened repositories of knowledge and wisdom. Critics of academia have generally missed the point that the entire institution needs to be restructured, toward a more philosophically oriented experience and de-compartmentalization. It is not multi-disciplinary inquiry that is required: so long as the plethora of disciplines remains part of the system, the same tensions will prevail. Rather, re-integration of the process of inquiry is required, where students and researchers are free to follow their fields of interest in a collegial relationship with their peers and mentors.

How far can knowledge take humanity? Can we aspire to a seat at the pinnacle of the mountain, where everything is in plain view? Stephen Hawking, one of the icons of the scientific community in the late 20th and 21st centuries, states twice in his work *A Short History of Time*, that mankind is on the cusp of knowing everything. He alludes to the creation of a model that explains all natural phenomena in the universe.

Is this possible? And how will we know when we get there? Will we be able to replicate the process whereby the stars and planets were formed, and how could it ever be confirmed? Is it possible, for example, for humanity to completely know itself? Yes, an eye can see itself through a reflected image, but quantum theory explains that our sensory information is not only subject to the problem of interference, but what's more, information is inherently subject to uncertainty.

The concept of Thomas Kuhn, that falsifiability is an essential condition for acceptance of any hypothesis, i.e. that a theory must be disprovable before it can be accepted, seems to place an impenetrable barrier between humanity and ultimate knowledge. Some characteristics of nature are not subject to disproof.

Additionally, we humans are caught up in our own petard, insisting that knowledge is only certifiable through the scientific method. This despite the fact that agriculturalists, for example, during many millennia improved their crops and livestock through 'unscientific' processes. Originally the seed pod of teosinte, which even now grows in its native habitat in the mountains of Mexico, was only a few centimeters in length, and was improved over a couple of millennia to the form it has today – maize or corn with seed pods up to 10 or 12 inches in length – and a staple for the world.

Some scientists attempt to reconnect with society after having been isolated and fed through the academic sausage grinder, particularly those immersed in issues and phenomena that bear directly on the conditions of human life and those species that have captured the public imagination. For most of them, it would be far better for the future of life if their learning had taken place in unstructured association with mentors and peers lured by the same flickering candle flame.

Science and technology ahead of itself

In the hands of a secure and mature species, knowledge can serve as foundation for social progress and the preservation of life. The divorce of science, along with derivative technology, from its 'parent' philosophy, is unfortunate. While scientific achievements have mesmerized most of humanity, our mythical propensities blot out the fact that the very future of life hangs in the balance. Rather than applying a sufficient portion of the intellectual power that has created microelectronics, global communications, space exploration and smart bombs to resolving the crises confronting all of life on Earth, the absence of a philosophical foundation in the pursuit of knowledge is very likely to have irretrievably fatal consequences.

Part III
The Road Ahead

Chapter 9
TO BE OR NOT TO BE

Nature has dealt humankind a joker, a flaw in its makeup that countervails against its extraordinary intellectual prowess. It is a kind of split personality, one supremely rational, the other imaginative and prone to fantasizing. For most of us, the left and right cerebral hemispheres each has primary control over different functions. The two hemispheres are connected by the equivalent of a coaxial cable, the corpus callosum, a band of nerves that provides channels of communication between them. That the two are not independent, and attempt to coordinate their functions, gives rise to much of the upheaval that humanity has created on Earth.[194] As a consequence the human animal is endowed with heightened self-awareness or self-consciousness employing both word (language) and a veritable toolbox of deeds (actions) to manipulate self-image to an extent far beyond the 'instinctive' mechanisms employed by our primate cousins, such as facial expression, posture and gestures.[195]

The tug of war that exists between the left and right hemispheres is suggested by their division of responsibilities: the left brain is the rational, logical, factual, comprehending, realistic, orderly and strategic partner, and has most of the verbal responsibility as well. The right brain is emotional, imaginative, impetuous, fantasy-prone.[196]

An individual interacts with the external world essentially through speech and actions. Ideas inspired by the right brain are communicated largely through verbal capacities of the left brain, which conditions the message according to its own priorities. Conversely, left brain-inspired activities are rarely 'pure' in the sense that coordination with the other hemisphere is usually unavoidable.

Genetic and cultural signatures of the individual human organism control the physical configuration and informational content of the brain. In *The Selfish Gene*, Richard Dawkins introduces the meme (pronounced *meem*), carrying concepts, skills and ideas instead of the gene's DNA building instructions. The meme resides in the brain of the individual human organism and is transmitted in the course of communication, with all of the nuances of traditional and body language available to this complex organism, or through communications media (for example a meme could be transmitted in writing). This is the cultural analog of the gene, with similar evolutionary properties. However, owing to imperfect processes of contemporaneous and intergenerational replication, transmission and reception, a meme can mutate so that it represents a potential cultural change, to be rejected or accepted based on its 'fitness'. In a manner similar to that of the gene in every living cell, the meme also resides in the material substance of the organism, most likely in the neuronal pattern of the brain.

So the individual presents to the world the behavioral consequences of her history, genes and memes, filtered by internal wiring that is itself derived from a combination of genetic inheritance and experience. In turn the individual receives feedback from the external environment, being altered in the process and responding in accordance with her genetic and cultural imperatives.

As a consequence, despite having at its disposal reliable information, and with the capacity to accurately analyze the consequences of one or another response to an external stimulus, the human organism will usually opt for a path that is not optimal regarding what is prescribed by the life force. The flaw gets in the way, either allowing the myth-laden right brain to choose a path according to its own criteria while its counterpart is slumbering from boredom – or permitting the rational left brain to choose a course, but all too often undermined by interference of its emotion and fantasy-laden partner. The result is that rarely, if ever, does the individual human being arrive at a sensible course of action.

Evidence that humans have rarely responded to their rational prodding is overwhelming. Consider for example, the decision of US leaders and a compliant populace to engage in war in Vietnam during the 1960's and 1970's. The recent history of Indochina at that time included the ouster of the hated French colonialists, who were defeated at Dien Bien Phu in 1953 and who had occupied at least part of the country since the mid 19th century, having been reinstated (with US complicity) after the Japanese occupation during WWII. Because the country was being supported by Cold War enemies of the US, it was easy for demagogues to stir the imaginations of Congressional leaders and the population in general, that the Vietnamese represented a clear and present threat, even though many experienced analysts identified the movement of the North Vietnamese to unify their divided country as purely nationalistic. Instead, the Vietnamese leaders, and particularly Ho Chi Minh, were successfully painted as communists, although it was clear that they were driven to the Russian bosom because they were so thoroughly rejected by those whom they sought as friends. This is truly ironic considering that the Vietnamese constitution was patterned after that of the United States. The entire episode was, in reality, a proxy global confrontation between Cold War adversaries, which itself is testament to the widespread predominance of completely irrational behavior. Over fifty thousand Americans and countless numbers of the people of Vietnam, Laos and Cambodia were sacrificed, and hundreds of thousands irreparably harmed, by this insanity.

In fact, at virtually any crossroads at which large numbers of people are poised, inevitably the path taken has been predominantly irrational.

No work has more clearly explained this phenomenon than that of Reg Morrison[197], *The Spirit in the Gene, Humanity's Proud Illusion and the Laws of Nature*[198]. On the surface, Morrison seems an unlikely candidate to peer with such acuity into the frailties of humanity. He is a photojournalist, untrained in the scientific disciplines that would ordinarily be considered prerequisites. That he is eminently competent in this role confirms the irrelevance of disciplinary certification for those examining critical issues of the day.[199] In his magnum opus, Morrison first probes the temporal panorama of life on Earth. The focus is on *H. sapiens* - modern humans - and our indispensable links to all other forms of life. He first examines the carnage wrought by our species since we assumed the status of "plague mammal" at the onset of agriculture some 10-12 thousand years ago. The exponential rate of growth of human populations during this period is characteristic of species under conditions of stress. The typical pattern is boom and bust, with the human population moving inexorably toward that eventuality.

Our encroachment upon and despoilment of habitats of other species not in a position to defend themselves, owing to our exponentially growing numbers and life style of consumption, has precipitated the highest rate of species extinction since the Cretaceous era of 65 million years ago when the dinosaurs disappeared. He recounts the litany of environmental abuses, placing all other life forms and us in peril. Global warming, with alarming possibilities for positive feedback as methane-laden polar ice caps melt, threatens inundation of the most fertile lands alongside watercourses. These are the collective human 'choices', which are almost certain to hasten our demise.

A warning signal of ultimate climax and crash typical of plague species is diminishing per capita human grain supply, which peaked in the mid-1980's. Since that time there has been steady erosion that technology will not be able to fix. In fact, technology has provided a false sense of security. The Green Revolution that averted a crisis in the 1960's provides the dangerous presumption, all too readily accepted, that it can be replicated whenever the need arises. But high yields have high costs. Applications of high rates of nitrogenous fertilizers and synthetic pesticides have resulted in other environmental problems – excessive nutrients, pesticides, erosion, acidification of soils, salinization (from excessive irrigation) and soil imbalances in micronutrients and trace elements. Biotechnology poses another set of dangers: emasculated viruses used to immunize crops have somehow recovered missing genes from transgenic host plants; food crops have been inadvertently pollinated by sterilized varieties.

Morrison places *H. sapiens* squarely within the animal kingdom, and disabuses us of the delusion of immunity from nature's imperatives, which derive from our history of the past 2.5 million years. Ice ages that occurred during this period were probably responsible for much of human evolution. After the eruption of Mt. Toba on the island of Sumatra about 70 thousand years ago, a six year long volcanic winter was followed by a millennium of ice, during which the human population probably fell to around 10-15,000 adults, according to genetic evidence, with summer temperatures about 12 degrees Centigrade higher than normal, which would have decimated, if not eliminated, populations in Europe and northern China.[200] Recession of the ice likely precipitated adoption of a survival strategy through evolutionary adaptations more attuned to warming temperatures and the developing savannah that replaced our ancient rain forest abode, a strategy that incorporated bipedalism, brain enlargement and language enhancements.

The need for a high level of social cohesion for a relatively weak and otherwise vulnerable animal required the development of a rational adjunct to the primordial perceptive faculties that supported survival of our primate ancestors. Language capacity was an early addition to the armor, perhaps a primitive form as early as 2 million years ago when our forebears were at the stage of *H. erectus*, adjusting to the hunter-gatherer lifestyle.

Because the language faculty is located in Broca's area of the left, rational hemisphere, vocalized perceptions emanating from the right hemisphere of the brain are mediated by our rational and loquacious left brain, which ghostwrites the right brain narrative, filling in the gaps and its own propaganda. This is the source of most primitive, mystical visions and spiritual fantasies within the human psyche, part of our evolutionary make-up that enabled us to survive over the millennia.

In all events, our neuronal circuitry retains its direct connection with our genes. In fact, Morrison attributes virtually all human behavior to genetic response, a position increasingly supported by current behavioral research. This was necessary to assure that our forebears and we would not be handicapped by excessive logic when unmediated genetic responses were demanded by the situation. "That is why, under the spell of our carefully programmed spirituality, we cannot help falling in love, yearning for sexual gratification, nurturing our children, forging tribal bonds, suspecting strangers, uniting against common enemies and on occasion laying down our lives for family, friends or tribe."

Surviving human genetic material, filtered through nature's sieve over the ages, provides the basis for the predominance of mystically inspired, irrational behavior. "There is little doubt that during the past 2 million years of human evolution the cold-blooded processes of Darwinian selection would have unerringly weeded out many a deep-thinker in favor of the wild-eyed fanatic – among tribal leaders especially. The clinical eye and the cool head would have its uses, but only as optional extras that could be called upon to solve tactical or technical problems and then be relegated to their usual subordinate role – just as they are today." One only has to regard humanity's resolution of critical contemporary issues of global import to confirm the subordinated status to which rationality been relegated.

This is the built-in flaw that assures our compliance with the natural flow of species that come and go. "Two million years ago, an animal that strayed a little too far from its ecological niche, judging from its lack of adaptive structures, appeared earmarked for extinction. But this versatile, resourceful survivor with the ability to reason, communicate and culturally modify its behavior, so cunning that it would eventually insulate itself temporarily from nature's shocks, was able to appoint itself as executor of its culture-driven evolution – creating, modifying and discarding other species. The most dangerous animal ever to walk the earth", even to itself.

However, our incapacity to make good choices is itself an illusion. Morrison adopts the material interpretation of our existence, dismissing the mind-matter duality of religionists, politicians, and most every flavor within the philosophical and scientific spectra. All of our physical and intellectual attributes are characteristics acquired in the process of natural selection.

After discussing how the forebrain area of our shrew-like ancient ancestors that originally processed the sense of smell eventually was converted to other types of sensory processing in humans, Morrison dismisses the possibility of free choice. "Prevailed upon by my informational "nose", *I too make choices I cannot help making, given the prevailing landscape of information* (italics added). Regardless of the careful reasoning I may marshal in support of my actions, the choices I make are ultimately animal choices. In fact, the only thing that distinguishes humans in the arena of animal behavior is our naïve belief that our decision-making processes are primarily cortical and rational and therefore unlike those of all other animals."

Each of us is an organism whose response to an external stimulus is determined by our genetic and experiential history. "We may agonize over alternative courses of action for as long as we like, using whatever combination of reason and intuition we feel is appropriate, but *our final decisions still represent the inevitable reactions of our particular genetic makeup to the peculiar patterns of perceived information investing us at the time*. In other words, *the choices we make are those we cannot help making in the circumstances* (italics added)."

Morrison cites the work of Thomas Bouchard of the University of Minnesota, who performed studies on identical twins behavior patterns. Identical twins are monozygotic, or genetic clones, having identical genetic composition. Bouchard's work indicates that *no dimension of our behavior is wholly immune to the effects of genetic expression* (italics added). "In fact", Morrison says, "I would suggest that the moment we accept that we are entirely normal animals, then no other reasonable conclusion is available to us. The differences and similarities in the behavior patterns of identical and fraternal twins *point unequivocally to the genetic origins of all human behavior and the very practical unity that exists between mind and matter* (italics added)." This implies that all human behavioral processes follow the dictates of natural systems (physical-chemical-biological).

The absence of choice does not imply a deadening determinism for human life. According to Morrison, "the uniqueness of our dictatorial genes guarantees our unpredictability and the ultimate failure of anyone who attempts to control our behavior. Thanks to the autonomy of our DNA, we remain indomitable and therefore free in the only sense that matters to us." However, if humans are only matter (not mind), inherent variability in physical processes - for example, the macroscopic effects of quantum uncertainty[201] - assures the unpredictability of individual or collective human fate.

As regards our future, it is not easy to be sanguine. We are handicapped by monumental misconceptions arising from our mystical predilections that assure nature's retribution. Contrary to common belief:

- A human organism is an integrated mind-body entity whose behavior is genetically driven, as any other animal, but mediated by the influence of culture.

- Although our self-consciousness provides the illusion of choice, we do the only thing we can do, as dictated by our genes and experience.

- The natural environment is chaotic and inherently unstable; much of evolution is comprised of adaptations to environmental change.

- Most environmental damage is the inevitable consequence of excessive numbers of humans, a phase in our species' population cycle.

- The rise and fall of population is a vital component of the evolutionary process and an essential element in nature's contract with a fertile, high-impact species such as *H. sapiens.*

- Environmental problems do not have technological solutions; all human activity – 'good' or 'bad' adds to the environmental debt (overexploitation of natural resources)[202].

Morrison alludes to Lovelock's Gaia hypothesis, which theorizes that Earth is a cosmic organism comprised of its biota (all of its organisms) and biosphere (the integration of all of Earth's ecosystems) continually interacting with other physical elements of Earth and the cosmos to maintain viable conditions for life. Our general failure to perceive the biosphere as an organism is a consequence of mystical beliefs and genetic response, made all the more difficult for us by the lack of temporal perspective - many natural processes have a time span far in excess of the human "three score and ten".

The fate of humanity was sealed by the confluence and interplay of language and spirituality, which not only compensated for physical shortcomings, but also was an evolutionary asset of revolutionary proportions. By selectively preserving the mystics among our ancient ancestors, evolution devised an insurance plan against everlasting success. Only our obsessive yearning for significance, spirituality and the supernatural, and consequent auto-adoration, could blind us to the dangers of overpopulation and environmental degradation and prevent us from taking corrective action.

" Let us recognize human mysticism for what it really is – the rusting Excalibur[203] of our species, an old and vital streak of genetic madness that once rescued our kind from the brink of extinction, took us to the moon, and will run us through with due dispatch when our play is done."

So what has humanity in store, for itself and the rest of life on Earth? It is difficult to be sanguine about our future, even in the relatively near term. Our numbers continue to grow by about 75 million per year, with no commensurate increase in the means of providing sustenance for the human population with already over 1 billion at the point of desperation. The suggestion of finding an alternative planet to host our starving minions is chimerical. Extinction of species continues at an alarming rate, while some who sense the significance of this loss seek to preserve them through study and confinement to artificial habitats. However, this is a mortal embrace, a kiss of death, as knowledge will ultimately be used to their detriment as the need for human 'lebensraum' takes precedence.

Morrison anticipates a sharp reduction in human numbers, as in a plague cycle, at some time in the 21st century. Although our spiritual side tells us that this would be a tragic and unthinkable outcome, particularly when we contemplate the fate of our own progeny, he suggests that there is no way out. Ontogenetic pressures in the human animal appear to preclude avoidance of this eventuality. His good news is that continued domination of the current strain of *H. sapiens* is detrimental to biodiversity, and would have the most devastating impact upon evolution itself.

The human plague may have been triggered by the advent of agriculture, and accelerated by the industrial revolution, but oil was undoubtedly the bullet in the barrel - probably two thirds of us are made of it. Exploitation of fossil fuels, just as any other natural phenomenon, was not written in the stars. Had this not occurred, the fury of the plague, if it is indeed to exact its toll in relatively short order, may well have been expressed in a more benign manner, so that a vestige of the humanity we know would end its tenure in some other way, maybe even in the inevitable fiery holocaust of the solar supernova.

Awareness of our 'condition' is the first and essential step to allowing a reasonable tenure on Earth for humanity and for the other species that share it with us. The essence of our condition is that we are not in control, but rather follow the dictates of our genes. There are too many of us, and our adverse impact on the biosphere too great, to allow a sustainable future for all of Earth's life forms.

The outgrowth of our condition is an array of behaviors, predicated on our genetic endowment and history. A few of our salient behavioral issues illustrate the need for modification:

- The process of adjusting the human population to

sustainable level is a race against time - will reproductive restraint and attrition occur quickly enough to avoid catastrophe?

- Will the order of our priorities place nurturing of youth at the top of the list, as the foundation for adjustments to all other behaviors threatening the future of life?

- Will responsibility rather than rights become the driving force behind administrative, legislative and judicial thought and action?

- Will sexual expression take on a more wholesome aspect, free from exploitation and destabilizing constraints?

- Will religionists and political operatives discontinue the practice of exploiting myths and superstitions?

- Will knowledge be pursued in a philosophical context, taking into account the full measure of our approach to learning, its applications consequences?

Humanity is out of control, as if a wire in nature's normally effective cybernetic system had come loose. Awareness of our condition as normal animals following the rules and dictates of nature, devoid of the illusion of choice and its malignant consequences that outsized consciousness has bestowed, offers the possibility of transcendence to a state of humility that appears essential to prevent further deterioration of our planet.

Will the metastatic malaise attributable to human behavior succumb in the end to nature's capacity to heal its wounds, or has the disease spread to the point of no return?

Is it too late in the game to alter the outcome? If what Morrison envisions comes to pass, and if humanity does not completely disappear from the face of Earth within this century, will the population emerging from the collapse have characteristics less dismissive of nature's imperatives, able to use its rational faculties to greater benefit of life? Or can the collapse be averted by a twist of fate that raises our species to the necessary level of awareness? In any case, vicissitudes of nature preclude prognostication.

Endnotes

Preface

1. The pickup basketball court serves well as a laboratory for the study of individual and group psychology.

2. Khayyam, Omar. *The Rubaiyat*. The Internet Classics Archive: http://classics.mit.edu/Khayyam/rubaiyat.html

Chapter 1 Introduction

3. Recent progress in mapping the genome may shed more light on ancestry of individuals and populations than has heretofore been possible.

4. Quote first used by Walt Kelly in a poster for Earth Day, 1970

5. Very late one night many years ago my wife and I came upon the wreckage of a convertible sports car under one of the elevated train lines in New York City. The car's tires were burning, and two young people were pinned into the front seat, a man and a woman, unconscious and apparently badly injured. Without hesitation, I quickly stopped my own vehicle, jumped out and pulled the woman out of the burning car while my wife ran to a nearby diner to call the police. The young man was completely pinned behind the wheel, so it was impossible to free him. This action was essentially instinctive, even though my thoughts were on imminent explosion of the vehicle. The irrepressible

force of culture appeared to have trumped genes. Fortunately the fire department arrived before the flames spread to the front seat, so the probably dead young man was not immolated. We didn't stay around to find out.

6.   James Carl Nelson, in his prodigiously researched history of doughboys of WWI in France, *The Remains of Company D*, confirms through their letters and other documentation that their predominant motivations were protection of family and country and abhorrence of totalitarianism.

7.   American service casualties: WWI (1914-1918) – 117,000 deaths and 204,000 wounded; WWII (1941-1945) – 292,000 KIA, 417,000 deaths, 670,000 wounded. Total military casualties for all countries: WWI 29.5 million; WWII 59 million, (http://www.infoplease.com/ipa/A0004619.html).

8.   Positions of some philosophers on the subject are discussed in Chapter 2 *A Matter of Choice*.

9.   See Bill McKibben, Eaarth, Times Books (2010), for a thorough and alarming survey of the environmental damage resulting from greenhouse gas emissions.

Chapter 2 A Matter of Choice

10.   Foundations in the writings of Soren Kierkegaard (1813-55), Friedrich Nietzsche (1844-1900) and Karl Jaspers (1883-1969)

11.   The *spirit* in this context refers to a moral and/or ethical quality divinely bestowed on the individual. This contrasts with the *spirit* or *élan* of Chapter 7, which refers to the essential life force of every organism.

12.   Acknowledgement of an interventionist deity is not intended, but the possibility is allowed that nature may have a way of bestowing moral fiber to an individual organism.

13.   There is a multiplicity of possibilities describing how an indeterminate or random process evolves over time, which can be expressed as a probability distribution. The distribution, if it is known, assigns probabilities to alternative outcomes.

14.   Peter Sterling and Robert G Smith. "Design for a Binary

Synapse". *Neuron*, Volume 41, Issue 3, 313-315, 5 February 2004

15. Jean Piaget, best known for his 20th century research into childhood developmental psychology.

16. The analysis of Reg Morrison (1999) supports the contention that the illusion of choice has significant consequences (see Chapter 9).

18. Albert Einstein, Banesh Hoffman (ed.) , Helen Dukas. *Albert Einstein, the Human Side – New Glimpses from his Archives*, p.60. Princeton: Princeton University Press, 1981

19. Thinking Allowed; Conversations On The Leading Edge Of Knowledge and Discovery; The Simple and the Complex, Part I: The Quantum and the Quasi-Classical with Murray Gell-Mann, Ph.D.; http://www.williamjames.com/transcripts/gell1.htm

20. Peter L. Bernstein, financial historian, economist and educator, wrote on the understanding of risk, arising from uncertainty in the outcome of any action.

21. See Morrison (1999)

Chapter 3 How Many of Us are Too Many?

22. International Monetary Fund, World Economic Outlook Data Forum, http://forums.imf.org/showthread.php

23. Global Policy Forum, General Trends and Statistics on Income Disparity, Development Report 1997, UNDP, http://www.globalpolicy.org/component/content/article/218-injustice-and-inequality/46629.html

24. David Cay Johnson. *"Income Gap Is Widening, Data Shows"*. NY Times, March 29, 2007

25. Many investigators have shown an inverse relationship between information dissemination and fertility. One relates televised soap operas in Brazil to fertility reduction: Eliana La Ferrara, Alberto Chong, Suzanne Duryea, *Soap Operas and Fertility: Evidence from Brazil*; Bureau for Research and Economic

Analysis of Development (BREAD) Working Paper No. 172, Duke University; March 2008

26. In an interview with Terrence McNally entitled "Globalization has Increased the Wealth Gap" in Jan. 2007, Nobel economist Joseph Stiglitz discusses how income disparities have widened as a result of globalization. http://www.alternet.org/story/45833/?page=1.

27. The relation between destitution and fertility is widely recognized by experts in the field. Two papers on the subject are (1) David Lackland Sam. "Value of Children: Effects of Globalization on Fertility Behavior and Child-Rearing Practices in Ghana", Research Review NS 17.2 (2001) 5-16. http://culturesofcare. uib.no/downloads/17_2/SAM_17.pdf, and (2) Gu Baochang, Zheng Zhenzhen, Wang Feng, Cai Yong. "Globalization, Policy Intervention, and Reproduction: Below Replacement Fertility in China". Paper prepared for presentation at the Population Association of America annual meeting, New York City, March 29-31, 2007; http://paa2007.princeton.edu/download.aspx?submissionId=70260

28. Global Issues, Dec. 2009, http://www.globalissues.org/article/4/poverty-around-the-world#WorldBanksPovertyEstimatesRevised

29. In June, 2010 the Chinese have begun to allow the value of their currency, the renminbi or yuan, to decrease in value relative to the U.S. dollar. This should tend to reduce the enormous trade surplus that the country enjoys, and possibly reduce their rate of economic growth as measured by the traditional standard of Gross Domestic Product.

30. Jeffrey D. Sachs (2005) convinced the former Soviet states to rapidly convert to market economies. Failure to allow time for adjustment created difficult conditions for Russia and particularly for the former republics, whose umbilical cords were severed precipitously.

31. ibid.

32. University Of Texas, Austin. "Extinction Rate Across The Globe Reaches Historical Proportions". *Science Daily*, 10 January 2002.

http://www.sciencedaily.com /releases/2002/01/020109074801. htm.

33. Victoria's Ecological Footprint, State Government of Victoria, June 2006

34. See David Pimentel and Mario Giampietro. "Food, Land and Population and the US Economy". Carrying Capacity Network, Washington, D.C. 1994

35. Global Food Trends – Overview, UN Office for Coordination of Humanitarian Affairs, 2010

36. Neil MacFarquhar. "Experts Worry as Population and Hunger Grow". NY Times, October 21, 2009. http://www.nytimes. com/2009/10/22/world/22food.html?hpw

37. Néfer Muñoz, Inter Press Service English News Wire, February 27, 2002

38. US Dep't of Agriculture. "Global Land Resources & Population Supporting Capacity". *American Journal of Alternative Agriculture*, 14:129-136, 1999

39. Has Oil and Gas Collapse Sealed Fate of Peak Oil? http:// www.321energy.com/editorials/simmons/simmons042909/ show042909.html?id=27

40. *The Economist*. "The IEA puts a date on peak oil production". Dec. 10, 2009

41. Tom Whipple. "The Peak Oil Crisis: Priorities". Falls Church News-Press, Apr. 9, 2009. http://www.energybulletin.net/ node/48577

42. Lester R. Brown, Earth Policy Institute. *Book Bytes*. "The Oil Intensity of Food", June 25, 2009

43. "Human Appropriation of the World's Fresh Water Supply". Global Change, 2006. http://www.globalchange.umich.edu/ globalchange2/current/lectures/freshwater_supply/freshwater. html.

44. UNEP/GRID-Arendal. "Water availability in Africa"; 2008

45. *Deforestation continues at an alarming rate*; FAO Newsroom; 2008

46. World Migration Report; Section 3: "International Migration Data and Statistics". International Organization for Migration (IOM), 2005

47. James G. Gimpel and Frank Morris. "Immigration, Intergroup Conflict, and the Erosion of African American Political Power in the 21st Century". *Center for Immigration Studies*, Jan. 2007. http://www.cis.org/AfricanAmericanPoliticalPower-Immigration

48. Lynching and Violence in American Culture. "Mexican Migrant Workers and Lynch Culture". CU-Dillard Collaborative Curriculum Partnership, 2004. http://amath.colorado.edu/carnegie/lit/lynch/migrant.htm

49. Quaker Witness, *American Friends Service Committee* newsletter, March 2010

50. Michael T. Klare is Professor of Peace and World Security Studies at Hampshire College. See "A Planet at the Brink: Will Economic Brushfires Prove Too Virulent to Contain?". Tuesday 24 February 2009. http://www.truth-out.org/022509B

51. Global Footprint Network; http://www.footprintnetwork.org/en/index.php/GFN/page/world_footprint/

52. Paul Chefurka. "World Energy and Population Trends to 2100". http://www.paulchefurka.ca/WEAP/WEAP.html

53. Median population figures of the UN Population Fund are: 2010, 6.8 billion, 1.1% growth (approx. 75 M per annum); 2050, 9.3 billion, .045% growth (approx. 42 M per annum)

Chapter 4 The Jewel in Society's Crown

54. Jean Leidloff (1986) explains adverse effects of a modern, "non-continuum" upbringing.

55. See http://www.infoplease.com/ipa/A0005074.html

56. Dr. Weikert's High/Scope Educational Research Foundation in Ypsilanti, MI focused on the value of pre-school education.

57. Posit Science. "A Conversation With Bruce McEwen" with

Simon Hansen, Ph.D. June 8, 2010. http://brainconnection. positscience.com/topics/?main=conv/mcewen

58. David A. Hamburg. "The American Family Transformed". *Society* (periodical), Volume 30, Number 2 / January, 1993. New York: Springer

59. Neal Halfon, Ericka Shulman and Miles Hochstein. "Brain Development in Early Childhood. August, 2001 http://www. healthychild.ucla.edu/Publications/Documents/halfon.health. dev.pdf

60. Synapses are specialized structures in the nervous system (in humans, the brain, spinal cord and retina) that permit neurons to pass signals to other cells. Neurons are core components of the nervous system, cells that process and transmit information through electrical and chemical signaling.

61. See, for example: Jacqueline S. Johnson and Elissa L. Newport. "Critical Period Effects in Second Language Learning: the influence of maturational state on acquisition of English as a second language". *Cognitive Psychology* 21, 1989

62. Tom DeLay, Op/Ed Washington Post Mar 27, 2000. "Why Kids Murder Kids: Removal of religious values from public life has left us without a moral foundation". p 27

63. As gleaned from a brief tenure as a school board member, the emphasis appears to be preparing children for roles in the economy, rather than as citizens of the community, state and world.

64. Highly controversial health care 'reform' legislation was passed by the US Congress and signed into law by President Barack Obama in March 2010, but it falls far short of a national commitment to comprehensive health maintenance for children, or for adults as well.

65. Jean Piaget (1896-1980), Swiss biologist and psychologist: development and learning model based on the child's construction of cognitive structures for understanding and responding to physical experiences.

66. Encyclopedia of Mental Disorders, http://www.minddisorders. com/index.html

67. Andrea Sedlak, et. al. (1996) compares abuse of children based on family income.

68. US Dept of Health and Human Services. "Child Maltreatment 2008" http://www.acf.hhs.gov/programs/cb/pubs/cm08/cm08. pdf

69. See Nancy Peddle, Ph.D., Ching-Tung Wang, Ph.D., Javier Diaz and Robert Reid. "Current Trends in Child Abuse: Prevention and Fatalities: The 2000 Fifty State Suvey". Working Paper Number 808. National Center on Child Abuse Prevention Research, September 2002

70. Dorothy Lewis, M.D. "From Abuse to Violence: Psychophysiological Consequences of Maltreatment". *Journal of the American Academy of Child and Adolescent Psychiatry*, 1993

71. See: Sarah Fass and Nancy K. Cauthen. "Who Are America's Poor Children?" National Center for Children in Poverty (NCCP), 2006

72. US Department of Agriculture. "Household Food Security in the United States, 2008". November 2009

73. In Marquette (Wis.) Tribune, Jan. 25, 2007

74. Stanford J. Newman, J.D., President of Fight Crime: Invest in Kids; "America's Child Care Crisis – A Crime Prevention Tragedy", Jan. 2000

75. US Environmental Protection Agency. "America's Children and the Environment (ACE)". November 2009. www.epa.gov/ envirohealth/children

76. PBS Frontline. "The Medicated Child". Report of November 2009. www.pbs.org/wgbh/pages/frontline/medicatedchild/

77. See: Pier Alberto Bertazzi1, Dario Consonni, Silvia Bachetti1, Maurizia Rubagotti, Andrea Baccarelli1, Carlo Zocchetti and Angela C. Pesatori. "Health Effects of Dioxin Exposure: A 20-Year Mortality Study". *American Journal of Epidemiology* Vol. 153, No. 11 : 1031-1044

78. U.S. Department of Health and Human Services, Substance Abuse and Mental Health Services Administration, Office of Applied Studies. Results from the 2008 National Survey on Drug Use and Health

79. See: Center for Disease Control (CDC). "Study on Overweight and Obesity, 2008". http://www.cdc.gov/obesity/data/trends.html

80. Judy Garland. "The Plot Against Judy Garland". *Ladies' Home Journal*, August 1967

81. Judy Garland. "By Myself". PBS American Masters, Feb. 25, 2004

82. Gerald Clarke. *Get Happy: The Life of Judy Garland*, p. 23. New York: Random House, 2001

83. Louis B. Mayer, according to Jane Ellen Wayne. *The Golden Girls of MGM*, p. 204. New York: Carroll and Graf, 2003

84. James Bone. "Drinking bleach and Being Bullied on 'Lord of the Flies' Reality Show". Time (London), August 25, 2007

85. Teresa Wiltz. "Child Advocates Question Safety of Reality TV". *Washington Post*, July 29, 2008

86. Kevin Sullivan, Washington Post Foreign Service. "Excel Africa". April 1, 2009. http://fr.excelafrica.com/showthread.php?t=9568

87. CNN Money Report. "The Changing Face of Poverty in America". January 2009

88. Octavio Blanco, CNN/Money. "The Changing Face of Poverty". New York, Dec. 30, 2004

89. John Biewen. "The Forgotten Fourteen Million". American Public Media, A Coproduction with National Public Radio, May 1999

90. Reeve Vanneman. "Sociology 441 – Stratification". University of Maryland, 2002. http://www.bsos.umd.edu/socy/vanneman/socy441/default.html

91. Koen Vleminckx and Timothy M. Smeeding, eds. *Child Well-*

Being, Child Poverty and Child Policy in Modern Nations. Bristol (UK): The Policy Press, 2001

92. Robert F. Drinan, "A Global Revolution for Children" in The Mobilization of Shame: A World View of Human Rights. Yale University Press, 2001, pp. 45-50.

93. Anne M. Veneman, UNICEF Executive Director. Presentation at 58th World Health Assembly. Geneva, May16, 2005

94. Amnesty International. "Child Soldiers". 2010. http://www. amnestyusa.org/children/child-soldiers/page.do?id=1051047

95. Coalition to Stop the Use of Child Soldiers. "Child Soldiers – Global Report 2008"

96. Tom Regan, Christian Science Monitor. "Report: Israeli soldiers used children as 'human shields'". March 9, 2007. http://www. csmonitor.com/2007/0309/p99s01-duts.html

97. Fathi Hammad, Hamas MP. "We Used Women and Children as Human Shields". Al-Aqsa TV (Hamas/Gaza) - February 29, 2008 - 00:49. http://www.memritv.org/clip/en/1710.htm.

98. CNN reported on June 10, 2010 that the Taliban in Afghanistan had executed a 7-year-old boy as a spy.

99. Shannon McManimon and Rachel Stohl. "Use of Children as Soldiers". Institute for Policy Studies, Foreign Policy in Focus. October 5, 2005. http://www.fpif.org/reports/use_of_children_ as_soldiers

Chapter 5 Rights are Wrong in Democracy

100. Instances of 'inalienable rights' being abrogated abound. For example, during the Bush administration in the US of 2000-2008, in defiance of the Bill of Rights, one could be spied upon without a court order; due process was denied in some cases; torture was permitted; wars could be undertaken without Congressional approval; enemies could be assassinated (see Robert Parry. "The End of Inalienable Rights". Consortium News, Jan. 24, 2006

101. For further discussion, see Will and Ariel Durant. *Rousseau and Revolution.* New York: Simon and Schuster, 1967

102. Center for Disease Control. "Data and Statistics, Deaths, 2006" http://www.cdc.gov/datastatistics/

103. ibid.

104. Garrett Hardin. "The Tragedy of the Commons" *Science*, December 13, 1968

Chapter 6 Sexual Repression and the Peeping Tom

105. U.S. Department of Justice, Bureau of Justice Statistics. "National Crime Victimization Survey", 1996.

106. U.S. Departments of Justice and Health and Human Services survey, released on 17 November 1998

107. National Victim Center. "Rape in America: A Report to the Nation"., 1992

108. See Brownmiller (1975), a report of findings of research by Dr. Menachiam Amir, Israeli criminologist, and the National Institute of Law Enforcement and Criminal Justice

109. See: Brown (2007), a gripping survey, from the perspective of Native Americans, of their virtual annihilation in the United States, primarily during the 19th century

110. See: Nesbitt (1996)

111. Alexis de Tocqueville (1835)

Chapter 7 Spirit, Religion and Politics

112. Freud identified the libido as the life force, assigning to it essentially a sexual connotation. Other students of the human psyche, e.g. Jung, broadened the concept to a more general creative drive of the individual. These are merely the human manifestations, however, of a characteristic shared by all of life.

113. The term is used as a synonym for the libido, but in the sense that Jung proposed, a life force that exists in every living thing, and not merely the sex drive.

114. See: Tattersall (1998). Dr. Tattersall was curator of the Museum of Natural History in New York

115. Dalai Lama. "Philosophical Questions on Consciousness". http://hhdl.dharmakara.net/hhdlquotes3.html#time

116. Herrmann Hesse. *Siddartha*. Scotts Valley (CA): Create Space, 2008

117. Dalai Lama, op. cit.

118. See, for example: Sue Taylor Parker; Robert W. Mitchell, Maria L. Boccia, et. al., eds. *Self-Awareness in Animals and Humans - Developmental Perspectives*. New York: Cambridge University Press, 1994

119. See, for example: Art Moore. "Sudan jihad forces Islam on Christians". March 04, 2002. http://www.wnd.com/?pageId=12985

120. For a scathing rebuttal, see Dawkins (2009)

121. In one formulation, the uncertainty in position and velocity of a particle of matter.

122. The idea behind putting 'science' and 'scientist' in quotations is explained in Chapter 8. Hereinafter, quotation marks are usually omitted.

123. Survey in *Nature*, 1997

124. Albert Einstein. From "Science, Philosophy and Religion, A Symposium", published by the *Conference on Science, Philosophy and Religion in Their Relation to the Democratic Way of Life, Inc.*, New York, 1941

125. Albert Einstein. "The Religiousness of Science". from *The World as I See It*. Minneapolis (MI): Filiquarian Publishing, LLC., 2006

126. See: Michael Brown. "World History Chart". http://www.creation-science-prophecy.com/timeline.htm

127. William Henry Green. "Primeval Chronology - Are There Gaps in the Biblical Genealogies?" Bibliotheca Sacra (April, 1890), 285-303, http://www.reasons.org/interpreting-genesis/adam-and-eve/are-there-gaps-biblical-genealogies

128. Lansing State Journal. "Crews find boy's body after 30 hours in well". March 21, 1998

129. As quoted in Heisenberg, Werner. *Physics and Beyond, Encounters and Conversations*. New York: Harper Torchbooks, 1971, p. 206

130. See for example: Thomas Whitfield Selover. "Hsieh Liang-tso And The Analects Of Confucius: Humane Learning As A Religious Quest". American Academy Of Religion. Oxford: Oxford University Press, 2005

131. See: Stanford University Encyclopedia of Philosophy. "Ancient Theories of Soul". http://plato.stanford.edu/entries/ancient-soul/

132. See: James Orr, John Nuelsen and Edgar Mullins, eds. *International Standard Biblical Encyclopedia*. Peabody (MA): Hendrickson Publishers, 1994

133. Christadelphians. "The Bible Meaning of Soul – An Animal Life or Body Subject to Death – not Immortal". http://www.learnbible.net/soul.html

134. See: Hastings Dictionary of the Bible. Peabody (MA): Hendrickson Publishers; abridged edition, 1989

135. Augustine. "On the Immortality of the Soul" (CE 387). http://puffin.creighton.edu/phil/Stephens/Augustine/On%20the%20Immortality%20of%20the%20Soul.htm

136. Lorenz, Hendrik. "Ancient Theories of Soul". Stanford Encyclopedia of Philosophy. Apr. 2009

137. See: Innvista: http://www.innvista.com/culture/religion/bible/contraot.htm, but typical of such lists published on the internet

138. Although religion is inherently predicated on fantasy, this would not necessarily be grounds for condemnation if devotees of ROs did not usually function in slavish obeisance to their holy edicts and canons, often obviating sensible solutions to societal issues.

139. Paul Tice. *Jumpin' Jehovah – Exposing the Atrocities of the Old Testament God* , 3rd ed. San Diego:The Book Tree, 2007: Quoting Steve Allen

140. Thomas Paine. "Of The Religion Of Deism Compared With The Christian Religion"

141. Thomas Paine. "The Age of Reason"

142. Solipsism – a philosophical concept that nothing exists outside of the mind, and that the claim to external knowledge is unjustified – a dangerous myth in Hitchens' view as a departure from reality.

143. See: Dawkins (2008), from Chapter 1, "A Deeply Religious Non-Believer"

144. See: Dawkins (2009), op. cit.

145. http://contenderministries.org/prophecy/endtimes.php

146. See: David Holwick. "Jehu: Fanaticism's Price". March, 1993 http://church.holwick.com/topical-sermons/119-old-testament-series/index.php

147. *Middle East Policy Council Journal*. Translation of April 24, 2002 al-Qaeda document. http://www.mepc.org/journal_vol10/0306_alqaeda.asp

148. Sheryl Henderson Blunt. "Election 2000: Partisanship in the Pews; Race: Religion Played Decisive Roles in the Presidential Vote". *Christianity Today*, April 2, 2001. http://www.christianitytoday.com/ct/2001/april2/15.29.html.

149. Ironically, the US backed president of Afghanistan, Hamid Karzai, was reported to be negotiating with Taliban terrorists because he has "lost faith in the US strategy in Afghanistan and is increasingly looking to Pakistan to end the insurgency", according to those close to Afghanistan's former head of intelligence services. See Reuters News Service. "Potential Allies: Karzai, Pakistan and the Taliban?". Jun 11, 2010 http://blogs.reuters.com/afghanistan/2010/06/11/potential-allies-karzai-pakistan-and-the-taliban/

150. Alan Cooperman and Thomas B. Edsall, Washington Post Staff Writers. Monday, November 8, 2004, Page A01

151. See: Laurie Goodstein. "Seeing Islam as 'Evil' Faith, Evangelicals Seek Converts" *New York Times*. May 27, 2003

152.   See, for example: Seth Mydans. Published in *NY Times*, January 10, 2010

153.   The use of gender (she/he) in describing a deity seems misplaced. Gods most likely do not have to resort to sexual means to reproduce or recreate, as the Romans apparently believed of their Pantheon. It would be a great disappointment to learn that the Romans were correct, but even if true, this doesn't apply to the common god of Christians, Jews and Muslims.

154.   Sam Harris; Letter to a Christian Nation – A Thesis on the End of Faith, Vintage, January 2008

155.   Carolyn Tuft. *St. Louis Post-Dispatch*, April 30, 2005

156.   Jonathan Wynne-Jones, Religious Affairs Correspondent, *The Telegraph*, Nov 29 2008 http://www.telegraph.co.uk/news/ newstopics/religion/3534960/Disney-accused-by-Catholic-cleric-of-corrupting-childrens-minds.html

Chapter 8 A Road Not Taken

157.   The term 'science' is intended to describe the activities of academic, industrial and government researchers who are engaged in the pursuit, acquisition and application of knowledge via the 'scientific method', involving observation, hypothesis and confirmation through experimentation.

158.   Michael Agnes. *Webster's New World Dictionary of American English*. New York: Pocket, 2003

159.   Some may bridle at the assertion that all quests for knowledge are ultimately utilitarian. This is consistent with a material view of existence, i.e. that humans are part and parcel of nature and driven by its forces, as is any other species, with choice, or free will, an illusion (see Chapter 3).

160.   See: Thomas Kuhn (1996), p. 88

161.   Andrew Janiak. "Newton's Philosophy". *Stanford Dictionary of Philosophy*. Oct. 2006. http://plato.stanford.edu/entries/ newton-philosophy/

162.   Qur'an 6:97

163. Nicolaus Copernicus. *Dedication of the Revolutions of the Heavenly Bodies to Pope Paul III.* (1543). The Harvard Classics. 1909–14.

164. Nicolaus Copernicus. *On the Revolutions of the Heavenly Spheres,* Preface. Amherst (NY): Prometheus Books (November 1995)

165. Kepler's interests extended into many other areas: his studies in optics resulted in discoveries concerning reflection, refraction and imaging. His book *Stereometrica Doliorum* was the basis of integral calculus later developed by Isaac Newton and Gottfried Liebniz. He used stellar parallax to measure the distance to stars, and revealed that the sun rotates around its own axis, among other mathematical and astronomical discoveries.

166. Sir Isaac Newton. *The Mathematical Principles of Natural Philosophy.* Andrew Motte, trans. London: H. D. Symonds, 1803

167. Sir David Brewster in *Memoirs of the Life, Writings, and Discoveries of Sir Isaac Newton,* (Volume II, Ch. 27) 1855

168. See: John van Wyhe. *The Complete Works of Charles Darwin Online.* "Charles Darwin: Gentleman Naturalist, A Biographical Sketch"; http://darwin-online.org.uk/darwin.html

169. Charles Darwin. *The Descent of Man* (Ch. XXI: General Summary And Conclusion).

170. See: The Stanford Encyclopedia of Philosophy: "Einstein's Philosophy of Science", Wed Feb 11, 2004. http://plato.stanford.edu/entries/einstein-philscience/#7

171. Albert Einstein. *The Born-Einstein Letters* (translated by Irene Born). Letter to Max Born (4 December 1926): New York: Walker and Company, 1971

172. Albert Einstein. "Physik und Realität". *Journal of The Franklin Institute,* 1936 221: 313-347, Jean Piccard, trans., *Journal of the Franklin Institute* 221: 348-382.

173. Albert Einstein, "Ernst Mach", *Physikalische Zeitschrift,* 1916 17: 101-104

174. Letter of Albert Einstein to Robert Thornton, December 7, 1944. http://open-site.org/Science/Physics/Modern

175. See: Philip Hunter. *European Molecular Biology Organization.* "Is political correctness damaging science?". 2005 May; 6(5), 405–407, http://www.ncbi.nlm.nih.gov/pmc/articles/PMC1299305/

176. See: Paul Arthur Schilpp, ed. *Albert Einstein: Philosopher-Scientist.* "Remarks Concerning the Essays Brought together in this Co-operative Volume." Evanston, IL: The Library of Living Philosophers, vol. 7, p. 665-688, 1949

177. Paul Arthur Schilpp, ed. *Albert Einstein: Philosopher-Scientist* (Living Philosophers Volume 7). New York: MJF Books, March 2001

178. Ronald William Clark. *Einstein: The Life and Times.* New York: Harper Perrenial, 2007

179. ibid, p. 752

180. Dr. Maury Seldin, Chairman of the Board of The Hoyt Group, Roots of Modern Disciplines, Philosophical Foundations, www.hoyt.org.

181. NationMaster. List of academic disciplines, http://www.statemaster.com/encyclopedia/List-of-academic-disciplines

182. World Health Organization, Chemical Hazards, http://www.who.int/ceh/risks/cehchemicals/en/

183. Monika Gisler and Didier Sornette. "Exuberant Innovations: The Apollo Program". *Society Journal*, Springer, Volume 46, Number 1 / January, 2009

184. ibid.

185. Positions of commentators on the manned space program are posted on a blog maintained by Stephen J. Dubner for the NY Times: "Is Space Exploration Worth the Cost? A Freakonomics Quorum". January 11, 2008. http://freakonomics.blogs.nytimes.com/2008/01/11/is-space-exploration-worth-the-cost-a-freakonomics-quorum/

186. Dubner, op. cit.: Mike Hollis, Jan 29 2010

187. NASA Solutions. http://techtran.msfc.nasa.gov/at_home.html

188. Dubner, op. cit. G. Scott Hubbard, professor of Aeronautics and Astronautics at Stanford University and former director of the NASA Ames Research Center, January 11, 2008

189. Extinction is inevitable, if not by our own hand then ultimately at the burnout of our sun a few billion years hence, when Earth will be swallowed up in the resulting supernova. But why rush it?

190. Jennifer Washburn. "Science's Worst Enemy: Corporate Funding". *Discover,* October 2007. http://discovermagazine. com/2007/oct/sciences-worst-enemy-private-funding

191. Alexander Pope (1688 – 1744) in "An Essay on Criticism", 1709

192. Deficiencies in the system of higher education is supported by the analysis of Jeff Schmidt (2000)

193. ibid.

Chapter 9 To Be or Not To Be

194. Julian Jaynes, in *The Origin of Consciousness in the Breakdown of the Bicameral Mind,* postulates that the human brain existed in a bicameral state within the last few thousand years, in which people were not conscious in the sense with which we are familiar. Rather, the impressions of the right brain were transmitted to the left via auditory hallucinations. It was only with the acquisition of metaphorical language that self-consciousness arose.

195. Some philosophers postulate a variety of self-conscious states, some more primitive and not necessarily reflective. Here the reference is to the reflective form of self-consciousness. For further discussion see Shaun Gallagher and Dan Zahavi. Stanford Encyclopedia of Philosophy. "Phenomenological Approaches to Self-Consciousness". August, 2006. http://plato. stanford.edu/entries/self-consciousness-phenomenological/

196. Much of what is known about the division of functions in brain

hemispheres is attributable to Roger Sperry, who won a Nobel Prize for his experiments in1973.

197. Morrison, op. cit.

198. Revised and republished in 2003 by New Holland Publishers, Sydney, as *Plague Species: Is it in Our Genes?*

199. Nevertheless, for some, doubts may be assuaged by the endorsement in his Introduction of Lynn Margulis, eminent biologist and professor of botany in the Department of Geosciences at the University of Massachusetts at Amherst.

200. Stanley H. Ambrose, (Department of Anthropology, University Of Illinois, Urbana, USA). "Late Pleistocene human population bottlenecks, volcanic winter, and differentiation of modern humans". *Journal of Human Evolution*, 1998 34, pp. 623-651

201. Heisenberg's Uncertainty Principle assures that complete knowledge of the state of a subatomic particle is not possible. The Copenhagen Interpretation of the principle, attributed to Neils Bohr and Max Born, are considered synonymous with indeterminism in physical processes.

202. The President of the Nature Conservancy, Mark R. Tercek, in the Spring 2010 issue of his organization's publication of the same name: "You need reliable science on which to base pragmatic conservation decisions that will yield tangible results." Nature did a reasonably good job for all but about the last 10 millennia, when humanity began to apply its science.

203. The sword of the legendary King Arthur of the Knights of the Round Table, with magical powers that could blind opponents with bright light.

Bibliography

Chapter 1 Introduction

Carroll, Lewis. *Through the Looking Glass*. Bel Air, CA: Hesperides Press, 2008

Dawkins, Richard. *The Selfish Gene*, 3rd ed. New York: Oxford University Press, 2006

Gregg, Allan. "A Medical Aspect of the Population Problem". *Science*, 121: 681-682, 1955 (with permission of the journal *Science*)

Knoll, Andrew (professor of biology at Harvard). "How Did Life Begin?". *NOVA*, July 1, 2004. http://www.pbs.org/wgbh/nova/beta/evolution/how-did-life-begin.html.

Lovelock, James. *Gaia: A New Look at Life on Earth*. New York: Oxford U. Press, 2000

McKibben, Bill. *Eaarth*. New York: Times Books, 2010

Morris, Desmond. *The Naked Ape*: A Zoologist's Study of the Human Animal. Los Alamitos (CA): Delta, 1999

Nelson, James Carl. *The Remains of Company D: A Story of the Great War*. New York: St. Martin's Press, 2009

Olson, Steve. *Mapping Human History – discovering the past through our genes*. New York: Houghton Mifflin Co., 2002

Chapter 2 A Matter of Choice

Bargh , John A. and Ezequiel Morsella. "The Unconscious Mind". Yale University, *Perspectives on Psychological Science*. 2008 Vol. 3, No. 1. p. 77

Bernstein, Peter L. *Against the Gods: The Remarkable Story of Risk*. Hoboken: John Wiley & Sons, 1996. quoted in NY Times July 10, 1994.

Brooks, Michael. *13 Things that Don't Make Sense*. New York: Doubleday, 2008

Einstein, Albert, Banesh Hoffman (ed.), Helen Dukas. *Albert Einstein, the Human Side – New Glimpses from his Archives*, p.60. Princeton: Princeton University Press, 1981

Hume, David (Erick Steinberg, ed.). *Enquiry Concerning Human Understanding: With A Letter from a Gentleman to His Friend in Edinburgh and Hume's Abstract of A Treatise of Human Nature.* Chapter 8 Liberty and Freedom. Hackett Publishing, 1993

Johnson, George. *Fire in the Mind; Science, Faith and the Search for Order.* New York: Vintage, 1995

Kowalski, Maria. "Hegel: Abstract Right and Duties to Self". Paper presented at the annual meeting of The Midwest Political Science Association, Palmer House Hilton, Chicago, Illinois, Apr 15, 2004. <http://www.allacademic.com/meta/p82865_index.html>

Popper, Karl R. *Conjectures and Refutations.* Abingdon (UK):Taylor and Francis, 2002

Rummel, R.J. *Understanding Conflict and War,* Vol I: The Dynamic Psychological Field, Chap 30, "Determinism and Free Will". Beverly Hills: Sage Publications, 1975

Viorst, Judith. *Imperfect Control: Our Lifelong Struggles with Power and Surrender.* New York: Simon and Schuster, 1998, p. 29

Watzlawick, Paul. *How Real is Real? Confusion, Disinformation, Communication.* New York: Vintage Books, 1976

Chapter 3 How Many of Us Are Too Many?

Carson, Rachel. *Silent Spring* (original release 1962). New York: Mariner Books, 2002

Sachs, Jeffrey D. *The End of Poverty: Economic Possibilities for Our Time.* New York: Penguin Press, 2005

Wilson, Edward O. *The Future of Life*. New York: Vintage, 2003

Chapter 4 The Jewel in Society's Crown

Hughes, Kent. *Building the Next American Century: The Past and Future of Economic Competitiveness*. Baltimore: The Johns Hopkins University Press, 2005

Koen Vleminckx and Timothy M. Smeeding, eds., Child Well-Being, Child Poverty and Child Policy in Modern Nations, The Policy Press, 2001

Kotulak, Ronald. *Inside the Human Brain – Revolutionary Discoveries of How the Mind Works*. Kansas City: Andrew McMeel Publishing, 1997

Leidloff, Jean. *The Continuum Concept*. Cambridge (MA): Da Capo Press, 1986

Magaloni, Beatriz. "Comparative Autocracy". *Research Frontiers in Comparative Politics*. Duke University, April 27-28, 2007

Schwartz-Nobel, Loretta. *Growing Up Empty – The Hunger Epidemic in America*. New York: Harper Collins Publisher, 2002

Sedlak, Andrea and Diane D. Broadhurst. US Dep't. of Health and Human Services. *Third National Incidence Study of Child Abuse and Neglect (NIS-3)*, 1996

Chapter 5 Rights are Wrong in Democracy

Samuel Elliot Morrison. *Oxford History of the American People*. New York: Oxford University Press, 1965.

Chapter 6 Sexual Repression and the Peeping Tom

Brown, Dee. *Bury My Heart at Wounded Knee, An Indian History of the American West*. New York: Holt Paperbacks, 2007

Brownmiller, Susan. *Against Our Will: Men, Women and Rape*. New York: Simon and Schuster, 1975, p. 183

de Tocqueville, Alexis. *Democracy in America*. London: Saunders and Otley, 1835-1840

Freud, Sigmund, (L. Menand, ed.). *Civilization and its Discontents*. New York: Norton & Co. Inc., 2005

Hamilton, Marcus J., Bruce T. Milne, Robert S. Walker, Oskar Burger and James H. Brown. The complex structure of hunter–gatherer social networks. Proceedings of the Royal Society, July 3, 2007. http://anthropology.missouri.edu/people/walkerpubs/complex4. pdf

Nesbitt, Richard E. and Dov Cohen. *Culture of Honor, the Psychology of Violence in the South*. Boulder (CO): Westview Press, 1996

Chapter 7 Spirit, Religion and Politics

Allott, Robin. "Time and Consciousness", delivered at European Society for the Study of Cognitive Systems, Wadham College, Oxford 26-29 August 2000

Dawkins, Richard. *The God Delusion*, Reprint edition. Wilmington (MA): Mariner Books, 2008

Dawkins, Richard. *The Greatest Show on Earth*, First Edition. New York: Free Press; 2009

Diamond, Jared. *Guns Germs and Steel*. New York: WW Norton & Co., 1999

Ehrman, Bart D. *Jesus, Interrupted: Revealing the Hidden Contradictions in the Bible (And Why We Don't Know About Them)*. First edition. New York: HarperOne, 2010

Harris, Sam. *Letter to a Christian Nation – A Thesis on the End of Faith*. New York: Vintage, 2008

Hitchens, Christopher. *God is Not Great – How Religion Poisons Everything,* 1st ed. New York: Twelve, 2009

Huller, Stephen. *The Real Messiah – The Throne of St. Mark and the True Origins of Christianity*. New York: Sterling Publ. Co., 2009

James, William. *The Principles of Psychology,* 1890; reprint New York: Dover, 1950

Jefferson, Thomas and Andrew A. Lipscomb, Albert Ellery Bergh, eds. *The Writings Of Thomas Jefferson V1: Containing His Autobiography, Notes On Virginia, Parliamentary Manual, Official Papers, Messages And Addresses, And Other Writings, Official And Private*, Vol. 10, pg. 379. Kila (MT): Kessinger Publishing, LLC, 2009

Kant, Immanuel. *Critique of Pure Reason,* translated by F. Max Muller. New York: Doubleday, 1966

Kimball, Charles. *When Religion Becomes Evil*. New York: HarperOne, 2003

Koch, Adrienne, ed. *The American Enlightenment: The Shaping of the American Experiment and a Free Society*. John Adams, "A Defense of

the Constitutions of Government of the United States of America"
[1787-1788]. New York: George Braziller, 1980, p. 258

Popper, K.R. *The World of Parmenides: Essays on the Pre-Socratic Enlightenment.* London: Routledge, 1998.

Ridley, Matt. *Genome - the Autobiography of a Species in 23 Chapters.* New York: Harper Collins Publishers, Inc., 1999

Sagan, Carl. *Billions and Billions.* New York: Random House, 1997

Stenger, Victor J. *God: The Failed Hypothesis - How Science Shows That God Does Not Exist.* Amherst (NY): Prometheus Books, 2008

Tattersall, Ian. *Becoming Human – Evolution and Human Uniqueness*, Chapter "Being Human". New York. Harcourt Brace & Co., 1998

Chapter 8 A Road Not Taken

Kuhn, Thomas. *The Structure of Scientific Revolutions*, 3rd ed. Chicago: University of Chicago Press, 1996

Schmidt, Jeff. *Disciplined Minds: A Critical Look at Salaried Professionals and the Soul-Battering System that Shapes their Lives.* Lanham (MD): Rowman & Littlefield, 2000

Chapter 9 To Be or Not To Be

Morrison, Reg. *The Spirit in the Gene, Humanity's Proud Illusion and the Laws of Nature* (with forward by Lynn Margulis). Ithica: Cornell University Press, 1999

Index